Justice Robert H. Jackson's Unpublished Opinion in Brown v. Board

Other Books by David M. O'Brien

Storm Center: The Supreme Court in American Politics, 11th edition

*Constitutional Law and Politics: Struggles for Power and Governmental
Accountability*, 10th edition

Constitutional Law and Politics: Civil Rights and Civil Liberties, 10th edition

Supreme Court Watch (annual, 1991–2015)

*To Dream of Dreams: Religious Freedom and Constitutional Politics in Postwar
Japan*

Animal Sacrifice and Religious Freedom: Church of Lukumi Babalu Aye v.
City of Hialeah

Judicial Roulette

*Congress Shall Make No Law: The First Amendment, Unprotected Expression,
and the U.S. Supreme Court*

Privacy, Law, and Public Policy

The Public's Right to Know: The Supreme Court and the First Amendment

What Process Is Due? Courts and Science Policy Disputes

Judges on Judging, 5th edition (editor)

The Lanahan Readings on Civil Rights and Civil Liberties,
3rd edition (editor)

Abortion and American Politics (coauthor)

Courts and Judicial Policymaking (coauthor)

The Judicial Process: Law, Courts, and Judicial Politics (coauthor)

Government by the People, 22nd edition (coauthor)

The Politics of American Government (coauthor)

*Judicial Independence in the Age of Democracy: Critical Perspectives from
around the World* (coeditor)

Views from the Bench: The Judiciary and Constitutional Politics (coeditor)

Justice Robert H. Jackson's Unpublished Opinion in Brown v. Board

David M. O'Brien

University Press of Kansas

Published by the University Press of
Kansas (Lawrence, Kansas 66045), which
was organized by the Kansas Board of
Regents and is operated and funded by
Emporia State University, Fort Hays
State University, Kansas State University,
Pittsburg State University, the University
of Kansas, and Wichita State University

Library of Congress Cataloging-in-Publication Data

Names: O'Brien, David M., author.
Title: Justice Robert H. Jackson's unpublished
opinion in Brown v. Board : conflict, compromise, and
constitutional interpretation / David M. O'Brien.
Description: Lawrence, Kansas : University Press of
Kansas, [2017] | Includes bibliographical references
and index.
Identifiers: LCCN 2017026726
ISBN 9780700625185 (cloth : alk. paper)
ISBN 9780700625192 (ebook)
Subjects: LCSH: Brown, Oliver, 1918–1961—
Trials, litigation, etc. | Topeka (Kan.). Board of
Education—Trials, litigation, etc. | Jackson, Robert
H., 1892–1954. | Judicial opinions—United States.
| Segregation in education—Law and legislation—
United States. | Discrimination in education—Law and
legislation—United States. | African Americans—Civil
rights. | Constitutional law—United States. | Justice,
Administration of—United States.
Classification: LCC KF228.B76 O27 2017 | DDC
344.73/0798—dc23
LC record available at https://lccn.loc.gov/2017026726.

British Library Cataloguing in Publication Data
is available.

Printed in the United States of America

10 9 8 7 6 5 4 3 2 1

For Claudine and our three children,
Benjamin, Sara, and Talia,
and our grandson, Isaac

Contents

Illustrations

Acknowledgments

First and foremost I am indebted to my wife, Claudine, for putting up with my research and writing while raising our three wonderful children. This book has its origins in research conducted over three decades ago for *Storm Center: The Supreme Court in American Politics,* now in its eleventh edition. In the process of working through the papers of justices and presidents, I acquired the basis for this book and became intrigued with Justice Robert H. Jackson's unpublished opinion in *Brown v. Board of Education.* For more than a quarter of a century, excerpts of that opinion have been included in my casebook, *Constitutional Law and Politics,* volume 2, *Civil Rights and Civil Liberties,* now in its tenth edition.

Hence, I remain grateful for all of the assistance over the years of the staffs at the Manuscripts Division of the Library of Congress, the Bancroft Library at the University of California, Berkeley, the Butler Library Oral History Division at Columbia University, the Dwight D. Eisenhower Presidential Library, the Harvard Law School Library, the Lyndon Baines Johnson Presidential Library, the Seeley G. Mudd Library at Princeton University, the Franklin D. Roosevelt Presidential Library, the Harry S. Truman Presidential Library, the Special Collections Library at the University of Kentucky, the Bentley Historical Library at the University of Michigan, the University of Texas Law School Library, and the Yale University Library's Manuscript and Archives Collections.

In addition, for further work on this book, I appreciate the assistance of Carol A. Leadenham at the Hoover Institution Archives, Amy Wheaton and Lesley Schoenfeld at the Harvard Law School Archives, and Cecilia Brown, special collections archivist, at the University of Virginia Law School Library, as well as the staff at Alderman Library, Joni Blackman at the Fention History Center, Jamestown, New York; Alexis Valentine at the Library of Congress, John Fields at the Supreme Court of the United States, and Sheryl Schutter at the Robert H. Jackson Center in Jamestown, New York.

Several scholars read portions or all of the book and deserve mention. I especially appreciate the time, trouble, and encouragement given by University of Chicago Law School professor Dennis H. Hutchinson, who kindly read and commented on (at times very rough) draft chapters. A former Ph.D. student and now the Robert H. Jackson Distinguished Professor of

Law at Albany Law School, Vincent M. Bonventre meticulously read and commented on every chapter. Two colleagues at the University of Virginia, Henry J. Abraham and James S. Todd, also read portions and kept me going. In addition, historian Melvin I. Urofsky and John Q. Barrett of St. Johns University Law School read the first chapter, previously published in *Journal of Supreme Court History,* for which I am grateful. I also appreciate the work of the University Press of Kansas's editor-in-chief, Joyce Harrison, and before her the encouragement of Fred M. Woodward and Michael Briggs, along with Karen Hellekson, copyeditor, Larisa Martin, production editor, and the editorial assistance of Cole Anneberg.

Of course, none of them bears responsibility for any remaining omissions, mistakes, or misinterpretations.

Introduction

A Story Retold

Brown v. Board of Education (1954) is widely recognized as one of the Supreme Court's most important decisions in the twentieth century, second perhaps only to *Marbury v. Madison* (1803). Justice Robert H. Jackson is generally considered one of the Court's most gifted writers. Much has been written about *Brown,* of course, but comparatively little on Jackson or his unpublished opinion in *Brown.*

The story of *Brown* has been told and retold in many ways, from different perspectives by historians, legal scholars, political scientists, and others. Some explain *Brown* in terms of historical currents and struggles,[1] the influence of World War II and the cold war on the justices,[2] and the role of social science in reconsidering the "separate but equal" doctrine in education.[3] Still others focus on the impact and problems of implementing *Brown*'s mandate.[4] *Brown* for some epitomizes the "hollow hope" of looking to the Court to forge social change[5] and a failure to address fundamental racial inequalities.[6] In hindsight, legal scholars have speculated about what the justices should have said in *Brown.*[7] However, insiders who participated in arguing what became a seminal ruling have offered their historical reflections.[8] So too have some of the justices who decided *Brown* left recollections in their correspondence, interviews, and memoirs.[9] Likewise, former law clerks, who witnessed aspects of the justices' decision making, have weighed in.[10]

Brown is placed in the canon of constitutional law by legal scholars on both the left and the right.[11] In a well-known article, Justice Felix Frankfurter's former law clerk, Alexander Bickel, however, argued that the "original intent" of the drafters of the Fourteenth Amendment provided no basis for the ruling, yet concluded the decision was morally right.[12] By contrast, Bickel's Yale Law School colleague and leading champion of a jurisprudence of "original intentions," ill-fated 1987 Supreme Court nominee Judge Robert H. Bork, condemned the Court for embracing moral philosophy and asserting its "virtually invulnerable" power over democratic self-governance. *Brown,* in his and other conservatives' view, was the height of judicial overreach and lack of "self-restraint."[13] Subsequent scholars have nonetheless tried to square *Brown* with the "original public understanding" of the Fourteenth Amendment,[14] though not without justified criticism of their historical revisionism.[15]

Much has also been written about the justices' decision making in *Brown,*

1

and their unanimity in particular.[16] Some scholars have speculated about how *Brown* might have been decided if Chief Justice Fred Vinson (1946–1953) had not died in the summer of 1953.[17] Even more praise Chief Justice Earl Warren (1953–1969) for leadership in obtaining a unanimous decision,[18] although he downplayed his role in that regard.[19] Numerous others consider *Brown* in light of the New Deal justices' antagonism over broader jurisprudential views,[20] along with how their deliberations may be explained from various other perspectives—judicial attitudes and alliances, concerns about the Court's institutional prestige, and strategic political considerations.[21]

Most interpretations and reinterpretations since Richard Kluger's definitive book, *Simple Justice: The History of* Brown v. Board of Education *and Black America's Struggle for Equality* (1975),[22] have (at least in part) turned on the availability of the private papers of justices who participated in deciding *Brown*, oral histories, and the papers of their law clerks and others. Besides interviews with former justices and law clerks, Kluger had access to the papers of Justices Harold Burton, Hugo L. Black, and Felix Frankfurter, as well as some of Jackson's papers. Later the papers of Chief Justices Fred Vinson and Earl Warren, along with those of Justices William O. Douglas, Stanley Reed, Sherman Minton, and Tom C. Clark, as well as their law clerks, became available at the Library of Congress, Harvard Law School, the University of Kentucky, and the University of Texas, as well as at presidential libraries. Kluger's own notes on interviews conducted for *Simple Justice* later also became available at Yale University. Subsequently, more oral histories of justices, former clerks, and others were made available at Columbia University, the University of Virginia, Princeton University, the University of Michigan, the Hoover Institution Archives, and elsewhere. All of these and other sources have enriched the story of *Brown* but also at times have led to conflicting historical accounts.

By comparison, Jackson received relatively less attention—though, of course, virtually all works dealing with *Brown* discuss him. There is only one major biography,[23] a couple of collections of reflections and his opinions,[24] and a much larger number of articles. Kluger, among others, drew attention to Jackson's unpublished opinion. It has remained a subject of speculation about its significance (sometimes mistakenly taken as a dissenting opinion), much excerpted[25] and analyzed, particularly in connection with the controversy over claims made by one of Jackson's clerks, William H. Rehnquist, during his 1971 and 1986 Senate confirmation hearings on his appointment to the Court and then as chief justice. That memo argued for upholding the "separate but equal" doctrine, which Rehnquist subsequently claimed reflected Justice Jackson's, and not his own, position.[26]

The story of *Brown* that I tell here is from the perspective of Jackson and his unpublished opinion, and as such, it is about both the decision and the justice. More importantly, it is about constitutional interpretation as well as the intersection of law and politics. It deals with the mind of a justice within the context of a Court deciding a seminal case as he wrestles with arguments over "original intent" versus a "living Constitution," the role of the Court, and social change and justice in American political life.

By no means was Jackson alone in withholding draft opinions. All justices have undoubtedly done so.[27] Indeed, his successor, Justice John Marshall Harlan, had his unpublished opinions bound and kept them in his chambers for reference.[28] Jackson's papers include a considerable number of suppressed drafts.[29] They register his struggles with competing arguments over constitutional interpretation and the role of the Court. They also reflect not only conversations with himself but also his thinking about fundamental issues of constitutional interpretation, law, and politics that still remain debated.

Jackson's unpublished opinion went through six drafts, changing in length, structure, and substantive focus. The length grew from fourteen to twenty-three pages as material was deleted, added, and elaborated. The first couple of drafts have only four sections, whereas the third has seven, and the fourth and fifth each have five. The final draft's four sections incorporate and reorganize material from earlier versions. The titles of sections also reflect his evolving thinking. The title of section 2, for instance, changes from "Constitutional Basis" in the first draft to "Basis for Existing Law for Decision" in the third and "Existing Law Does Not Condemn Segregation" in the fourth and fifth; in the final draft, it becomes "Does Existing Law Condemn Segregation?" In addition, from the first to the last, the tone and analysis grow less pessimistic and more reconciled to the result. Throughout, he remained anxious about the ruling and the problems of compliance and implementation—less so than Frankfurter or Reed, but more so than Black or Douglas.

Moreover, Jackson revised drafts at critical times. The first was drafted on December 7, 1953, two days before the second round of oral arguments in *Brown*. Written without the assistance of law clerks, it reaches conclusions contrary to some of their later recommendations and subsequent recollections. Most significantly it makes clear that for him the decision was a foregone conclusion. "The Constitution," Jackson stated, "this morning forbids" segregation that had previously been constitutionally sanctioned. Although finding a "judicial basis" for the ruling "dubious," he was confident that segregated schools could no longer stand. Conceding that constitutional interpretation is political, he stood apart from some other justices who denied or refused to acknowledge that fact. What continually and deeply troubled him (and others on the bench) was not only the justification for applying the guarantees of the Fourteenth Amendment but also how much flexibility and guidance should be given for achieving desegregation. The outcome was nevertheless certain, even before conference discussions with Chief Justice Earl Warren presiding (as a recess appointee). That does not mean the decision would have been unanimous had Chief Justice Vinson not died before a final vote was taken, only that a solid majority—including Jackson—initially supported the eventual result.

In January 1954, after the second round of oral arguments, the draft was revised twice more. The fourth draft, written on February 15, 1954, notably again refers to "today's decision," even though the decision in *Brown* would not come down until May 17, 1954. The fifth draft, written on March 1, 1954, the same day the Senate unanimously confirmed Warren as chief justice, was followed two weeks later by the sixth and last revision.

This retelling of the story of *Brown* weaves together judicial biography, legal history, judicial politics, and debates over constitutional interpretation, along with the role of the Court in American politics. In Part I, Chapter 1 discusses Jackson's background, rise to the Court, judicial philosophy, and advocacy of judicial self-restraint. Chapter 2 examines his relations with other justices, their backgrounds and positions, and their relative contributions to reaching a unanimous decision in *Brown*. Chapter 3 deals with Jackson in chambers and relationships with law clerks. More specifically, extensive discussion is devoted to the controversy over Rehnquist's memo on *Brown* and Jackson's decision to withhold publication of the draft opinion. Chapter 4 analyzes Jackson's drafts and his coming to terms with problems of constitutional interpretation in justifying *Brown*. Finally, Chapter 5 concludes with a reconsideration of some criticisms and misunderstandings of Jackson's unpublished opinion and offers a final assessment.

Part II includes the final draft of Jackson's unpublished opinion, followed by the Warren Court's opinions in *Brown v. Board of Education of Topeka, Kansas,* and *Bolling v. Sharpe* for comparison, as well as a timeline of developments and decision making leading to the Court's landmark ruling.

PART ONE

CHAPTER ONE

He Travels Fastest Who Travels Alone

When moving into the marble temple in 1941, Justice Jackson brought a framed 1919 *Life* magazine photograph of a man working alone at his desk. The caption read, "He travels fastest who travels alone," from "The Winners" in *The Story of the Gadsbys* (1888), by English poet Rudyard Kipling (1865–1936). Jackson lived by that motto. It reflected his upbringing and symbolized his career and life's pursuits.

He acquired the photograph years earlier when working as an apprentice in Frank Mott's law office in rural Jamestown, New York. Mott, a cousin of his mother, oversaw his study of the practice of law. Mott also introduced him to Franklin D. Roosevelt, at the time a state senator and rising star in New York Democratic politics. In the following decades, along with building a lucrative legal practice, Jackson became increasingly active in Democratic politics and close to Roosevelt, who rose to the governorship in 1928 and to the White House after the 1932 presidential election. In 1934, Roosevelt persuaded him to join the New Deal administration. Jackson's career in public service was then meteoric. Within seven years, he moved from working as general counsel for the Internal Revenue Service (1934–1936), to an assistant attorney general for the tax and antitrust divisions in the Department of Justice (1936–1937), to serving as solicitor general (1938–1940), to attorney general (1940–1941), and, at age forty-nine, to a seat on the Supreme Court (in 1941, in which he remained until his death on October 9, 1954).

Always a loner (except with family and close friends), Jackson was complex and paradoxical. He had "a dialectical mind," recalled Paul A. Freund, a longtime Harvard Law School professor who had clerked for Justice Louis D. Brandeis (1916–1939) and worked with Jackson in the solicitor general's office.[1] He was ambitious and proud. He could be morally uncompromising in taking positions, yet also often pragmatic. Politically astute, he nonetheless appeared at times quixotic, or at least difficult to decipher. Although fiercely independent, Jackson still had a keen sense of community. Highly ambitious in both law and politics, as well as deeply concerned about his place in history, he was a "country-gentleman lawyer" who achieved national and international prominence.

While basically self-taught, he was erudite and eloquent. Like most New Deal liberals battling with the conservative majority on the pre-1937 Court, he was associated with "judicial self-restraint"—a label that, after *Brown*, conservatives would embrace in attacking the liberal "judicial activism" of the Warren Court (1953–1969). Although concerned about the institutional prestige and the prudential limits of the Court's power, he remained no less committed to the exercise of judicial review and its role in balancing competing interests between the nation and the states and those of individuals and minorities against majoritarian democracy, or when representative government failed, even if that meant overruling precedents when protecting unpopular groups against popular laws.[2]

An Outsider Inside

Jackson was born in 1892 in Spring Creek, Warren County, Pennsylvania, to a family of yeomen farmers of Scottish-Irish heritage. Five years later, the family moved to Frewsburg, New York, a village near upstate Jamestown. There he grew up and spent the next two decades in private practice and Democratic politics. His family was "uncompromisingly" Democratic, a minority in a virtually all-white rural Republican community. (There was only one black family in his community, and Jackson never experienced segregation firsthand until he moved to Washington, D.C., in 1934.) His family was also Presbyterian, although they were not regular churchgoers like their neighbors. He was later introduced to the Eastern philosophy of theosophy and other universalist faiths of spiritual colonies in late nineteenth-century upstate New York, like Harmonia, six miles south of Jamestown.[3]

Tolerant of others but staunchly independent, Jackson recalled, his family largely lived "independent of community life" and "never looked to others for support or even companionship." In a candid oral history interview, he described his family as having "a certain detachment from other people, a certain self-reliance and self-dependence in them that did not care very much what other people thought, or did, or said. . . . They were individualists of the strongest kind . . . [and] were self-sufficient and self-reliant, believed it was up to them to take care of themselves, sought no help and taught, insofar as they consciously taught anything, thrift, industry, and self-reliance."[4]

Jackson was even more revealing about the influences on his early life when he drafted (but never completed) an autobiography. In it, he recalled growing up in a different America—one reminiscent of the nineteenth century in which communities were small, rural, and revolved around strong and self-supporting Yankee farmers. That life had quickly receded after World War I; then, in the years after World War II, it had become transformed by increasing urbanization and the growth of a national integrated economy, oriented toward the accumulation of wealth, along with greater

Frewsburg, New York, 1908. Courtesy of the Fenton Historical Center

social stratification. His reflections are worth quoting because they reveal the complexity of his thought and sense of being torn between "two worlds" throughout his life:[5]

I have lived much of my life in a time and an environment that was truly and deeply democratic—democratic in an economic and social as well as in a political sense. That kind of society has largely passed, and I am from the last generation to have had that experience and to have felt the influence of that kind of democracy. The great change in the life I knew dates from World War I. Before that we lived in a fool's paradise perhaps—but it was the nearest Paradise that most of us ever knew.

Really fundamentally democratic life existed in this country only in communities made up of small, self-sufficient, family-operated farms. These predominated in a belt extending from the coasts of New England through New York, Pennsylvania and Ohio and into the northern Mississippi Valley. . . . The farms of which I speak had rarely over two hundred acres and usually about half that. . . . The design was to be self-sufficient, . . . to depend on markets for cash as little as need be, resorting to them mainly to dispose of surplus above farm needs. Those farms provided a living and a way of life. Their owners were both producer and consumer; they were labor and capital in a unit. . . . The source of well being on these farms was the labor of the family applied to the soil. No great accumulation is possible in this economy and none was expected. . . . Our general level of existence was to be independently poor.

Looking back, even as he was personally driven and rose to the height of the legal profession, Jackson observed: "Our statesmen, lawyers, judges, and leaders no longer come from this socially classless society. They come, instead, from one side or the other of the railroad tracks, often with bitterness from the wrong side or superciliousness from the right side. No longer do they come from homes where they were taught respect both for labor and for property which it produces." By contrast, he was comfortable with the "rugged individualism" of the late nineteenth century. As he said in a letter to his biographer, he was "an individualist of the school of [Ralph Waldo] Emerson. Self-reliance, self-help and independence of other people I believe to be the basis of character and essential to success."[6]

After graduating from Frewsburg High School in 1909, he took a daily trolley five days a week for a year to attend Jamestown's high school, from which he graduated in 1910. There, he was on the debate team and greatly influenced by two teachers, Mary Willard and Milton J. Fletcher. They introduced him to the classics and taught history and economics; they also encouraged him to go to law school. After graduation, over the objections of his father, who wanted him to become a doctor, Jackson began an apprenticeship with Mott.

Although Jackson did not go to college, he was not "a rare exception, having become a lawyer without attending law school."[7] In fact, he attended Albany Law School for a year, and along with his first year as an apprentice, he met the school's requirements for its two-year degree. Jackson was not yet twenty-one years old, and under the school's charter, he was therefore given a diploma of graduation, instead of a degree, in 1912. Years later, in 1941 he delivered Albany Law School's commencement address and was awarded an LL.B. degree, and another decade later the law school conferred an honorary LL.D. degree upon him.

While in Albany Jackson also regularly listened to oral arguments before the state's highest court, the New York Court of Appeals, widely considered among the nation's finest tribunals, in no small measure because of the quality of advocacy of the New York bar. This increased his zeal for advocacy and debate. After the year, he returned to Mott's law office for another year before passing the New York bar exam.[8]

Jackson largely learned the skills of lawyering through apprenticeship and self-study, like most members of the Court throughout the nineteenth century. Roosevelt never completed law school but passed a bar exam. His first appointee to the Court, Justice Hugo L. Black, had a law degree from the University of Alabama but had not gone to college. Roosevelt's second appointee, Justice Stanley Reed, attended Columbia and the University of Virginia law schools but did not graduate. Neither did Justice James Byrnes.

Jamestown, New York, 1909. Courtesy of the Fenton Historical Center

Other justices that Jackson argued before and joined on the bench did have degrees from prestigious schools: Chief Justice Harlan F. Stone and Justice William O. Douglas had both graduated from Columbia, and Justice Felix Frankfurter had graduated from Harvard. With the exception of Chief Justice Fred Vinson, whose degree was from Centre College, President Harry Truman's appointees were also graduates of distinguished schools: Harold Burton graduated from Harvard, Tom C. Clark from the University of Texas, and Sherman Minton from Yale. Still, it was not until 1957 (after

Jackson's death) that all nine sitting justices had formal law degrees. Jackson was thus not exceptional in this regard. For Roosevelt and Truman, personal friendship and rewarding party faithful and liberals—liberals from across the broad spectrum of the New Deal coalition—were more important in making judicial appointments than their nominees' legal backgrounds.[9]

In private practice and later in the government, Jackson continued to relish advocacy. As he once explained, "I like the combat. I always liked the underdog's side, but I had no great emotion about it and no conviction that the underdog is always right, like some people think. . . . My people never looked down on anybody; never had any bitter experiences; I never needed anything that I didn't have. I was never a crusader. I just liked a good fight."[10] While taking pride in being a "country lawyer," his legal practice in fact included banks, corporations, railroads, and wealthy individuals. Yet the legal practice was actually built on a diverse clientele of individuals and businesses. None of them, he estimated, made up more than 5 percent of his income. He found that gratifying for it "laid the foundation of financial independence which is an important asset in public office, relieving one of fear of loss of office and contributing a general sense of security."[11]

He amassed considerable wealth in Jamestown, and his legal reputation grew even greater after moving to the District of Columbia and joining Roosevelt's administration in the Department of Justice. One of his earliest cases commanding national attention was the successful prosecution of millionaire Andrew Mellon for tax evasion. Later he would take a year's leave from the high bench to serve as chief prosecutor at the Nuremberg war crimes trial of Nazi leaders (1945–1946), the first war crimes trial. His opening and closing arguments commanded worldwide attention.

Even before becoming solicitor general, Jackson had argued fourteen cases before the Court. As solicitor general and attorney general, he argued another twenty-five cases, winning nineteen. Including rearguments, he appeared before the Court forty-four times.[12] He cherished serving as solicitor general, claiming it was "the most enjoyable period of my whole life,"[13] though he likewise felt serving as Nuremberg's chief prosecutor was "infinitely more important than my work on the Supreme Court."[14]

Unquestionably a skilled advocate, he was clear, concise, confident, relaxed, and invariably commanded a "bird's-eye view" of cases. He was so outstanding that Justice Brandeis reportedly said he should be "Solicitor General for life."[15] He nonetheless remained an ambitious loner. As one of his assistants in the solicitor general's office, and later a federal judge, Charles E. Wyzanski Jr., observed: "He never had a team nor did he ever evoke that kind of team loyalty in spite of the admiration of everybody who played with him had for him as a player."[16] Another assistant, Paul Freund, agreed, fondly remembering his "gift of phrase" and quick wit during oral arguments.[17] In short, Jackson wrote and argued with grace, lucidity, and clarity; he also had a flair for turning a phrase and drawing on his command of literary classics.

Moreover, Jackson never participated in moot courts (as most attorneys now regularly do), and he rarely even discussed preparations in advance of oral arguments. He maintained a disciplined, hardworking pace that most attorneys today would find exceptionally grueling; he once argued seven cases in ten days. As a result, Jackson ranked among the most notable members of the Court's bar in the twentieth century, including John W. Davis (1873–1955), who argued a record 140 cases and defended segregated schools in South Carolina's companion case to *Brown v. Board*.[18]

Along with relishing advocacy, Jackson invariably celebrated the "country lawyer," the solo practitioner. He lamented how in the early twentieth century legal practice was moving toward large corporate law firms, along with greater specialization, as well as toward more law schools.[19] The experience of learning law through apprenticeship and in a generalist practice, he thought, taught much about "the structure of society and how its groups interlock and interact, because [the lawyer] lives in a community so small that he can keep it all in view." Accordingly, the country lawyer understood "how disordered and hopelessly unstable [society] would be without law." For him, law was "like a religion, and its practice was more than a means of support; it was a mission."[20]

As a young attorney active in Democratic politics, Jackson stood out in Jamestown's Republican Party–dominated community. Yet that never hurt his legal practice. Years later, he remained an outsider inside Franklin Delano Roosevelt's Ivy League–dominated inner Democratic circle. As he reflected,[21]

> I was never strictly a New Dealer in the sense of belonging to the crowd of young college men that came to Washington and formed a sort of clique. I wasn't a member of the so-called "brain trust." I never even went to college. Neither was I one of the political group, for I never had served in the political national committee, run for office, had a political following or any of that sort of thing. I was pretty much outside of all those groups and yet friendly with many of the members of all of them.

In sum, although Jackson grew up in rural New York and rose to the top of the legal profession, he never forgot his roots, all the while ambitiously pursuing legal and political acclaim. He remained "by temperament an individualist,"[22] driven, disciplined, and self-reliant.

On the high bench, Justice Jackson was no less independent. He was neither a team player nor concerned about building coalitions. Indeed, he rarely went to lunch with his brethren on oral argument days. He once told a law clerk that all Chief Justice Vinson wanted to talk about was baseball and bridge.[23] His former law clerk and later justice and chief justice (1972–2005), William H. Rehnquist, remembered him as "maintaining throughout his life a sturdy independence of view [that] took nothing on someone else's say-so."[24] As Jackson explained, "The court functions in a way that is pleasing to an individualist. Each justice has his own office and his own staff. It's a completely independent unit."[25] Not surprisingly, he found life in the marble temple most congenial, even though he often warred with friends and foes on the bench.

In his short time on the bench, Justice Jackson delivered 154 opinions announcing the opinion of the Court, 46 concurring opinions, 115 dissenting opinions, and another 15 separate opinions concurring and dissenting in part.[26] Among his most notable opinions for the Court was *Wickard v. Filburn* (1942).[27] Writing for the Court, Jackson again transcended the localism of his farming heritage in defending the New Deal vision for the government's role in leading a national economic recovery from the Great Depression. He was always more a small "d," rather than a big "D," Democrat. In *Wickard,* he confidently upheld the Agricultural Adjustment Act of 1938, a key piece of New Deal legislation authorizing the executive branch to set quotas for farmers' crops—crops entirely grown and consumed on individual farms—in order to stabilize prices in the country. In affirming Congress's broad power to regulate interstate commerce under Article I of the Constitution, and the aggregation principle underlying a national economic common market, *Wickard* underscored the post-1937 Roosevelt Court's deference to Congress over national economic regulation. Moreover, *Wickard* stood the test of time, even though the Court under Chief Justices Warren E. Burger (1969–1986), William H. Rehnquist (1986–2005), and John G. Roberts Jr. (2005–) later moved in the direction of curbing such assertions of congressional power.[28]

No less memorable are his opinions striking down compulsory flag-salute statutes in *West Virginia State Board of Education v. Barnette* (1943);[29] concurring with a still widely cited pragmatic analysis of presidential power in the famous "Steel Seizure case," *Youngstown Sheet & Tube Co. v. Sawyer* (1952);[30] and dissenting from the majority's upholding of the government's relocation and internment of Japanese Americans during World War II.[31]

Justice Jackson's opinions from the bench remain widely admired, no less than his oral advocacy and extrajudicial writings. His style, Freund ob-

Franklin Delano Roosevelt and Jackson just after taking the judicial oath, July 11, 1941. Courtesy of the Library of Congress

served, was "artistry. He had style to delight, grace and power of expression to captivate . . . [along with gusto] for the swordplay of words."[32] Philip Kurland, a University of Chicago Law School professor who had clerked for Justice Frankfurter and who later planned a biography of Jackson, likewise praised his work as "probably the best writing that a Justice of the Supreme Court has ever produced."[33] One of Jackson's own law clerks characterized his writing as "incisive and effective. He did not employ purple prose or picturesque language. His strength was in his ability to utilize clear, expressive, distinctive language appropriate to the particular occasion."[34] Jackson was "gifted and beguiling," "ineluctably charming," a "naturalist." In Justice Frankfurter's words, "He wrote as he talked, and he talked as he felt. The fact that his opinions were written talk made them as lively as the liveliness of his talk."[35]

His literary flair and the ability to turn a phrase have rarely been matched on the Court. In his first term on the Court, for instance, the Court struck down California's statute making it a misdemeanor for anyone knowingly to bring or assist a nonresident indigent into the state.[36] The state aimed during the Great Depression to keep out Midwestern dust bowl indigents. The majority invalidated the law for imposing a burden on interstate commerce. But in his first opinion, concurring with the Court's ruling, Jackson contended the decision should rest on the "almost forgotten" Fourteenth Amendment's privileges and immunities clause. The amendment's recognition of the right of citizenship included the right to travel. Drawing on ancient and more recent times, he succinctly stated, "If national citizenship means less than this, it means nothing." He reminded the Court and the country that "the power of citizenship as a shield against oppression was widely known from the example of Paul's Roman citizenship, which sent the centurion scurrying to his higher-ups with the message: 'Take heed what thou doest: for this man is a Roman.'" Unless the Court was willing to say citizenship means at least that much, he concluded, "then our heritage of constitutional privileges and immunities is only a promise to the ear to be broken to the hope, a teasing illusion like a munificent bequest in a pauper's will."

Throughout his career, he was an active speaker, campaigner, and writer.[37] The year he was appointed to the Court, his first book, *The Struggle for Judicial Supremacy: A Study of a Crisis in American Power Politics* (1941), appeared. The book was written while he served as solicitor general and attorney general, and it reviewed and challenged the Court's pre-1937 defense of the old constitutional order against the rising progressive political tide and the battle over Roosevelt's Court-packing proposal to increase the number of justices from nine to fifteen in order to secure a majority favorable to upholding New Deal programs. The lesson Jackson drew from that epic battle and the Court's "switch in time that saved nine" (further discussed in Chapter 2)—abandoning its jurisprudence of laissez-faire capitalism—was that if the Court gets too far out of step with the country or goes too fast, it will experience a backlash. Although judicial supremacy remained central to the rule of law, he understood that the power of judicial review in the long run rests, in the words of Chief Justice Edward Douglas White (1910–1921), "solely upon the approval of a free people."[38]

While on the bench, among other extrajudicial publications, he published *Full Faith and Credit: The Lawyer's Clause of the Constitution* (1946), and two books on the Nuremberg trials, *The Case Against the Nazi War Criminals* (1946) and *The Nürnberg Case* (1947). In addition in the early 1950s, he worked on a manuscript on Roosevelt that appeared posthumously, *That Man: An Insider's Portrait of Franklin D. Roosevelt* (with John Q. Barrett; 2003). Another book, *The Supreme Court in the American System of Government* (1955), was published shortly after his death in 1954, at age sixty-two. It was prepared as three lectures on the Supreme Court: (1) "as a Unit of Government," (2) "as a Law Court," and (3) "as a Political Institution." They were to be given as the Godkin lectures at Harvard in 1954–1955. Significantly, they were also written in the spring and summer of 1954, while he was working on the last draft of his unpublished opinion for *Brown v. Board*. That book thus reflects his final thinking about the role of the Court as a legal and a political institution, as well as implicitly his ultimate reflections on its role in the desegregation controversy.

The Supreme Court in the American System of Government was a kind of bookend to the earlier *Struggle for Judicial Supremacy*. In both, as in his unpublished *Brown* opinion, he acknowledged that major constitutional cases and controversies are inexorably "political." As he candidly put it: "Any decision that declares the law under which a people must live or which affects the powers of their institutions is in a very real sense political."[39] At the same time, he never doubted when the Court's rulings went too far or too fast—whether in the direction of waging a rearguard action (as against the New Deal before 1937) or fighting in the vanguard (as with rulings like *Brown*)—the Court invites confrontation and popular demands for curbing its power. That was the lesson of the 1937 "constitutional crisis" and the basis for his profound concerns about the Court's taking the lead on school desegregation. Indeed, recalling Roosevelt's battle over the Court, he emphasized that "not one of the basic power conflicts which precipitated the Roosevelt struggle against the judiciary has been eliminated or settled, and the old conflict between the branches of Government remains, ready to break out again whenever the provocation becomes sufficient."[40] For that reason, he repeatedly warned against the Court seizing "the initiative in shaping the policy of the law."[41]

When it came to constitutional interpretation, Jackson was neither an "absolutist" nor an uncompromising libertarian, like Justices Black and Douglas.[42] Rather, like the others on the Roosevelt Court, he was a legal realist and was not averse to the liberal legalism that swept legal education and the profession in the first half of the twentieth century.[43] American legal realism debunked the traditional view, as Holmes put it, that judges are mere "oracles of the law"[44] who discover and declare law as "a brooding omnipresence in the sky."[45] Instead, legal realism taught that judges in fact "make law" and that the law has an indeterminacy or underdeterminacy. As Chief Justice Stone, a Republican and considered a judicial conservative, reflected in a letter to Princeton's constitutional historian, Edward Corwin, "I always thought the real villain in the play was [Sir William] Blackstone, who gave to both lawyers and judges artificial notions of the law which, when applied to constitutional interpretation made the Constitution a mechanical and inadequate instrument of government."[46]

Justice Frankfurter elaborated (although rarely publicly articulated) that view in a rather snide letter to his frequent antagonist and the standard-bearer of "absolute literalism," Justice Black:[47]

I think one of the evil features, a very evil one, about all this assumption that judges only find the law and don't make it, often becomes the evil of a lack of candor. By covering up the law-making function of judges, we miseducate the people and fail to bring out into the open the real responsibility of judges for what they do. . . .

That phrase "judicial legislation" has become ever since a staple of a term of condemnation. I, too, am opposed to judicial legislation in its invidious sense, but I deem equally mischievous—because founded on an untruth and an impossible aim—the notion that judges merely announce the law which they find and do not themselves inevitably have a share in the law-making. The difficulty comes from arguing in terms of absolutes when the matter at hand is conditioned by circumstances, is contingent upon the everlasting problem of how far is too far and how much is too much.

For Frankfurter, the issue was not whether judges make law, but when, how, and how much. He concluded by quoting Justice Holmes's quip: "'They can do so only interstitially; they are confined from the molar to molecular motions.' I used to say to my students that legislatures make law wholesale, judges retail."

Justice Jackson was even more publicly candid about judges making law and rendering political decisions than Frankfurter and some later justices. As Justice Antonin Scalia (1986–2016), for example, though an ardent proponent of a jurisprudence of "original intent" or "original textualism," was once compelled to acknowledge: "I am not so naive (nor do I think our forebears were) as to be unaware that judges in a real sense 'make' law. But they make it *as judges make it,* which is to say *as though* they were 'finding' it—discerning what the law *is,* rather than decreeing what it is today *changed to,* or what it will *tomorrow* be."[48]

Moreover, unlike Scalia and some other justices, Jackson did not seek reassurance with purported reliance on the framers' "original intent" or the pretense of "strict constructionism." His widely cited concurring opinion in the "Steel Seizure Case" remains illustrative and highly regarded. There, Justice Black, writing for the Court, rejected President Truman's claim of inherent power to seize steel mills in the interest of "national security" during the Korean War in order to prevent the stoppage of steel production which might hinder war efforts. Jackson, however, distanced his pragmatic position from Black's absolute "literalism," just as he also did with respect to interpreting the scope of the Fourteenth Amendment's due process clause.[49] Hence, in *Youngstown Sheet & Tube,* he observed: "Just what our forefathers did envision, or would have envisioned had they foreseen modern conditions, must be divined from materials almost as enigmatic as the dreams

Joseph was called upon to interpret for Pharaoh. A century and a half of partisan debate and scholarly speculation yields no net result but only supplies more or less apt quotations from respected sources on each side of any question. They largely cancel each other." Not to leave it at that, tongue in cheek, he cited contradictory statements on presidential power by Alexander Hamilton versus James Madison, Professor William Howard Taft versus President Theodore Roosevelt, and Professor Taft versus President Taft. In his unpublished opinion in *Brown,* he would likewise find the record of the drafting and ratification of the Fourteenth Amendment ambiguous and inconclusive, revealing little definitive except that it was "a passionate, confused, and deplorable era."

Claims to "strict constructionism" or "literalism" were deemed not merely indeterminative but often misleading. Jackson ridiculed such claims for actually leading to the "loose and irresponsible use of adjectives [that] colors all non-legal and much legal discussion of presidential powers. 'Inherent' powers, 'implied' powers, 'incidental' powers, 'plenary' powers, 'war' powers and 'emergency' powers are used, often interchangeably and without fixed or ascertainable meanings."[50] In addition, in his pragmatic and prudential fashion, he emphasized that governing "does not and cannot conform to judicial definitions of the power of any of its branches based on isolated clauses or even single Articles torn from context. While the Constitution diffuses power the better to secure liberty, it also contemplates that practice will integrate the dispersed powers into a workable government." Along similar lines, in writings off the bench, Jackson was both a careful literary stylist and an occasionally seemingly unpredictable pragmatic balancer. In his view, as explained in the Godkin lectures, the Court has a crucial "political function" in reconciling competing constitutional values:[51]

> In a society in which rapid changes tend to upset all equilibrium, the Court, without exceeding its own limited powers, must strive to maintain the great system of balances upon which our free government is based. Whether these balances and checks are essential to liberty elsewhere in the world is beside the point; they are indispensable to the society we know. Chief of these balances are: first, between the Executive and Congress; second, between the central government and the states; third, between state and state; fourth, between authority, be it state or national, and the liberty of the citizen, or between the rule of the majority and the rights of the individual.

While principled and always concerned about the role of the Court, Jackson was also pragmatically tactical and strategic in his thinking. As he once candidly explained the use of dissenting opinions often requires distorting precedents and the majority's opinion in order to blunt the force of its ruling, "The technique of the dissenter often is to exaggerate the holding of the Court beyond the meaning of the majority and then to blast away at the excess. So that the poor lawyer with a similar case does not know whether the majority meant what it seemed to say or what the minority said it meant."[52]

Furthermore, he was especially frank about "how thin is the line that separates law and politics."[53] In the Godkin lectures as well as his unpublished opinion in *Brown,* he elaborated by quoting Justice Benjamin Cardozo (1932–1938) about the difference between sitting on the New York Court of Appeals and on the Supreme Court: "[The New York Court of Appeals] is a great common law court; its problems are lawyers' problems. But the Supreme Court is occupied chiefly with statutory construction—which no man can make interesting—and with politics." Justice Cardozo, according to Jackson, acknowledged that the Court was a political institution, not in the "sense of partisanship but in the sense of policy-making."[54] So too, in the chapter "Government by Lawsuit" in *The Struggle for Judicial Supremacy,* did Jackson acknowledge the limitations of lawsuits and legal procedures for forging public policy while at the same time embracing the inevitability of exercising such power in deciding constitutional controversies.

Jackson's understanding of the intersection of law and politics thus differed significantly from Frankfurter's. Their differences bear emphasizing because both remain known for advocating judicial self-restraint. As New York Court of Appeals judge Charles D. Breitel once perceptively observed, "The two of them often reached the same views and the same conclusions and the same results in cases, but by entirely different ways."[55] Both agreed that constitutional law, in Frankfurter's words, "is not at all a science, but applied politics."[56] Likewise, in the Godkin lectures, Jackson candidly admonished: "Only those heedless of legal history can deny that in construing the Constitution the Supreme Court from time to time makes new constitutional law or alters the law that has been. And it is idle to say that this is merely the ordinary process of interpretation."[57]

Still, they did not share a "common eye," and they therefore drew different conclusions about the role of the Court. How could they, Frankfurter noted, given "the great differences in [their] backgrounds"? One "was a child of the country" and rural America, the other of "the big city" and an immigrant. One was self-trained, the other Harvard educated. More importantly, one took great pride in his celebrated art of advocacy, while the other was a self-consumed academic—a lifelong professor. As Frankfurter concluded in a rather self-serving tribute after Jackson's death, "The function of the advocate is not to enlarge the intellectual horizon. His task is to seduce, to seize the mind for a predetermined end, not to explore paths to truths. There can be no doubt that Jackson was specially endowed as an advocate."[58]

On the bench, Frankfurter's brand of "judicial self-restraint" was exemplified in championing jurisdictional "standing doctrines" such as mootness, ripeness, and "political questions."[59] He did so in order to delay or avoid deciding cases that might spark political controversy. Not surprisingly, he pushed for delays in deciding *Brown* and other segregation cases. He perhaps took too seriously and too far his beloved Justice Brandeis's admonition: "The most important thing we do is not doing."[60]

By contrast, while advocating judicial self-restraint, Jackson openly admitted what the Court was doing and why—namely, resolving conflicts in constitutional politics by balancing competing interests. Even before going to the Court, Jackson diverged from Frankfurter's stance. In his first book, published the year he joined the Court, Jackson took aim at an essay written by Frankfurter while still at Harvard before his own appointment to the Court. In "The Supreme Court of the United States" (1939), Frankfurter praised "elaborate and often technical doctrines for postponing if not avoiding constitutional adjudication." He viewed "prolonged uncertainty [as] less harmful than 'the mischief of premature judicial intervention,'" by which the "Court's prestige within its proper sphere would be inevitably impaired."[61] Jackson responded to the contrary:

> Must we choose between *"premature judicial intervention"* on the one hand and *"technical doctrines for postponing if not avoiding constitutional adjudication"* on the other? If that were our choice I would think Mr. Frankfurter had chosen wisely. But need we be gored by either horn of such a dilemma? Can we not establish a procedure for determination of substantial constitutional questions at the suit of real parties in interest which will avoid prematurity or advisory opinions on the one hand and also avoid technical doctrines for postponing inevitably decisions? Should we not at least try to lay inevitable constitutional controversies to early rest?[62]

Jackson's and Frankfurter's views on the role of the Court and exercise of judicial review were subsequently put into bold relief in the second flag-salute decision, *West Virginia State Board of Education v. Barnette* (1943). There, writing for the Court, Jackson overruled *Minersville School District v. Gobitis* (1940).[63] In *Gobitis,* Frankfurter had delivered the Court's opinion, with only Justice Stone dissenting, upholding compulsory flag salutes at the beginning of each school day over the First Amendment objections of Jehovah's Witnesses. Within three years after *Gobitis,* Roosevelt elevated Justice Stone to chief justice and appointed Justices Jackson and Byrnes; the latter was replaced a year later by former liberal law school professor Wiley Rutledge. Justices Black, Douglas, and Frank Murphy, who had joined Frankfurter's majority in *Gobitis,* switched their positions in *Barnette.* Now chief justice and commanding a majority, Stone assigned the Court's opinion to Jackson. Notably, Jackson based the Court's decision on the First Amendment guarantee for freedom of speech, along with religious freedom. He eloquently explained:

> The very purpose of a Bill of Rights was to withdraw certain subjects from the vicissitudes of political controversy, to place them beyond the reach of majorities and officials and to establish them as legal principles to be applied by the courts. One's right to liberty and property, to free speech, a free press, freedom of worship and assembly, and other fundamental rights may not be submitted. . . .
>
> If there is any fixed star in our constitutional constellation, it is that no official, high or petty, can prescribe what shall be orthodox in politics, nationalism, religion, or other matters of opinion or force citizens to confess by word or act their faith therein. If there are any circumstances which permit an exception, they do not now occur to us.
>
> We think the action of the local authorities in compelling the flag salute and pledge transcends constitutional limitations on their power and invades the sphere of intellect and spirit which it is the purpose of the First Amendment to our Constitution to reserve from all official control.[64]

Not to be outdone, dissenting Frankfurter issued (ironically) an impassioned, highly personal appeal to his ideal of judicial impartiality and "self-restraint" that warrants quoting:

> One who belongs to the most vilified and persecuted minority in history is not likely to be insensible to the freedoms guaranteed by our Constitution. Were my purely personal attitude relevant I should wholeheartedly associate myself with the general libertarian views in the Court's opinion. . . . But as judges we are neither Jew nor Gentile, neither Catholic nor agnostic. We owe equal attachment to the Constitution and are equally bound by our judicial obligations whether we derive our citizenship from the earliest or the latest immigrants to these shores. . . . The duty of a judge who must decide which of two claims before the Court shall prevail, that of a State to enact and enforce laws within its general competence or that of an individual to refuse obedience because of the demands of his conscience, is not that of the ordinary person. It can never be emphasized too much that one's own opinion about the wisdom or evil of a law should be excluded altogether when one is doing one's duty on the bench.[65]

Jackson would have none of that. He ridiculed Frankfurter's claim that "national unity [inspired by mandatory saluting of the flag] is the basis of national security." With his typical flair, Jackson countered, "Freedom to differ is not limited to things that do not matter much. That would be a mere shadow of freedom. The test of its substance is the right to differ as to things that touch the heart of the existing order." He cautioned against Frankfurter's uncritical deference to legislative majorities by recalling the Romans' attempt to ban Christianity and, alluding to the more recent experience in Nazi Germany, observed: "Those who begin coercive elimination of dissent soon find themselves exterminating dissenters. Compulsory unification of opinion achieves only the unanimity of the graveyard."[66]

PRINCIPLED PRAGMATISM

Despite his soaring prose in *Barnette*, Jackson was by no means a libertarian, unlike like his and Frankfurter's frequent foes, Justices Black and Douglas. In *Barnette*, he did not single out the Jehovah's Witnesses for special treatment because their religious beliefs outweighed all societal interests. Concurring in a decision handed down the same term as *Barnette*, upholding an ordinance forbidding the ringing of household doorbells, even for religious purposes, by the Jehovah's Witnesses, Jackson made his view clear: "The First Amendment grew out of an experience which taught that society cannot trust the conscience of a majority to keep its religious zeal within the limits that a free society can tolerate. I do not think it any more intended to leave the conscience of a minority to fix its limits. Civil government cannot let any group ride roughshod over others simply because their 'consciences' tell them to do so."[67] In opposition to the "absolutism" of Justices Black and Douglas, he underscored the importance of balancing individuals' interests against governmental authority by weighing "the realities of life in those communities."[68] Moreover, he did so in other decisions rejecting religious minorities' objections, for example, to ordinances forbidding children from selling religious literature on the city street.[69] Rather than simply deferring to majoritarian democracy, as Frankfurter was so inclined to do, Jackson did so out of a nostalgic sense of community and democratic self-governance in rural America.

In addition, Jackson astutely understood that the reach of constitutional principles must be tempered by pragmatism. In another notable example, he dissented from Justice Douglas's opinion for the Court, overturning a conviction for breach of peace and extending First Amendment protection to an inflammatory anti-Semitic speech criticizing racial groups before a large crowd in an auditorium that police believed would incite violence. In *Terminiello v. Chicago* (1949),[70] Jackson famously observed, "If the Court does not temper its doctrinaire logic with a little practical wisdom, it will convert the constitutional Bill of Rights into a suicide pact." In such circumstances, like Justice Oliver Wendell Holmes (1902–1932), Jackson would have weighed the individual's freedom of expression against the interests of the community, and decide whether there was a "clear and present danger."[71]

As their opinions in *Barnette* highlight, Frankfurter's and Jackson's understanding of judicial self-restraint differed fundamentally in the deference accorded to legislative majorities. Their rival understandings of judicial self-restraint registered not only differences in candor but ultimately in their particular visions of the role of the Court. Frankfurter's far more deferential stance toward the operation and outcomes of majoritarian democracy led him to embrace the "passive virtues"[72] of the exercise of judicial review. Majoritarian democracy for Jackson, however, remained much more subject to constitutional constraints. Consequently, for him, the Court plays a pivotal role in overseeing constitutional balances between the majority and minorities. In other words, sometimes the Court had "a duty to decide"[73]— even politically explosive controversies like that presented in *Brown v. Board of Education*.

Along with his literary flair and commitment to pragmatically balancing competing interests, Jackson was inclined to quote, paraphrase, or draw allusions to classical literary works in support of his positions and when challenging others on the Court. Dissenting in *Everson v. Board of Education* (1947),[74] for instance, he criticized the reasoning of Justice Black's opinion for the Court by quoting the poem "Don Juan" (1819) by British Romantic poet Lord Byron (1788–1824). In *Everson* Justice Black invoked the "high wall" metaphor of the separation of church and state in holding that, under the Fourteenth Amendment, the First Amendment (dis)establishment clause limits the states, no less than the federal government. Yet his opinion for a bare majority concluded that a New Jersey program of paying for the transportation of students to parochial schools did not run afoul of the wall of separation. Instead, busing was an "indirect benefit" and primarily benefited the children. Jackson and three other dissenters, however, maintained that there should be a "strict separation" between government and religion. In his words, "The case which irresistibly comes to mind as the most fitting precedent is that of Julia who, according to Byron's reports, 'whispering "I will ne'er consent,"—consented.'"

In another case, Jackson mischievously quoted "Lycidas" (1637) by John Milton (1608–1674). Regarding the judicial mind and his colleagues, Jackson wrote, "If fame—a good public name—is as Milton said the 'last infirmity of a noble mind,' it is frequently the first infirmity of a mediocre one."[75] Years later, he drove home the need for judicial humility, reminiscent of the position laid out in *The Struggle for Judicial Supremacy*, with the quip, "We [judges] are not final because we are infallible, but we are infallible only because we are final."[76]

Notably, Jackson frequently and fondly drew on a poem by Matthew Arnold (1822–1888), a late Victorian writer. He does so in the opening sentence of the draft opinion prepared for, but not delivered, in *Brown v. Board*. "Since the close of the Civil war," Jackson wrote, quoting Arnold, "the United States has been 'hesitating between two worlds—one dead, the other powerless to be born.'" In addition, the title of chapter 3 of *The Struggle for Judicial Supremacy* is "The Court Hesitates Between Two Worlds." Arnold's poem, "Stanzas from the Grande Chartreuse" (1855), reads,

> Thinking of his own gods, a Greek
> In pity and mournful awe might stand
> Before some fallen Runic stone—
> For both were faiths, and both are gone.
>
> Wandering between two worlds, one dead,
> The other powerless to be born,
> With nowhere yet to rest my head,
> Like these, on earth I wait forlorn.[77]

Undoubtedly Jackson found the metaphor appealing for a number of reasons. It was also apt in a number of ways. The Civil War failed to resolve the country's racial problems. Slavery ended, yet segregation remained. Desegregation appeared only dimly on the political horizon, with integration far beyond that. Born in the nineteenth century and confronting *Brown* in the mid-twentieth century, Jackson looked backward, but also forward to the twenty-first century. The nineteenth century was the age of "separate but equal," constitutionally sanctioned by the Court in *Plessy v. Ferguson* (1896).[78] *Brown* presented a historic turning point, the most controversial decision in the twentieth century. Jackson foresaw the pushback—decades of resistance and potential for disaster by judicial decree comparable to, if not surpassing, the 1937 constitutional crisis—a crisis self-inflicted by the Court during its pre-1937 opposition to the New Deal and other progressive legislation. Still, he looked beyond to the inexorable changes transforming the country. He foresaw, as it were, a future that would include the likes of Tiger Woods and President Barack Obama.

CHAPTER TWO

Nine Scorpions in a Bottle

Jackson moved into the new building housing the modern Supreme Court as Roosevelt's eighth appointee. Chief Justice William Howard Taft (1921–1930) envisioned a building symbolizing the Court's institutional independence and prestige. When he lobbied Congress to fund the project, however, other justices balked.[1] Justice Louis D. Brandeis (1916–1939) thought it more important than symbolism for the Court to sit, as it had for three quarters of a century, at the center of the Capitol, in the old Senate chamber. Brandeis and others also abhorred the opulence of the design, which they called "the Taj Mahal."[2] Taft died before the building's completion in 1935, and Chief Justice Charles Evans Hughes (1930–1941) later referred to it as simply "a place to hang my hat." Justice George Sutherland (1921–1938) reportedly remarked that the justices "will look like nine beetles in the Temple of Karnak."[3] Although the Hughes Court held its sessions there, all the justices except Sutherland and Owen Roberts continued to work in their home offices. Even after Harlan F. Stone was elevated from associate to chief justice in 1941, he continued working primarily at home. Not until the Vinson Court (1946–1953) did all nine justices regularly work in the Court's new temple of justice, behind the Capitol on One First Street.

From the outside, the marble temple symbolizes the Court's institutional independence and the stability of the law. Ironically, though, New Dealers such as Jackson were battling a politically conservative bloc on the Court over its invalidation of Roosevelt's early New Deal programs. Roosevelt's Court-packing plan, which would have expanded the number of justices from nine to fifteen in order to secure a favorable majority, failed after the Court's "switch in time that saved nine" in May 1937. Nevertheless, it signaled the end of the old constitutional order.[4]

In *The Struggle for Judicial Supremacy,* Jackson reflected on the 1937 constitutional crisis and how to reconcile judicial review with democratic governance. He found no reason to believe in a permanent reconciliation. Even with the president's power of judicial appointments, many justices only become disappointments for their presidential benefactors. "Why is it," he wondered, "that the Court influences appointees more consistently than appointees influence the Court?" Institutional and procedural pressures, he concluded, push "towards a conservativism which only the most alert Justices will sense and only the most hardy will overcome."[5]

During his last term on the bench, however, Jackson offered a contrasting view. In the first of three posthumously published Harvard Godkin lectures, he shared his final thoughts on the Court's internal operations, which he thought actually operated like nine little law firms.[6] "The fact is that the Court functions less as one deliberative body than as nine, each Justice working largely in isolation. . . . These working methods tend to cultivate a highly individualistic rather than a group viewpoint."[7] Always a lone wolf, he relished the idea that "the court functions in a way that is pleasing to an individualist. . . . A justice might be in this building and work for a week and never see any associate."[8]

Subsequent justices would sound the same refrain. Justice John M. Harlan (1955–1971), who succeeded Jackson on the bench, likewise observed, "Decisions of the Court are not the product of an institutional approach. . . . They are the result of merely a tally of individual votes cast [at conference]."[9] When Potter Stewart (1958–1981) joined the bench, he expected to find "one law firm with nine partners, if you will, the law clerks being the associates." But Harlan told him, "No, you will find here it is like nine firms, sometimes practicing law against one another."[10] Even Frankfurter emphasized that the Court was "an institution in which every man is his own sovereign."[11] On another occasion, he even dismissed phrases such as "the Court as an institution" and "the Court as a team player" as question-begging clichés.[12]

During Jackson's short tenure, the justices indeed appeared like "nine scorpions in a bottle."[13] That was a fitting characterization because the tradition of institutional opinions for the Court, projecting consensus, was breaking down. Individual opinions— concurring, dissenting, or separate (in part concurring and dissenting) opinions—were on the rise. With the publication of increasing numbers of individual opinions, the norm governing institutional opinions became devalued. Throughout the nineteenth and early twentieth centuries, unanimous opinions announcing the Court's decisions accounted for 80 to 90 percent of all opinions annually handed down. In other words, beginning with the Court under Chief John Marshall (1801–1835), most opinions were unanimous. Very few concurring or dissenting opinions were written. That changed dramatically in the 1930s, when the percentage of unanimous opinions for the Court of the total opinions annually issued declined considerably. This continued through the rest of the century, rarely rising above 50 percent (Figure 2.1).[14] Disagreements within the Court thus became more publicly expressed—and pronounced.[15]

In his pioneering work, *The Roosevelt Court: A Study in Judicial Politics and Values, 1937–1947* (1948), C. Herman Pritchett highlighted the rise of individual opinions that accompanied the arrival of Roosevelt's appointees.

Figure 2.1. Percent of unanimous opinions for the Court of the total opinions issued, 1801–2015. From David M. O'Brien, *Storm Center: The Supreme Court in American Politics,* 11th ed. (W. W. Norton, 2017), 282.

"Looking backward," Pritchett pointed out, "the 1941–42 term was definitely a turning point for the Roosevelt Court." Disagreement rates had increased. The percentage of unanimous opinions for the Court plunged from 81 percent of the total opinions issued in Chief Justice Hughes's last term to 67 percent in Stone's first term as chief justice in 1941. Moreover, the percentage continued to fall sharply throughout Stone's chief justiceship (1941–1946) and persisted throughout the tenure of his successors, Chief Justices Fred Vinson (1946–1953) and Earl Warren (1953–1969), as well as thereafter (as shown in Figure 2.2).[16]

Pritchett offered a number of explanations, but he identified the 1941 term with Stone's debut as chief justice as pivotal. Compared with his predecessor, Stone failed as a task and social leader within the Court.[17] By all accounts, Chief Justice Hughes's photographic memory and personal charisma had made him a respected task and social leader. Although he defended dissenting opinions, Hughes maintained that unanimity was critical for public confidence in the Court's decisions and that dissents were best reserved for exceptional cases.[18] As he once put it to Stone regarding a draft dissent that he himself had written, "I choke a little in swallowing your analysis; still I do not think it would serve any useful purpose to expose my views."[19]

On the other hand, Stone viewed the value of consensus very differently. As an associate justice, he was annoyed with Hughes's running conferences

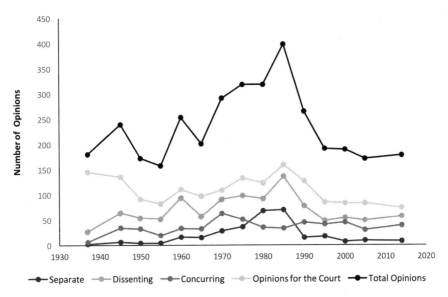

Figure 2.2. Opinion writing, 1937–2015. From David M. O'Brien, *Storm Center: The Supreme Court in American Politics*, 11th ed. (W. W. Norton, 2017), 282.

"much like a drill sergeant."[20] As chief justice, Stone by contrast encouraged lengthy discussions, even at the cost of prolonging conferences. That in turn reinforced divisions and resulted in carrying unfinished business over to another conference. Personally inclined to debate every point, Stone was not disposed to cut short debates erupting between Black and Frankfurter or Jackson. Consequently, as Justice Douglas observed, the justices were "almost in a continuous Conference."[21]

Even Frankfurter, always concerned about the Court's lack of collective deliberation, found Stone's conduct of conference discussions overwhelming. He proposed limiting them to four hours so that "the discussion should be by fresh and not fatigued minds."[22] Although the proposal fell flat, Frankfurter persisted in proposing such rules during the Warren Court in an annual memorandum from 1951 until his last term in 1961.[23] But he succeeded only in further distancing the others.[24] In particular, Douglas protested, "I, for one, could not agree to give anyone any more control over when I vote than over how I vote."[25] Likewise, Black favored flexibility, stressing, "The majority, I suppose, could not by mechanical rules bind individual Justices as to their exercise of their discretion."[26]

Undoubtedly Chief Justice Stone played a part in the erosion of the institutional norm of unanimous opinions for the Court. But there was more to it than that. Concurring opinions, for one thing, were on the rise before Stone's chief justiceship.[27] Also, the proportion of unanimous decisions began dropping during the last four years of the Hughes Court. Notably, this coincided with the arrival of Roosevelt's first five appointees: Black, Reed, Frankfurter, Douglas, and Murphy.[28] The arrival of the New Deal justices brought the full force of American legal realism and liberal legalism to the Court. Roosevelt's appointees not only constituted a majority, but they also embodied the intellectual forces of a generation of progressives revolting against the formalism of the old conservative order. American legal realism, to be sure, was not so much a school of thought as a movement embracing a range of diverse positions on judging and legal reform.[29] Still, legal realism, in acknowledging that justices were making law, made consensus more difficult and raised the premium on justifying individual and collective decisions.

In addition, before 1937, the Court appeared divided between a bare conservative majority and four liberal-leaning dissenters. Afterward, although dominating the post-1937 Court, Roosevelt's appointees were not of one mind. Instead, they almost immediately split into two camps: Frankfurter, Reed, and Jackson stood for judicial restraint, while Black, Douglas, Murphy, and Rutledge pushed toward what many regarded as liberal judicial activism. In time, the justices became further fragmented; they increasingly articulated their disagreements and defended their distinctive views in individual concurring and dissenting opinions.

Neither Chief Justice Stone nor Vinson proved capable of ending the battles on the bench or the appearance of the Court as sharply divided and openly in discord.[30] When the matter of multiple opinions was raised at conference—as well as in the press—not only were Black and Douglas defensive, but also their rival, Frankfurter, explained himself in a two-page letter to Vinson. "I adhere to the view, which Jefferson so convincingly expressed," Frankfurter wrote, "that were it possible to dispose of the business of the Court and to express individual views on constitutional issues that would be most desirable." Vinson responded that his concern was that multiple opinions were often confusing for lower courts and the public. Vinson thanked Frankfurter for the "lecture," adding that he had "misjudged me and set up a strawman to attack." Vinson, underscoring the individualism and isolation accompanying the Court's functioning like nine little law firms in its marble temple, continued, "I would have preferred to have had it face-to-face."[31] Not surprisingly, individual opinions became the new norm. It continues with justices as ideologically opposed as Antonin Scalia (1986–2016) and Ruth Bader Ginsburg (1993–), or even those similarly inclined such as Scalia and Justices Clarence Thomas (1991–) and Samuel Alito (2006–), defending dissenting and concurring opinions.[32]

Against the historical background of the rise of individual opinions and the demise of institutional opinions with their facade of consensus, the Warren Court's unanimity on such a momentous decision as *Brown* inevitably loomed large. The Warren Court's ostensible consensus, though, remains misleading in a number of ways. A kind of myth about the leadership of Chief Justice Warren, for instance, was perpetuated.[33] At the same time, Chief Justice Vinson's reputation was further disparaged. Most significantly, perhaps, the important role of Frankfurter and Jackson in pushing for delay and more deliberation, instead of rushing to judgment and simply tallying votes, also was often underestimated.

On the basis of the accounts reflected in different justices' conference notes and correspondence, some scholars have reinforced the myth. They have speculated that a bare majority in *Brown* might have upheld the doctrine of "separate but equal" (with Vinson, Reed, Frankfurter, Jackson, and Clark in the majority) over four dissenters (Black, Douglas, Burton, and Minton).[34] Alternatively, some have surmised that there were five votes (Black, Douglas, Frankfurter, Burton, and Minton) to invalidate segregated schools, with four possible dissenters (Vinson, Reed, Jackson, and Clark).[35] Still others have contended that without Warren's arrival, the vote might have been 6 to 3 (with Vinson, Reed, and Clark unwilling to find segregation unconstitutional)[36] or split, with four for desegregation (Black, Douglas, Burton, and Minton), two opposed (Vinson and Reed), and three who were "ambivalent" (Frankfurter, Jackson, and Clark).[37]

In light of these competing narratives, Jackson's relationships with the other justices and their internal deliberations remain crucial for understanding his draft opinion and his decision to withhold its publication. Within the context of the Vinson and Warren Courts' deliberations, it becomes clear that the outcome in *Brown* was not "scarcely imaginable," as Frankfurter claimed. Instead, it was virtually "inevitable," as Minton, Clark, and even Reed later recalled.[38] The direction and unanimity of prior Vinson Court desegregation rulings and the justices' prolonged deliberations over *Brown* make this clear. As Frankfurter himself told Harlan, "I do not rate unanimity as high as perhaps all the rest of my brethren do. Indeed, I don't rate it very high except in circumstances like those in the Segregation Cases."[39]

The fact that Jackson never contemplated a dissent is further underlined by the wording and substance of his unpublished opinion. *Brown* would likely have been 8 to 1, with only Justice Reed dissenting, if not unanimous. Indeed, in spite of Frankfurter's expressed fears in correspondence suggesting that *Brown* might have come down to a 6–3 or 5–4 vote, years later in a 1958 letter to Judge Learned Hand, he proclaimed—counterintuitively and self-contradictorily—that the decision would have been unanimous even if

Justice James Byrnes (1941–1942) had remained on the bench (notably after as South Carolina's governor he had vehemently attacked the Court for its ruling in *Brown*).[40] In Frankfurter's words: "On the basis of some of the attitudes that he manifested during the short single term that Jimmy Byrnes was on the Court, I am bold enough to believe that even Byrnes, had he stayed on the Court, would no more have dissented than Reed or Tom Clark dissented."[41]

ROOSEVELT REMAKES THE COURT

During Franklin Delano Roosevelt's first term, a bare conservative majority invalidated most of the early New Deal program. The so-called Four Horsemen—Justices Sutherland, James McReynolds (1914–1941), Pierce Butler (1923–1939), and Willis Van Devanter (1911–1937)—voted together in consistently opposing progressive state and federal regulations, and they regularly arrived at the Court in the same car. At the other end of the spectrum were Justices Stone and Benjamin Cardozo (1932–1938), who followed Brandeis in supporting progressive legislation. Finally, there were Chief Justice Hughes and Justice Roberts (1930–1945), the actual swing votes, though the latter more often cast the crucial fifth vote to strike down progressive legislation. Roberts, however, changed his mind and abandoned the Four Horsemen in *West Coast Hotel v. Parrish* (1937),[42] with the resulting Court's decision to uphold Washington state's minimum wage law. Two weeks later, in *National Labor Relations Board v. Jones & Laughlin Steel Corporation* (1937),[43] Roberts voted to affirm a major piece of New Deal legislation, the National Labor Relations Act.[44]

The Court's 1937 "switch in time that saved nine" was widely speculated to have been due to Roosevelt's Court-packing proposal, announced after Roosevelt's landslide reelection in November 1936. Even though those rulings did not come down until the spring, Roberts in fact had switched his vote at conference in December 1936, two months before Roosevelt's Court-packing plan was announced in February 1937. The switch of a bare majority to uphold progressive state legislation and New Deal programs came after Roosevelt announced his Court-packing plan due to the time it takes to draft opinions for the Court, circulate them to other justices, and for dissenters to write their opinions, before all opinions are finalized. Still, the reversal of the Court's position contributed to the Democratic-controlled Senate's rejection of Roosevelt's plan in May. Moreover, Justice Van Devanter resigned shortly thereafter, at the end of the term, partly because of new legislation permitting justices and judges to retire with full pay at age seventy after fifteen years of service.

It was then that Roosevelt made his first appointment to the Court. He remained angry at the Senate for defeating the Court-packing plan and at the Court for destroying early New Deal programs. Roosevelt thus nominated Senator Hugo L. Black, who had led the unsuccessful fight for the plan to pack the Court. Black had denounced the "judicial usurpation" of power by a bare majority—Justices Butler, Van Devanter, McReynolds, Sutherland, and Roberts. Quoting Chief Justice Hughes's observation that "the Constitution is what the Judges say it is," Black charged that it was more accurate to say "The Constitution is what five of the Supreme Court Judges say it is, and what four of the Supreme Court Judges say it is not."[45]

Roosevelt, recalled Jackson, wanted to "humiliate [the Senate and the Court] at a single stroke by naming Black." Because the Senate would only refuse to confirm one of its own in the most extraordinary circumstances, it had to "swallow hard and approve," Jackson observed. As he further observed, "The Court would be humiliated by having to accept one of its most bitter and unfair critics and one completely alien to the judicial tradition."[46]

Black, born in Clay County, Alabama, in 1886, had always regarded himself as a country boy. After graduating from the University of Alabama, he spent much of his early career in private practice, though always staying active in local Democratic politics. During Senate confirmation hearings on his nomination to the Court, rumors circulated that he had been a member of the Ku Klux Klan in the mid-1920s. At that time, it was essential for Democrats to win election in the Deep South. When evidence of his membership surfaced after the Senate's confirmation, Black went on national radio explaining, though not apologizing for, his KKK membership. Although Roosevelt denied any knowledge of the association, he must in fact have known. Indeed, Black left a note in his private papers to "correct for posterity any idea about Pres. Roosevelt's having been fooled about my membership in the Klan."[47]

On the Court, Black was pretty much a loner. Other Roosevelt appointees tended to be as well, but Black had the disposition of a street fighter when staking out his positions. Even Douglas, with whom he was most closely aligned,[48] once revealed: "Actually, personally, Black and I have never been very close. I very, very seldom see him. . . . It is just more happenstance, I think, that we have found generally some kinship."[49] Minton called Black a "demagogue" after he made, as Minton saw it, "one of his inflammatory outbursts at Conference."[50] Justice Arthur Goldberg (1962–1965), an experienced labor negotiator before he was appointed to the Court by John F. Kennedy, recalled, "When Hugo was in agreement, he was a sober fighter. . . . When he was in disagreement, he was a terrible and vigorous adversary. He was a gut fighter."[51] Likewise, Jackson confided to columnist Arthur Krock, "You can't just disagree with him. You must go to war with him if you

The Supreme Court building, completed in 1935. Photograph by Theodor Horydczak, collection of the Supreme Court of the United States

disagree."[52] Of course, as noted in Chapter 1, Black and Jackson feuded over the chief justiceship in 1946. Whether they maintained "mutual distain,"[53] or over time became "friendly,"[54] any reconciliation certainly came too late.[55]

When Frankfurter arrived at the Court, there was almost immediately a clash of personalities and judicial philosophies between him and Black. Their backgrounds were as different as those of Black's and Jackson's. Black was a populist Southern politician, while Frankfurter, an Austrian-born Jewish immigrant, was a Harvard Law School professor and a leading liberal academic. They embodied the tensions between politics and law, and those tensions underlay their battles on the bench. Almost immediately Frankfurter rubbed Black and others the wrong way. Moreover, his tendency to monopolize conferences and lectures particularly disturbed Black and Douglas.[56] On at least one occasion, Black and Frankfurter nearly came to blows at conference.[57] On another occasion, Douglas recalled, Frankfurter so infuriated Chief Justice Vinson that he stood up and left the conference table, heading around the room shouting "No son-of-a-bitch can ever say that to Fred Vinson."[58]

Black and Frankfurter's antagonisms were not just personal but were profoundly philosophical. They initially came to the fore in *Bridges v. California* (1941),[59] over the First Amendment's protection for freedom of expression. There, Black directly challenged the former law school professor's constitutional theories, in advocating "absolutism" or "literalism"—the "natural meaning" of constitutional provisions.[60] By contrast, Frankfurter abhorred "absolutes" and followed his judicial idol, Justice Holmes, in arguing for a "balancing" of First Amendment freedoms against governmental and other interests.[61] Black's vigorous defense of "absolutism" led him in more liberal, rights-defending directions, giving rise to the joke that before going to the Court, he dressed in white robes to scare blacks, and afterward he wore black robes to scare white people.[62]

The fundamental disagreements between Black and Frankfurter over constitutional interpretation famously carried over into fights over whether the Fourteenth Amendment's due process clause incorporated guarantees of the Bill of Rights, thereby making them applicable against the states. The two justices—and their former law clerks, since turned law school professors—waged war both on and off the bench. In separate opinions and law review articles, they sparred over the history and "original intent," or the "original public understanding," of the Thirty-Ninth Congress's passage of the Fourteenth Amendment.[63] Ironically for Black, the amendment meant precisely what it said, regardless of the political consequences. Frankfurter was skeptical of legal certainty, and he was preoccupied with federalism as well as with the political consequences of the Court's rulings extending the guarantees of the Bill of Rights to the states.

Adamson v. California (1947)[64] perhaps epitomizes the depth of their disagreements, along with the fragmentation of the Roosevelt Court. At issue was whether the Fifth Amendment guarantee against compulsory self-incrimination applied to the states through the Fourteenth Amendment. Writing for the Court, Justice Reed held that it did not. Frankfurter concurred, contending that all due process required was "fundamental fairness," determined on a case-by-case basis. Black, joined by Douglas and Rutledge, sharply dissented. He advocated the "total incorporation" of all the protections enumerated in the Bill of Rights. In a separate dissent, Murphy and Rutledge went further in arguing for "total-incorporation-plus" other unenumerated rights. These would include the "right of privacy," which, after Frankfurter's retirement and over Black's stinging dissent, was recognized in *Griswold v. Connecticut* (1965).[65] In *Griswold,* they undoubtedly would have for once agreed, though for entirely different reasons.

In addition to his position that the Fourteenth Amendment provided for the "total incorporation" of the Bill of Rights, Black had no doubt about racial segregation being wrong and "contrary" to the amendment's equal protection clause. Segregation was "a hangover of the Civil War" and "a badge of inferiority." But along with other justices, he was deeply troubled in *Brown* about extending precedents running against the separate but equal doctrine to primary and secondary schools. He foresaw a backlash, especially in the South. There schools might be closed. South Carolina's governor (and former justice), James Byrnes, threatened just that. Violence and massive resistance would certainly follow the Court's ruling. Never underestimating the difficulties of achieving compliance, Black worried about what kind of remedial decree should be handed down. For that reason, he initially argued against turning *Brown* into a class-action lawsuit, which would render the lower courts battlegrounds over implementation of the ruling. He favored leaving the matter to be fought out on a case-by-case basis, school district by school district. Nor was he alone in expressing those concerns. Reed also raised the issue during the first round of oral arguments. Jackson struggled with the problem when drafting his unpublished opinion. In fact, for that reason, he urged colleagues to postpone a decision on the scope of a remedial decree until after hearing rearguments. That resulted, at Frankfurter's suggestion, in the decree for compliance "with all deliberate speed" in *Brown II* (1955).[66] Decades later, Black regretted the course taken in *Brown II*. In a television interview, extraordinary at the time, he said that the phrase "all deliberate speed" actually slowed integration.[67] A year later, in *Alexander v. Holmes County Board of Education* (1969), the Court unanimously held that the time for "all deliberate speed" had run out.[68]

Although a champion of "absolutism" or "textualism" and one of the most libertarian justices on the Court for much of his tenure, Black delivered the Court's opinion upholding the evacuation and internment of Japanese Americans during World War II in *Korematsu v. United States* (1944). Notably, Jackson dissented and sharply criticized the sanctioning of "a military expedient that has no place in law under the Constitution." Nonetheless, Justices Black and Douglas never regretted their decisions, and decades later the latter explained: "The decisions were extreme and went to the verge of wartime power; and they have been severely criticized. It is, however, easy in retrospect to denounce what was done, as there actually was no invasion of our country. . . . But those making plans for defense of the nation had no such knowledge and were planning for the worst."[69]

By the 1970s, some of the justices' private papers also were becoming available to historians, political scientists, and other researchers. Much to Black's chagrin, some scholars seized on Justice Harold Burton's rather cryptic conference notes of discussions about *Brown*.[70] In particular, political scientist Sidney Ulmer wrote an article attempting to reconstruct the justices' decision making in *Brown*. Ulmer concluded Black initially held back on declaring segregated schools unconstitutional. In correspondence between the two, Black refuted Ulmer's reconstruction and refused any further correspondence.[71] Ulmer notably failed to pay attention to the last line in Burton's summary of conference votes: *"Rev."* That is, Black had initially voted in *Brown* to reverse the lower court's upholding of segregated schools. Black remained so angry with Ulmer's account that he had his son destroy some of his private papers pertaining to *Brown* before the collection went to the Library of Congress. As he told his son, "Good Lord, Son, you of all people know how false that is."[72]

Roosevelt's subsequent appointments all turned on support for the New Deal and on personal connections. When conservative justice Sutherland retired in 1938, Roosevelt momentarily considered nominating another senator, either South Carolina's James Byrnes (who was later appointed in 1941) or Indiana's Sherman Minton (who had to await President Harry Truman's selection in 1949). But Roosevelt worried about taking too many supporters from the Senate. Attorney General Homer Cummings urged him to elevate Solicitor General Stanley Reed, who had defended the constitutionality of the early New Deal before the Court. Reed was from a border state, Kentucky, and Roosevelt initially thought, "Well, McReynolds is from Kentucky, and Stanley will have to wait until McReynolds is no longer with us." Cummings countered that McReynolds was "closely identified with New York city" because of his earlier law practice, and that Reed's record justified his nomination. Roosevelt ultimately agreed: "Tell Stanley to make himself so disagreeable to McReynolds that the latter will retire right away."[73] Jackson speculated that Roosevelt also wanted to elevate Reed because of his legal credibility and his confirmability, especially after the KKK controversy that arose with Black's appointment.[74]

Reed, born in Minerva, Kentucky, in 1884, lived the life of a Southern squire, mostly in Mayville, once a center for the slave trade, surrounded by cotton and tobacco farms. Although he never earned a formal law degree, he received BA degrees from both Kentucky Wesleyan and Yale colleges, and he attended law schools at the University of Virginia and Columbia; he also read law at the Sorbonne in Paris. After military service during World War I, Reed went to Washington, D.C., initially during the administration of Republican president Herbert Hoover, and remained in Roosevelt's. He found the district congenial, living in the Mayflower Hotel, which was located at the center of the country's segregated capital.

Reed embodied the cultural attitudes of the old South even more so than Black or Vinson (a fellow Kentuckian, but from the Northern, pro-Union part of the state). While defending New Deal programs, Reed remained a cultural conservative who placed liberty above equality, continuity over sudden change, and the will of the people over what he called "krytocracy"—a term he used, according to a law clerk in the 1953 term, John D. Fassett,[75] as a label for government by the judiciary. Of course, that was a kind of clarion call for New Dealers battling the pre-1937 Court.

On the Court, Reed was often torn between his better angels and cultural heritage. That was especially true when it came to segregation. Accustomed to segregation, he struggled with how to deal with challenges coming to the Court. Between 1945 and 1953, he amassed four boxes of articles and correspondence on the subject.[76] He had law clerks compile statistics and research other nations' and international laws pertaining to segregation.[77] "Of course," he told a clerk, "the Constitution does not permit discrimination." But in his view, "segregation" did not mean "discrimination."[78] He thought social assimilation over time, not the courts, should resolve the segregation problem. In a 1950 speech, he made his position clear: in theory, equality was recognized "at the birth of our nation," and educational opportunities should now be considered "a common birthright in our country." He nonetheless warned, "We must guard well that our individual constitutional liberties are not lost in a stampede toward mass equality."[79]

In his first term on the Court, Reed voted to strictly enforce the doctrine of "separate but equal." He joined Chief Justice Hughes's opinion in *Missouri ex rel Gaines v. Canada* (1938),[80] holding that Missouri's denying blacks admission to its state law school, but providing them funding to go to out-of-state schools, violated the Fourteenth Amendment guarantee for equal protection. Although not entirely "in sympathy with the Court's treatment of the problems" of racial segregation, as Justice Burton recorded in his conference notes,[81] Reed wrote the Court's opinion in *Smith v. Allwright* (1944),[82] striking down Texas's "white primary" law that excluded blacks from voting in the Democratic Party's primaries, and thereby effectively disenfranchised them.

Reed also joined the unanimous decision in *Sweatt v. Painter* (1950),[83] holding that the denial of admission to the University of Texas Law School and the state's creation of a separate all-black law school ran afoul of the "separate but equal" doctrine. Likewise, he joined the Court's opinion in *McLaurin v. Oklahoma State Regents* (1950),[84] in which Chief Justice Vinson held that requiring a black graduate student to sit apart from whites in classes, the library, and cafeteria violated the Fourteenth Amendment.

Reed also joined unanimous rulings against segregation in train dining cars,[85] including that of a District of Columbia Reconstruction-era municipal ordinance barring discrimination in restaurants, which was deemed enforceable despite its being ignored for eighty years.[86] Yet after the latter decision, *District of Columbia v. John R. Thompson Co., Inc.*, Reed (in)famously remarked, "Why—why, this means that a nigra can walk into a restaurant at the Mayflower Hotel and sit down to eat at the table right next to Mrs. Reed!"[87] A few years earlier, when law clerks proposed inviting the Court's black messengers to an annual Christmas party, Reed refused to attend. He told Frankfurter that "this is a private matter" and that he could do as he pleased.[88] Consequently, the party was scuttled.[89] Ironically, the very next year, 1948, Frankfurter hired the Court's first black law clerk, William Coleman.

At the first conference discussion of *Brown* in 1952, Reed unambiguously voted to uphold segregated schools. He did not view segregation as discriminatory per se; rather, he saw it as a benefit for both races. Moreover, as he saw it, segregation was gradually disappearing and "we must allow time"—perhaps ten years in Virginia and fifteen to twenty in Kentucky and other border states. While agreeing that "the meaning of the Constitution is *not* fixed"—*Plessy*'s "separate but equal" doctrine might have been right at the time but not now—Reed argued against the Court declaring segregated schools "*no longer* permissible" or a denial of either equal protection or due process.[90]

A year later, at a conference with Chief Justice Warren presiding, Reed reiterated that segregation was not based on "racial inferiority, but on racial differences." According to Reed, it "protects people against the mixing of races." He still saw no equal protection problem. In fact, he noted that enforcing equal protection had resulted in "less facilities for Negroes." For him, this was basically a question of due process, not equal protection. Furthermore, since the adoption of the Fourteenth Amendment, Congress had sanctioned segregated schools in the District of Columbia. This was a matter for Congress to decide, not for "the Court to say it was or has become *un*constitutional."[91]

Subsequently, Reed sketched on a yellow pad the outlines of a dissenting opinion along the same lines. He never circulated it to other justices, but he did share it with his clerks.[92] He initially thought that Vinson, and perhaps Jackson, might refuse to overrule *Plessy*. But even before Vinson's death in September 1953 and Warren's appointment, he told a clerk "*they* know *they* have the votes and *they* are determined to resolve the issue."[93]

Chief Justice Warren thus proceeded patiently, without pushing for a vote and without any accusation or incriminations, framing the matter as a fundamentally moral issue and insisting on gradualism.[94] He also spent time going to lunch with Reed and Burton, discussing the need for unanimity. Finally, in late spring 1954, in the presence of a clerk in Reed's chambers, Warren said,

"Stan, you're all by yourself in this now. You've got to decide whether it's really the best thing for the country." The clerk, George Mickum, recalled that Reed put the tentative dissent aside, because as a Southerner, it would only have given "a lot of people a lot of grist for making trouble."[95] Although Justice Douglas in his autobiography claimed Jackson was the last holdout,[96] in an earlier interview, he remembered Reed telling him simply, "I am not going to stand out."[97]

When the justices entered the crowded courtroom on opinion day to announce the decision in *Brown,* Thurgood Marshall knew the decision was unanimous. As Marshall later recalled, "That old cracker [Reed] would not look me in the eye."[98] When Warren read the Court's opinion, tears ran down Reed's cheeks, according to Mickum.[99] A few years later, in 1957, Reed retired and moved to New York City, where he lived in a hotel until he died in 1981.

Although Reed joined the Court in 1938, his fellow Kentuckian, Justice McReynolds, did not retire until 1941. By then, pressures had built for an appointee from the West. Also in 1938, Justice Cardozo died. His vacancy appeared hard to fill. "Cardozo was not only a great Justice, but a great character, a great person and great soul . . . held in reverence by multitudes of people," Attorney General Homer Cummings observed, and "whoever followed him, no matter how good a man he might be, would suffer by comparison."[100] Roosevelt had contemplated appointing Frankfurter to Brandeis's seat, and earlier, he had unsuccessfully urged him to become solicitor general. "I want you on the Supreme Court, Felix," Roosevelt told him, "but I can't appoint you out of Harvard Law School. What will people say? 'He's a Red. He's a professor. He's had no judicial experience.' But I could appoint you to the Court from the Solicitor General's office."[101] Then, when Cardozo died, Roosevelt at first told Frankfurter, "I've got to appoint a fellow west of the Mississippi—I promised the party leaders he'd be a Westerner next time."[102] A number of Westerners were considered, but each was deemed unacceptable. In the end, Frankfurter was named despite criticism that it again put two Jews (as had been the situation with Brandeis and Cardozo sitting on the high bench) and an excessive number of justices from the Atlantic seaboard on the Court.

An immigrant born in Vienna, Austria, in 1882, Frankfurter taught at Harvard Law School after working in the Woodrow Wilson administration, as did Roosevelt and Jackson. He was a well-known liberal, supporting the New Dealers' attack on the conservative pre-1937 Court. After his appointment in 1939, however, he became a conservative champion of judicial self-restraint, often siding with Jackson but occasionally squaring off on opposite sides.[103] Within the Court, Frankfurter remained the consummate academic. He was a meddlesome backbiter, professing detachment and devotion to putting the rule of law above politics. Yet he failed to practice what he preached. On the contrary, he was passionate and arrogant, often petty, and an activist relishing in political intrigue. In short, he was paradoxical, self-serving, and self-contradictory.

Frankfurter portrayed himself as above politics, but in fact he was consumed by it. He remained actively involved in politics both on and off the bench.[104] Like other Roosevelt appointees, he continued to advise the president[105] while disingenuously criticizing the extrajudicial activities of others like Douglas. Frankfurter, for instance, once hypocritically proclaimed, "When a priest enters a monastery, he must leave—or ought to leave—all sorts of worldly desires behind him. And this Court has no excuse for being unless it's a monastery."[106]

He earnestly aspired to carrying on the Holmesian mantle of judicial self-restraint. But Holmes was an agnostic ironist, not a crusader, while Frankfurter was a political enthusiast. Holmes actually abided by "judicial self-restraint." As Judge Learned Hand told a clerk, "Frankfurter hasn't supreme self-restraint. He's learned a good deal of it. But he hasn't it," as a result of his political passions.[107]

Frankfurter referred to opponents—Black, Douglas, Murphy, and Rutledge—as "the Axis."[108] Although he tried to foster friendship with flattery, he had a penchant for ridiculing them behind their backs, even colleagues who sided with him. "The problem with Stanley [Reed]," he once said, "is that he doesn't let his law clerks do enough work. The trouble with Murphy is that he lets them do too much of the work."[109] Those justices were not unaware of his duplicity. As Reed remarked, "The trouble with Felix is that he never considers that he might be wrong; if you don't agree with Felix, you must be either stupid or dishonest!"[110]

From the perspective of other justices, in Douglas's words, Frankfurter "used his law clerks as flying squadrons against the law clerks of other Justices and even against the Justices themselves. Frankfurter, a proselytizer, never missed a chance to line up a vote."[111] His clerks were referred to as "Frankfurter's happy hot dogs." Besides encouraging them to talk with other chambers' clerks and report back to him, he had them prepare lengthy memoranda, such as Alexander Bickel's ninety-one-page examination of the history of the Fourteenth Amendment and the segregation cases.[112] Frankfurter also tended to try to dominate conference discussions and consumed large segments of oral arguments with questions, thereby exasperating attorneys and other justices.[113] He was also notoriously slow in circulating draft opinions, once conceding, "The elephant's period of gestation is, I believe, eighteen months, but a poor little hot dog has no such excuse."[114]

Not surprisingly, Frankfurter tried to manipulate not only clerks but other justices, particularly when they were new. He immediately sought to bring Vinson into his fold, but "within six weeks [he] couldn't wait to find a case in which he could vote against him."[115] Their relations quickly wore thin. When told of Vinson's death by former clerk and Deputy Solicitor General Philip Elman while walking from Union Station to the Court, Frankfurter sarcastically remarked, "I'm in mourning." He then grabbed Elman's arm, looked him straight in the eye, and said, "Phil, this is the first solid piece of evidence I've ever had that there really is a God."[116] Frankfurter's relationship with Earl Warren fared no better. In fact, he was actually furious over Warren's appointment as chief justice: "Just [another] politician."[117] Nonetheless, Frankfurter immediately sought to bring him "into his influence," but within a few years, their relationship "turned to resentment and bitterness."[118]

Some legal historians claim that the "decisive breach between Warren and Frankfurter came with *Cooper v. Aaron*" (1958).[119] That case involved violent protests over admitting a few blacks to the high school in Little Rock, Arkansas, which led to President Eisenhower's ordering the National Guard to enforce a desegregation order. Frankfurter worried Warren's attitude was "more like that of a fighting politician than that of a judicial statesman."[120] Moreover, he insisted on filing a concurring opinion in order to lecture Southern lawyers—some of whom were former Harvard students—about the legitimacy of *Brown*. That, however, broke with the unanimity, which he had earlier argued was crucial, in *Brown* and previous rulings on desegregation. As a consequence, all nine justices agreed to sign the Court's opinion in *Cooper v. Aaron* in order to underscore their continued unanimity in spite of his concurrence.[121]

Still, other scholars put the split between Warren and Frankfurter a few years earlier, in the 1954–1955 terms.[122] In particular, Frankfurter's invoking jurisdictional technicalities in order to avoid challenges to antimiscegenation laws, in cases like *Naim v. Naim*,[123] and which was not addressed until after he retired, in *Loving v. Virginia* (1967),[124] led Warren to consider him "a shameless hypocrite."[125] Ironically, Warren subsequently developed a close relationship with a former student of Frankfurter, Justice William J. Brennan Jr. (1956–1990).[126] Later, Warren said: "All Frankfurter does is talk, talk, talk. He drives you crazy."[127] Even one of Frankfurter's favorite and former law clerks, Alexander Bickel, apparently agreed. In Bickel's words, "He was the most unscrupulous debater alive; there were no holds barred."[128]

When it came to segregation and *Brown*, Frankfurter attempted to put off dealing with the matter as long as possible. Years before, during a conference discussion of *Sweatt v. Painter* (1950), he agreed that the creation of an all-black law school, instead of admitting blacks to the University of Texas Law School, was unconstitutional. But he warned, "We should abstain from saying anything about segregation as such."[129] The "momentum of history" and "deep feeling" of the people should resolve the problems of segregation, not the Court. A constant refrain was "The Court is not saved from being oligarchic because it professes to act in the service of humane ends."[130]

The forces of history were more important, in Frankfurter's view, than rulings by the judiciary. For that reason, he sought to avoid the issue of miscegenation in *Naim v. Naim,* maintaining that equal protection had no "fixed formula defined with finality at a particular time."[131] Nor, as Frankfurter insisted, did *Brown* proclaim a general principle of equality or a "neutral principle"[132] of law, as he made clear in exchanges with Judge Learned Hand, which drove the latter to finally agree the only "single absolute is there are none."[133] Frankfurter advocated gradualism and a "bare bones decree" that, he acknowledged, would unfold "responsibility upon the lower courts . . . without any guidelines for them except our decision of unconstitutionality [and] result in drawn-out, indefinite delay without even colorable compliance."[134] The Court, Frankfurter contended, "does its duty if it gets effectively underway the righting of a wrong. When the wrong is deeply rooted state policy the court does its duty if it decrees measures that reverse the direction of the unconstitutional policy so as to uproot it 'with all deliberate speed.'"[135]

So too did Frankfurter argue against expressly overruling *Plessy* in *Brown.* He fought with his main antagonist, Justice Black, who voted to overrule *Plessy,* though warning it might "mean the end of political liberalism in the South" and the Klan "riding again."[136] Frankfurter, more than all the other justices, except Reed, feared the political ramifications of doing what was right. Consequently, he pushed to delay taking a vote, initially partly because he thought that Vinson, Reed, and possibly Clark would vote to affirm *Plessy.* He urged a unanimous decision, but one that did not expressly overturn *Plessy* and that did not treat *Brown* as a "class action" lawsuit or order immediate relief.[137]

Did Frankfurter make a major contribution in persuading Vinson and Warren to postpone a formal vote, hearing rearguments, and later hearing arguments, as Jackson insisted, on the matter of a remedial decree? Some Court watchers conclude, "There is no question that the grand strategist in all of this inside the Court was FF."[138] Others are more doubtful.[139] Warren himself—admittedly, long after being at odds with Frankfurter and his own retirement—attributed the unanimity in *Brown* to Justices Black, Reed, and

Clark. These were the three Southerners who knew the most about segregation as a way of life and about the inexorable opposition to its death blow.[140]

As with Frankfurter's appointment, geography did not dissuade Roosevelt from filling Brandeis's seat in 1939 with another Easterner, his securities and exchange commissioner, William O. Douglas. Although born in Minnesota in 1898 and growing up in Oregon, he graduated from New York City's Columbia Law School, and after a year in private practice, he taught at the Columbia and Yale law schools. He thus had ties to the West—but more importantly, he had intellectual and personal appeal. Frank Murphy, who replaced Cummings as attorney general, urged the president to disregard pressures for a Westerner. "Members of the Supreme Court are not called upon nor expected to represent any single interest or group, area or class of persons," he emphasized. "They speak for the country as a whole."[141] Douglas claimed Connecticut as his legal residence because he taught at Yale before joining the SEC. He later recalled, "When Roosevelt named me he didn't name me from the State of Washington, but he stuck to the record and named me from Connecticut."[142] Unlike Reed—but like Black, Frankfurter, and Jackson—Douglas was another Horatio Alger story. He was confirmed at the age of forty-one, one of the youngest justices.

On and off the Court, Douglas was fiercely independent, an iconoclastic loner, a lover of the wilderness, and a prolific writer, publishing numerous books on his travels around the world and politics at home and abroad.[143] He was at least initially close to Jackson, even when they disagreed.[144] That was not so with Frankfurter, whom Douglas considered timid, tortured, and intellectually dishonest almost from the outset, but especially after sharply splitting with Frankfurter, as did Jackson, in the second flag-salute case.[145]

Douglas wrote his own opinions, usually in longhand, quickly and with minimal editing and with little assistance from his law clerks. As a result, in the words of one former clerk, some "opinions often read like rough drafts."[146] While they lacked Jackson's flair, his opinions were notable for their clarity, conciseness, and directness. Like Jackson's clerks,[147] some of Douglas's clerks found him distant and indifferent,[148] while others adored him.[149] Douglas's biographers, like those of other justices, were mixed, some critical and others celebratory.[150]

When it came to segregation, Douglas firmly maintained that it was obviously unconstitutional. Even when the justices in conference discussed *McLaurin v. Oklahoma State Regents* (1950), dealing with racial segregation in graduate schools, he made clear that "we should overrule *Plessy.*"[151] Subsequently, during the first conference discussion on *Brown*, he reiterated, "Segregation is a very simple constitutional question for me. No classifications on the basis of race can be made."[152] He staunchly opposed Frankfurter's and Jackson's advocacy of foregoing a vote and scheduling rearguments. Douglas particularly disdained Frankfurter's voting to avoid taking other segregation cases. In his view, Frankfurter "was very frightened, very uncertain, very unsure, very hesitant to walk up to the major issue of the racial problem of our time."[153]

By Douglas's count, there was a solid majority, composed of Vinson, Black, Burton, Minton, and himself, for striking down segregation laws. Justices Reed, Frankfurter, Jackson, and perhaps Clark were more or less opposed and pushed for gradualism.[154] According to Douglas, whereas Vinson was cautious and open to Frankfurter's arguments, Warren was a "real statesman." That is because, in Douglas's view, he had been a successful politician and proceeded carefully in order to forge common ground and consensus for a unanimous decision in *Brown*.[155]

When Pierce Butler, a Midwesterner, died in 1939, there was even more pressure to appoint a Westerner and a Catholic. Butler was Catholic, and Catholics were a crucial part of the New Deal coalition. Roosevelt settled on Attorney General Murphy. He was a Catholic, an affable "Irish mystic," and a former governor of Michigan. Murphy's Midwestern Catholic background, however, was only a politically useful rationalization. No less important was that morale within the Department of Justice under Murphy was abysmally low. Murphy was not equipped to handle the demands of being attorney general. Roosevelt was not unaware of Murphy's faults. Jackson, then an assistant attorney general, warned him, "Mr. President, I don't think that Mr. Murphy's temperament is that of a judge." But Murphy's elevation to the Court was also politically opportune. As Roosevelt explained to Jackson, "It's the only way I can appoint you Attorney General."[156]

Roosevelt promised to appoint Jackson chief justice if he accepted the attorney generalship. Jackson reluctantly agreed. Then in 1941, McReynolds retired, and Chief Justice Hughes informed Roosevelt that he was stepping down at the end of the term. Roosevelt thus had the opportunity to fill two more seats and to appoint Jackson. Hughes suggested to Roosevelt that the chief justiceship should go to Stone. He had long aspired to it and was disappointed when his friend, President Herbert Hoover, passed him over in appointing Hughes. Frankfurter preferred Jackson, but he agreed that Stone was "senior and qualified professionally to be C.J." Frankfurter also told Roosevelt that elevating Stone, a Republican, would inspire confidence in him "as a national and not a partisan President."[157] In July, Roosevelt nominated Senator James Byrnes for McReynolds's seat, Stone for chief justice, and Jackson to fill the resulting associate justice vacancy.

When trying to mollify Jackson, Roosevelt told him that Stone was within a couple of years of retirement, explaining, "I will have another chance at appointment of a Chief Justice, at which time you'd already be over there [in the Court] and would be familiar with the job." At the time, the arrangement appeared politically advantageous: "One Republican for Chief Justice and two Democrats will not be too partisan."[158] As fate would have it, however, Roosevelt made his last appointment a little over a year later in 1943, nominating Wiley Rutledge, a Westerner and law school professor, to replace Byrnes, who left the Court to go back into the administration. Finally, Rutledge got his seat and served until 1949, when he stepped down. Roosevelt's successor, President Truman, then named Sherman Minton to fill that seat.

Truman Follows Suit

When Roosevelt—"That Man,"[159] as Jackson affectionately referred to him—died less than three months into his historic fourth term in 1945, Vice President Harry S. Truman assumed the presidency. "Give 'Em Hell Harry" followed Roosevelt's example when selecting justices, rewarding personal friends and the party faithful—indeed, so much so that critics charged him with cronyism. His appointees, however, tended to be more conservative and generally sided with Reed, Frankfurter, and Jackson rather than Black or Douglas.

Within a year of his presidency, Truman named Democratic senator Harold Burton to fill conservative justice Roberts's seat. During his first term, Burton dissented alone in *Morgan v. Virginia* (1946),[160] in which Reed, writing for the Court, overturned a statute mandating segregation in train passenger cars as an unconstitutional burden on interstate commerce. Burton contended that any unequal treatment was neither an "undue burden" nor outweighed state and local interests. Otherwise, he generally sided with the most liberal justices in cases dealing with race despite voting with anti–civil libertarians in other civil rights cases.[161]

Justice Burton explained, a little after the first conference discussion of *Brown*, in a letter to Frankfurter: "I doubt that it can be said in any state (and certainly not generally) that compulsory 'separation' of the races, even with equal facilities, *can* amount to an 'equal' protection of the laws in a society that is lived and shared so *'jointly'* by all races as ours is now."[162] In the first conference discussion of *Brown*, Burton thought that the threshold had been crossed in *McLaurin v. Oklahoma State Regents* and *Sweatt v. Painter* (1950).[163] He had no doubt that segregation violates equal protection. Moreover, he remained steadfast. At the 1953 conference with Chief Justice Warren presiding, Burton argued that there was no choice but to act, and that the Fourteenth Amendment required uniform practices among the states.[164]

Chief Justice Stone's death in 1946 presented a ready-made controversy over a successor. The Roosevelt Court was badly divided. Disputes between Black–Douglas and Frankfurter–Jackson were deep-seated, ideological, personal, and increasingly public.[165] After Stone died, as senior associate justice, Black temporarily assumed the responsibilities of the chief justice in presiding over conferences and oral arguments. Jackson, long laboring under Roosevelt's promise to make him chief justice, became vindictive. He convinced himself that his rival, Black, would be named chief justice. Truman's assurances that he had not talked with Black failed to reassure him. And Jackson later became convinced that Douglas had lobbied against him.[166] While serving at Truman's behest as chief prosecutor of Nazi war criminals in Nuremberg, Germany, Jackson sent a telegram to the House and Senate judiciary committees in which he attacked Black for failing to recuse himself in a case involving a former law partner. Jackson thereby further publicly aired their animosities.[167]

Outraged by the Black–Jackson public feuding, Truman lamented, "The Supreme Court has really made a mess of itself."[168] Disgusted, he decided to name Fred Vinson, an old friend and experienced politician, with an allegedly "uncanny knack of placating opposing minds."[169] As William Rogers, former Reed law clerk and President Eisenhower's attorney general, later observed, "Fred Vinson would not have been on the Court but for the fact that he was a successful politician."[170]

Like Reed, Vinson was a Kentuckian, though from the northeastern pro-Union part of the state. He was a staunch New Deal Democrat. Roosevelt had appointed him to the court of appeals for the District of Columbia Circuit in 1937. Vinson resigned in 1943, when Truman appointed him as director of the Office of Economic Stabilization; Truman later moved him to a series of other administrative positions, before elevating him to the Court. As chief justice, Vinson was not highly regarded by some colleagues—in fact, he was subsequently derided. Douglas, for one, deemed him "mediocre."[171] Frankfurter, his chief antagonist, considered him "confident and easy-going and sure and shallow," someone who in conferences dealt "with complicated matters on a surface basis."[172] The fairest assessment, perhaps, is that of historian Melvin Urofsky: "Given another line up at a different time, Vinson might well have been considered a good chief, but he proved unable to control or guide his colleagues."[173]

In no small part due to Frankfurter's comments in correspondence and in his diaries, which first became available in the Library of Congress and at Harvard Law School, Vinson has been portrayed as opposed to the eventual ruling in *Brown*.[174] Yet that misses the mark. Vinson was a social progressive, a pragmatist who favored gradualism. He definitely was not a revolutionary like Douglas. Nor was he interested in legal theory. As one former law clerk put it, he "reacted suspiciously to the grand generalization."[175]

When it came to race relations, Vinson was a cautious progressive. He joined the majority in *Shelley v. Kraemer* (1948),[176] barring states from enforcing restrictive covenants. Indeed, he delivered the Court's opinion in a companion case.[177] Likewise, he wrote for the Court in *Sipuel v. Board of Regents, University of Oklahoma* (1948),[178] which overturned a state law requiring segregated education. He did the same in *Sweatt v. Painter* (1950), invalidating Texas's creation of an all-black law school rather than integrate the University of Texas Law School at Austin, its flagship law school.

Notably, at the conference on *Sweatt*, after reviewing prior desegregation rulings, he stated, "It may be that *now* we should expand the Constitution. . . . As a matter of policy, no great harm would result from the mingling of races in professional schools. But I don't see how we can draw the line there. I can't distinguish professional and elementary schools."[179] Notably, he also delivered the Court's opinion in *McLaurin v. Oklahoma State Regents* (1950), leading the conference discussion and stating firmly, "There is color discrimination in their treatment of Negroes. I reverse [the lower court]. . . . Negroes are entitled to enter the university without restriction if they are admitted at all."[180]

When it came to the first conference discussion of *Brown*, Vinson dismissed Jackson's initial view that the matter was a "political question" best left to Congress. He did not "think much of the idea that it is for Congress and not for us to act. If they *do not act,* this leaves us with it." Agreeing with Jackson, he did believe that "it would be better if Congress would act," but he added that it "probably will *not* act for the states."[181]

In sum, as Newton Minow, a former Vinson clerk in the 1951–1952 term, recollected, "Had Chief Justice Vinson lived one more year the Court would have acted as it eventually did in the *Brown* case. Of that I have no doubt. And with the same unanimity."[182]

Truman had the opportunity to appoint two more justices. In 1949, he elevated his attorney general, Tom C. Clark, to replace Justice Murphy and federal appeals court judge Sherman Minton to fill Rutledge's seat. Clark was born in Texas in 1899; he went to college and law school there before

Justices Hugo Black, Robert H. Jackson, and Felix Frankfurter at the funeral of Chief Justice Vinson. Getty image

working in private practice for over a decade. In 1937 Roosevelt appointed him to the Department of Justice, where he rose to become attorney general in the Truman administration. He served on the Court until 1965 when his son, Ramsey, was named attorney general by President Lyndon B. Johnson.[183] Minton, a Midwesterner born in Indiana in 1890, attended Indiana and Yale law schools. He spent much of his early career in private practice before being elected to the Senate in 1935. Minton served there until 1941, when Roosevelt appointed him to an appellate court. Eight years later, Truman elevated him to the highest court in the land.[184]

Truman viewed "Tom Clark [as his] biggest mistake. No question about it." Truman later bluntly claimed, "It's just that he's such a dumb son of a bitch."[185] Historians have portrayed Clark as a holdout in *Brown* and indifferent to civil liberties.[186] But that is far from the truth. He was actually a Southern progressive. He was anxious and hesitant, to be sure, as were Jackson and virtually all of the others, about the scope of the segregation rulings and the foreseeable problems with compliance. Yet as attorney general, Clark had represented the Truman administration in arguing that racially restrictive covenants were unconstitutional; he signed on to Truman's

Presidential Civil Rights Committee's report, *To Secure These Rights;*[187] and he further publicized arguments against housing discrimination in *Prejudice and Property.*[188]

Clark foresaw the eventual ruling in *Brown* and its ramifications. He was a realist and a gradualist who thought ruling against segregation "must be done carefully or it will do more harm than good."[189] In a 1950 memorandum to the justices on segregated graduate schools in *Sweatt* and *McLaurin,* he argued against applying or adhering to *Plessy*'s doctrine of "separate but equal." But he also opposed abandoning that doctrine as applied to primary and secondary schools, even though that was unnecessary for the Court to consider at the time. Although Clark "would not approve *Plessy* in any manner," he was against expressly overturning *Plessy*. Nonetheless, he acknowledged the Court would be perceived as implicitly doing precisely that, and he observed, "then let it [*Plessy*] fall as have many Nineteenth Century oracles."[190] During subsequent conference discussions of *Sweatt,* Clark did not see how the Fourteenth Amendment applied to graduate schools but not to elementary and secondary schools. While stressing, "I don't want [the decision] to affect elementary schools," he, along with Vinson, Frankfurter, and Jackson, thought it was "important to have as many of us as possible in this opinion."[191]

Years later, Clark said that he considered *Plessy* to have been basically overruled by *Sweatt* and *McLaurin.*[192] He also dismissed the conventional criticism of Vinson having stalled or evaded the crucial question of whether the "separate but equal" doctrine remained constitutional. Such criticism, in his words, was "all tommy rot, just pure and simple. When I came here . . . *all* of us thought the climate was just not ripe for change. We often delay adjudication. It's not a question of evading at all. It's just the practicalities of life—common sense."[193]

Justice Minton, Frankfurter observed, was "an almost pathological Democrat," while Douglas considered him "Mr. Mainstreet."[194] Like Black and Burton, but unlike Frankfurter and Jackson, Minton was a politician. As a senator, he had supported an antilynching bill advanced by the NAACP. When questioned about that, he responded, "I am interested in states' rights; but I am much more interested in human rights."[195] When asked to testify before the Senate Judiciary Committee's hearings on his nomination to the Court to explain his support for Roosevelt's Court-packing plan, he refused, responding simply, "That record speaks for itself."[196]

Minton shared the caution of Jackson, Frankfurter, and others about *Brown,* but he was more resolute than Clark or Vinson. At the first Vinson

Court conference discussion, at which as the junior justice he was the last to speak, he stated firmly, "We are confronted with a body of law that lays down separate but equal. We have chipped and chiseled it away in *Sweatt* and *McLaurin*. Classification by race does not add up. It is *not reasonable. It is invidious* and it can't be maintained. . . . *Segregation is per se unconstitutional. I am ready to vote now.*"[197] Later, when Warren became chief justice and *Brown* was reargued, he did not waver.[198] He was convinced segregation was psychologically detrimental, just as Thurgood Marshall and the NAACP Legal Defense Fund had argued. All the while, he was nevertheless resolved to the fact that desegregation and integration would take a long time. Looking back on his seventieth birthday in 1960, he regretfully observed: "I doubt if I'll live to see the end of segregation."[199]

EISENHOWER, EARL WARREN, AND *BROWN*

Chief Justice Warren's appointment stemmed from the 1952 Republican Party convention. Shortly after the presidential election, Eisenhower told Warren he would have the "first vacancy" on the Court. Later in the summer of 1953, Eisenhower persuaded him to leave the California governorship to become solicitor general for the avowed purpose of his gaining experience arguing cases before the Court. When Vinson unexpectedly died, the chief justiceship was immediately offered to him.[200] Eisenhower was committed to appointing Warren because he "was firmly convinced the prestige of the Supreme Court had suffered severely in prior years, and that the only way it could be restored was by the appointment to it of men of nationwide reputation, of integrity, competence in the law, and in statesmanship." As California's favorite-son candidate for the presidency in 1952, Warren had "national stature." In Eisenhower's view at the time, he had "unimpeachable integrity," "middle-of-the-road views," and "a splendid record during his years of active law work" as state attorney general.[201] Years later, however, Eisenhower, echoing Truman's disappointment with his own appointees to the Court, called Warren's appointment the "biggest damn fool mistake I ever made."[202]

Warren, a big bear of a man with great personal charm, was a more successful politician than Vinson. He was a pragmatic progressive and another political Horatio Alger. Warren, born in 1891 in Los Angeles, had devoted his life to public service. After graduating from the University of California and Boalt Hall Law School, then serving in the army during World War I, Warren rose through the ranks to state attorney general and then governor from 1942 to 1953, before going to the Court. At the time, he was also considered a staunch "law and order" man, not a "liberal judicial activist," since he had presided over the evacuation and internment of Japanese Americans

The Warren Court in 1953–1954. Photograph by Hessler Photographers, collection of the Supreme Court of the United States

in California during World War II, which by a 6 to 3 vote was upheld in *Korematsu v. United States* (1944).

When Warren first arrived as chief justice, he was unprepared and unfamiliar with the Court's ways. Black, as senior associate justice, led the first several conferences, while his antagonist,[203] Frankfurter, immediately sought to bring Warren into his orbit. Warren gradually came into his own at conference. Although more of a skilled politician than a legal scholar, he had firm moral convictions and greater intellectual ability than many critics have granted. Despite his accomplishments, Warren was remarkably self-effacing. He was "the first to say that he was no legal scholar."[204] But he cared deeply about equality, education, and young people. During oral arguments, for instance, his trademark question from the bench was "Yes, but is it fair?"[205]

When it came to *Brown,* Warren stayed the course set by the Vinson Court. After the rearguments held in December 1953, he began the conference discussion by stating simply, "The previous plan was to discuss these cases informally in view of their importance, and that no vote be taken at this time. I favor that idea of delay—there is great value in unanimity and uniformity, even if we have some differences."[206] He was considerably more determined, skilled, and patient in achieving the ultimate result than Vinson. He thus took time to discuss *Brown* "from week to week . . . in groups, over lunch, and in conference. It was," he recalled, "too important to hurry it."[207]

Whenever possible, Warren typically sought to achieve unanimity, but especially so in *Brown*. Still, he always gave credit for the unanimous decision in that landmark ruling to the justices from the Deep South.[208] That is partially the reason, along with Warren's nonaccusatory, narrow, and straightforward opinion, why Jackson withheld publication of his separate opinion.

Whether unanimity in *Brown* was as crucial as the justices thought, even in light of their otherwise increasingly internal fragmentation and the filing of more individual concurring and dissenting opinions, remains debatable. In retrospect, perhaps, as Justice John Paul Stevens (1975–2010), who clerked for Rutledge, once remarked, a nonunanimous decision might have been preferable. Southerners might have felt that at least some justices understood their traditions as well as the inexorable opposition to ending segregation.[209]

In the end, despite ensuing criticism and massive resistance to the ruling in *Brown*, Chief Justice Warren dismissed charges of "judicial activism." "Some people think *Brown* was revolutionary," but he countered, "I see it as evolutionary in character. Just look at the various cases that had been eroding *Plessy* for so many years. . . . It was natural, the logical and practically the only way the case could be decided."[210] Jackson thought similarly.

Chapter Three

Justice and Company

Within the Court, Jackson found another struggle between "two worlds."[1] The Court was in a jurisprudential transition from its pre-1937 conservative stance against progressive legislation to the post-1937 Roosevelt Court's deference to Congress in defense of the New Deal. After the move into the "marble temple" in 1935, the Court was also undergoing an institutional transformation. Besides individual justices' separate opinions becoming more highly prized than institutional opinions for the Court,[2] work in the marble temple was different and on the verge of becoming more bureaucratic, with more law clerks and delegation of opinion writing.[3]

In his Godkin lectures,[4] Jackson expressed concerns about the growing role of law clerks. He did not think judging was a staff job, and he deplored the trend toward that. Accordingly, he invariably wrote the first draft of all his opinions, delegating little to clerks, reminiscent of the practice of most justices before the move into the marble temple. Only a few others—like Justices Black and Douglas, and later Justices John Paul Stevens (1975–2010) and David H. Souter (1990–2009)—continued the former tradition of writing all (or almost all) first drafts.

Most of Jackson's colleagues, as well as most subsequent justices, delegated opinion writing to clerks. As Justice Reed, for one, lamented, it would "be nice if we could write the way we think."[5] But in Reed's chambers, as in others, clerks "had the first word and [the justice] had the last word."[6] Indeed, clerks for Justice Murphy were snidely referred to as "Mr. Justice Huddleson" and "Mr. Justice Gressman."[7] According to William H. Rehnquist, that was for the most part true in other chambers during his clerkship with Jackson. Years later, when he himself sat on the Court, he likened the justices' chambers to "opinion writing bureaus."[8] Justice William J. Brennan Jr. went even further, referring to his opinions as the product of "the Brennan chambers," explaining, "I say from 'the Brennan chambers' because, as [nineteenth-century English philosopher and legal reformer Jeremy] Bentham said, 'the Law is not the work of judge alone but of judge and company.'"[9]

Chief Justice Warren's chamber was no exception. He relied extensively on clerks for drafts and revisions, though he did the first draft in *Brown*. "The Chief is not a good writer," one of his clerks recalled. "His first drafts are commonly very bad. Happily, however, he is quite willing to accept criticism or, indeed, to have his clerks reject the whole thing in toto."[10] Another former Warren clerk, Jesse Choper, recalled that clerks "ordinarily composed a first draft of an opinion, almost always assigned by the Chief to the clerk who had written the bench memo in the case."[11]

In a remark abandoning and contradicting an earlier claim that clerks wielded too much influence,[12] Justice Rehnquist observed, "I don't think people are shocked any longer to learn that an appellate judge receives a draft of a proposed opinion from a clerk."[13] As chief justice, Rehnquist revealed that he gave clerks ten days to do a first draft, before "reworking" it—conceding that his contributions to some opinions were minor, while for others they were major.[14] Likewise, Chief Justice John J. Roberts Jr. (2005–), who clerked for Rehnquist, has adopted the same practice.[15]

Over the last half century, not only has more opinion writing been delegated but also the number of law clerks has grown. It went from one to two for each justice to three to four, with a fifth for the chief justice. Their role in the opinion-writing process became institutionalized to the point, as one former clerk put it, that the Court became "clerk driven."[16] Even in the early 1950s, when Rehnquist clerked, the role of clerks in the opinion-writing process was beginning to grow and becoming controversial. Still, one of Frankfurter's former clerks, Alexander M. Bickel, defended the trend: "The day of the single, unassisted practitioner is over, and so is the day of the unassisted judge."[17]

Jackson's observations about the modern Court functioning like nine little law firms, and especially his concerns about the growing reliance on law clerks, provide a context for appreciating the significance of his unpublished opinion in Brown. First, it reveals Jackson's thinking unfiltered and unencumbered by the influence of clerks. Second, it reflects his intellectual struggles with fundamental questions of constitutional interpretation. In doing so, it contributes to contemporary debates over competing theories of constitutional interpretation. Finally, it further discredits claims made by Rehnquist during his 1971 Senate Judiciary Committee's confirmation hearings on his nomination as associate justice and those same claims made at the 1986 hearings on his elevation to chief justice. On both occasions, Rehnquist contended that a 1952 memo on Brown that he wrote as a clerk, arguing against overruling Plessy v. Ferguson's doctrine of "separate but equal," reflected Jackson's views, not his own. But Jackson's unpublished opinion, along with other evidence, makes abundantly clear, contrary to Rehnquist and some scholarly speculation, that Jackson never planned on dissenting in Brown. For these reasons, Jackson's working relationship with his clerks is important and sheds light not only on the controversy over Rehnquist's claims but also on Jackson's decision to withhold publication of the draft opinion.

Jackson and His Clerks

Like other justices at the time, Jackson had only one clerk each term until 1949 when, after Congress authorized a second, he hired two. However, after the 1952 term, during which Rehnquist and Donald Cronson clerked for him, he returned to employing only one, E. Barrett Prettyman Jr. Prettyman and another former clerk, James M. Marsh, speculated that was due to tensions among Rehnquist, his co-clerk, and Jackson himself.[18] Jackson, though, appeared open to hiring another clerk for the second half of the 1953 term, but he changed his mind because Prettyman proved so capable and congenial.[19] Moreover, although clerkships typically last for only one term, Jackson and some others kept theirs for two or more. Justice Murphy kept Eugene Gressman for five years, and Justice Owen Roberts (1930–1945) had a husband-and-wife team as his clerk and secretary for fifteen years.

Jackson's selection of clerks was eclectic and egalitarian, especially by contemporary standards. Most clerks today are recent graduates of Harvard, Yale, or another top-ten law school, and have already clerked for a federal appellate court "feeder" judge. Similarly, Jackson's first three clerks were graduates of Harvard. But his clerk during the 1947 and 1948 terms, James M. Marsh, attended law school at night at Temple University. Marsh came to know the justice while arranging for Temple's law review to publish articles by Jackson on the Nuremberg trials.[20] Jackson hired him even though he thought it might pose a problem because his chambers would be operating "without even one college degree." As he explained: "I do not have a degree. My secretary doesn't have a degree, and you do not have a degree. . . . So I would be compounding a weakness."[21] He nonetheless hired Marsh. Subsequently, Jackson rationalized his selection of law clerks in a letter to a law school dean, telling him most of the justices hired clerks who graduated from particular law schools they favored. But he frowned on that and was open to taking clerks from various schools. "There are other things in the world that count besides marks," he wrote, "and good common sense and agreeable ways have their value."[22]

Another Jackson clerk, Phil C. Neal, was recommended by the justice's son, William E. Jackson, a classmate at Harvard Law School. Neal was at the top of his class and president of the *Harvard Law Review*. He clerked for Jackson in the 1943 and 1944 terms and then recommended his replacement. After the clerkship, Neal eventually joined the faculty of Stanford Law School and later became dean of the University of Chicago Law School.

At Stanford, Neil came to know Rehnquist and recommended him to Jackson for a clerkship. Beginning in 1948, Jackson annually went to the Bohemian Grove in Montre Rio, California. The Bohemian Club—an all-

male club of influential businessmen, educators, lawyers, and politicians, in-
cluding former president Herbert Hoover—gathered for a few weeks each
August in the woods of northern California for relaxation and socializing.
In the summer of 1951, after his Bohemian Club retreat, Jackson went to
Palo Alto to dedicate a new law school building. There he was introduced to
Rehnquist, who was taking summer classes.

In *The Supreme Court: How It Was, How It Is,* Rehnquist recounts his interview with Jackson and his later receiving a letter in November telling him
that having only one clerk was not quite working out, and additional assistance might be needed. Rehnquist recalled telling Jackson that because he
was taking classes in the summers, he would graduate ahead of schedule
in December. According to Rehnquist, Jackson "requested that I come to
Washington on February 1, 1952, and plan to serve as his clerk from then
until June 1953. I was surprised and delighted to receive this offer, and accepted it immediately."[23]

In fact, after their meeting in August, Rehnquist immediately lobbied for
the clerkship in letters. Jackson responded in September, telling him that he
would probably not decide until the spring. Rehnquist wrote again, insisting
on knowing whether a decision could be made earlier because he was graduating in December and already had job offers in California. In Rehnquist's
words, "I trust you can see my point of view when I say that I am hesitant
to decline an attractive vested interest on the chance of a mere expectancy
materializing. Or, in non-legal terminology, a bird in the hand is worth two
in the bush."[24]

A little over a week later, Jackson replied that he was managing well with
one clerk but that he might "need an additional clerk by the first of March."
He also reminded Rehnquist of the importance of taking the California bar
exam after graduating, admonishing him that it "would be unwise to pass up
the first opportunity to try for the bar." Undeterred, Rehnquist wrote back
to explain, "I am available as of January 1; your letter spoke of March 1 as
the optimum time for you, but suggested that I should take the bar exam
if possible." The exam was not until April, which Rehnquist ventured was
probably too late. Reiterating that he wanted to come as soon as possible,
Rehnquist added he could always take the D.C. exam. He then followed
with another letter even before Jackson responded. This letter told of his
decision not to take the California exam. Rehnquist now explained that he
had "never been sold on California as a place to either live or practice." He
was now contacting firms in Arizona and New Mexico. Moreover, this time,
he proposed arriving on January 25, 1952. Jackson relented. Rehnquist thus
began midterm, serving through the following term until June 1953.[25]

Jackson's hiring of Rehnquist's co-clerk, Donald Cronson, was no less peculiar; the latter was even more self-promoting. A graduate of the University of Chicago Law School, Cronson arranged to meet Phil Neal, who was in Chicago visiting relatives during the Christmas holidays in 1947. Although they had just met, Neal agreed to send a letter of introduction to Jackson, recommending Cronson as "exceptionally intelligent and a pleasing person" who admired the justice's Nuremberg prosecutions.[26] Unsuccessful in his quest to meet Jackson, Cronson went to work on Wall Street. But he nevertheless mounted a five-year letter-writing campaign that, by 1952, he termed his "annual application." Jackson finally relented and hired Cronson for the October 1952 term,[27] during which the initial arguments were heard in *Brown*.

On arriving at the Court as Jackson's clerk, Rehnquist discovered that his primary task was writing memoranda on petitions for certiorari (known as cert. memos) on cases requesting the Court to grant review. Like most other justices, Jackson gave clerks an "office memo" detailing their duties and responsibilities. It provided specific instructions for preparing cert. memos. For example, the memos should concisely state the facts, the lower court's ruling, the questions presented, the names of the judges, and a recommendation about whether to grant the petition to hear a case.[28] At first Rehnquist found it daunting. He recalled that it "seem[ed] like a lot of responsibility for a brand-new law clerk."[29] Yet he soon got the hang of it. Another duty of clerks was maintaining the chamber's library. They were responsible for inserting all advance sheets of statutes and opinions into their appropriate series collections. But they had no access to the files of written communications with other justices or draft opinions unless they had the approval of Jackson's secretary, Elsie Douglas.

In a separate memo, Jackson underscored the need for confidentiality. "At the Supreme Court the office of each Justice functions as a separate unit, so far as its work is concerned. Not only is all of the Court work highly confidential, but tentative plans or opinions are not to be prematurely disclosed, *even to other offices*."[30]

As for opinion writing, Jackson typically wrote first drafts except, James Marsh recalled, in cases "not involving any controversial social or political issues." In those few instances, Jackson "would allow a law clerk to draft an opinion."[31] Likewise, Rehnquist noted that first drafts were done by a clerk in only one or two cases each term, adding, "If the clerk were reasonably faithful to his instructions and reasonably diligent in his work, the Justice could be quite charitable with his black pencil and paste pot."[32]

Notably, Frankfurter told Philip Kurland, one of his former clerks and University of Chicago Law School professor, that in writing Jackson's biography he should consult with Marsh and Prettyman, along with Elsie Douglas, for details about Jackson's opinion-writing process.[33] Frankfurter was consumed with history and getting the record straight, especially for his judicial icons—Justices Holmes, Brandeis, and Jackson, as well as Judge Learned Hand. He arranged for their private papers to be given to his former clerks turned professors—among them Mark De Wolf Howe, Bickel, Kurland, and Gerald Gunther—so they could write definitive judicial biographies.[34]

Marsh provided perhaps one of the best accounts of Jackson's opinion-writing process and use of clerks:[35]

> He has a natural flair for writing, but the smoothness of his opinions comes as much from working over as from his natural style and ability. We would often go through 4 or 5 typewritten and hand-corrected drafts before sending anything to the printer—and then three or four versions were printed before we circulated anything to the Brethren. . . . [He] of course writes the draft, gives it to me for suggestions, criticisms, and checking; I have an absolutely free hand to do whatever I will with it, and buy what he likes, discarding the rest.

Similarly, Frankfurter told Kurland, "Jackson was one of the few members of the Court who was eager for suggestions, even in style, although he was by long odds the most literarily gifted member on the Court and the most deeply versed in English literature, which enabled him to command so easily apt quotations."[36]

REHNQUIST AND JACKSON

Almost a year after the clerkship ended, Rehnquist wrote Jackson about his life and legal practice in Arizona. He had followed the justice's opinions and was surprised to find he agreed "with most everything you have done, and how well you seem to get along without me." Reflecting on his clerkship, Rehnquist noted that he felt at first, "Why, hell, that didn't teach me anything about practicing law." But rather condescendingly, he admitted, "One does pick up from a clerkship some sort of intuition about the nature of the judicial process."[37]

His last letter to Jackson expressed disappointment about Warren's appointment as chief justice. Lack of both legal experience—in spite of having been California's attorney general—and "the ability to think and write about law" made him unsuited. Warren's opinions struck Rehnquist as "not very good." However, he did grant that "one should not hold that against him; may be writing opinions is an act for which the knack is acquired."[38]

After the ruling in *Brown* and Jackson's death, Rehnquist was even more candid about Jackson in a 1955 letter to Frankfurter. In his book, *The Supreme Court: How It Was, How It Is,* he recounts his uneasiness about first com-

William H. Rehnquist, who clerked in 1952–1953, with Justice Jackson. C. George Niebank Jr. Collection

ing to the Court from a law school out West that did not yet have a national reputation. He felt out of his element. After meeting Frankfurter, the well-known former Harvard Law School professor, however, he was reassured and tremendously drawn to him. Frankfurter's willingness to debate legal and political issues was impressive, and Rehnquist thrived on that.[39] Before law school, Rehnquist earned an MA in political science at Harvard. During the 1952 term, a presidential election year, he came to know Frankfurter even better, and he appreciated that his "good friend Alex Bickel," who clerked for Frankfurter, had brought the justice to a party celebrating his engagement.[40]

Rehnquist's letter, along with other correspondence, however, was stolen from Frankfurter's papers in the Library of Congress sometime in the early 1970s.[41] It remains missing. Not until 2010 was it brought to light in a lecture by Prettyman.[42] After Jackson's death, Prettyman then clerked for Frankfurter, who asked for his thoughts on how to respond to Rehnquist's letter. In October 1955, Prettyman sent Frankfurter his reactions to Rehnquist's assertions that Jackson peaked as solicitor general, his judicial opinions didn't "seem to go anywhere," and he had a "tendency to go off half-cocked, and the justice never became close to him."[43]

Prettyman's response offered four counterpoints. First, the assertion that Jackson did not have a lasting influence was "foolish." As for the justice's going off half-cocked, Prettyman conceded that Jackson occasionally changed his mind. But he made two caveats: First, Jackson was not stubborn about switching initial positions after fully considering the facts and good oral arguments. And second, many of his "'flash' decisions were actually grounded on a lot more than appeared on the surface." The third criticism—that he was unpredictable and "you just can't figure him out," which was repeated in the *New York Times*'s obituary—made Prettyman "slightly ill." The very idea that a justice had to stick to a particular philosophy, regardless of where it leads, was "repulsive." Finally, as for never feeling a personal friendship, Prettyman acknowledged that Jackson was extremely complicated and a loner. But Prettyman still recognized "the small signs that meant friendship." Years later, Prettyman more frankly concluded, "Rehnquist had never much liked Jackson."[44] Nor was Prettyman alone in that view of Rehnquist's assessment of Jackson.[45] Likewise, Paul Freund, who worked with Jackson in the solicitor general's office, recalled that he "did not wear his heart on his sleeve or expose the deepest recesses of the spirit to the outside gaze."[46]

Whether Frankfurter responded to Rehnquist's letter remains unknown, along with whether it was lost in the theft of the justice's Library of Congress papers. In any event, besides Prettyman's letter, another important memo, written in December 1955, remained in Frankfurter's papers at Harvard Law School. That memo—with the author's name redacted, though it was probably from Harvard Law School professor Paul Freund, who clerked with Justice Brandeis in 1932–1933 and remained in close contact with Frankfurter—was from "a leading lawyer who in his day was one of the most esteemed of Mr. Justice Brandeis's law clerks."[47] The memo certainly reflected the views of Brandeis, who opposed the construction of the new building and refused to move in when completed. Like some other justices, Brandeis continued working with a clerk in his home office.[48]

In the memo, Brandeis's former clerk decried the erosion of the tradition of law clerks' confidentiality. Once strong but giving way, the tradition of confidentiality imposed a "moral obligation," which meant that "gossip about or any discussion of the Court's work with outsiders [was] absolutely not to be tolerated." That tradition had been reinforced by the fact that, before the marble temple, clerks worked in their justice's home offices and, except on decision days, rarely met as a group.

Pinpointing a source of disclosures and speculation in the press about the Court's work, the memo presumably from Freund highlighted the changed working conditions in the Court's new building. Clerks regularly met for lunch, socialized more frequently, and increasingly discussed pending cases.

Their lunchtime conversations, combined with their inexperience in D.C., made them targets of "sophisticated newspaper commentators or reporters," like Drew Pearson and Robert S. Allen.[49] Hence, gossip and rumors spread outside of their justices' chambers to those of others and into the press.

The memo was not merely nostalgic but prophetic. Rehnquist's 1952 memo to Jackson, arguing that *Plessy* "was right and should be re-affirmed," concluded with a confession: "I realize that it is an unpopular and unhumanitarian position, for which I have been excoriated by 'liberal' colleagues."[50] Not only does the use of first person belie Rehnquist's subsequent claims that the memo reflected Jackson's (not his) views. It highlights the insight of the former Brandeis clerk's complaint about too much gossip among the clerks, as well as with outsiders, after the Court moved into the marble temple. Rehnquist, however, had an entirely different view. He always enjoyed debating with other clerks about legal and political issues, including pending cases.[51]

The memo from Brandeis's former clerk was prophetic in another respect. Within the next year, in May 1956, former justice James F. Byrnes blasted the Warren Court's ruling in *Brown* in a *U.S. News & World Report* article, "The Supreme Court Must Be Curbed." Byrnes attacked the Court for imposing its own legal policy, unsupported by precedents, but instead based on the work of psychologists and sociologists. Byrnes also cited a recent article by Alexander Bickel, "The Original Understanding and the Segregation Decision," which was originally written as a memorandum while clerking for Frankfurter and which circulated to the other justices. Although he agreed with the ruling in *Brown*, Bickel concluded that the Fourteenth Amendment was not intended to apply to school segregation. Byrnes in turn criticized the Warren Court for saying that the evidence for the amendment's application to segregated schools was "inconclusive." He maintained that the Court should have acknowledged—like Bickel and Jackson—that legislative history conclusively established that the original understanding of the Fourteenth Amendment was that it did not apply to segregated schools.[52]

Coming from a former justice, Byrnes's article gave legitimacy to the mounting opposition threatening the Court's institutional prestige. Before Roosevelt appointed him to the bench in 1941, he had been a longtime member of Congress and supporter of the New Deal. Even while on the bench, he remained actively engaged with Roosevelt's White House on legislative matters.[53] After resigning from the Court a mere one year later, he became secretary of state and then governor of South Carolina. In his gubernatorial campaign, he ran on a promise to keep schools segregated but to make them equal. Byrnes maintained a close relationship with Frankfurter, and in correspondence, he made clear that he believed the Court would exceed its authority if it struck down segregated schools. He also warned that some public schools would close instead of integrate.[54]

Byrnes's frontal assault had to be answered, though not by a sitting justice. Alexander Bickel responded in June 1956, in another issue of *U.S. News & World Report,* with an article, "Frankfurter's Former Clerk Disputes Byrnes's Statement." But Bickel's article did not lay to rest the controversy over the Court as an institution and the influence of its clerks.

Little more than a year later, *U.S. News & World Report* published an exposé of "The Bright Young Men Behind the Bench." It probed the growing criticism that justices relied too much on clerks.[55] Focusing on the role of clerks in opinion writing, it included an interview with retired justice Sherman Minton. Besides having them write cert. memos, Minton said he usually prepared a first draft and then had the clerks go over it. If their comments or criticisms appeared valid, the opinion was rewritten.[56] The *New York Times* followed with another article, taking issue with other reports: "It has been suggested that the clerks have an important influence on the court, but former clerks say in persuasive language, that nothing could be further from the truth."[57]

A few months later in *U.S. News & World Report,* Rehnquist then entered the fray with an article, "Who Writes Decisions of the Supreme Court?" No former law clerk under his own name had publicly discussed their work so recently after clerking. Despite being guarded in describing writing cert. memos and working on draft opinions, there was no mistaking Rehnquist's bottom line: when the Court considered *Brown,* "the political cast of the clerks as a group was to the 'left' of either the nation or the Court." Although conceding that fellow clerks did not make a "conscious" effort to impose their ideological bias, Rehnquist nonetheless charged that "unconscious bias" crept into many of his fellow clerks' cert. memos. Moreover, he asserted that a majority of the clerks had "extreme solicitude for the claims of Communists and other criminal defendants."[58]

Not surprisingly, Rehnquist's public charges contributed to the growing unease in many quarters about the apparently increasing role of law clerks, and the growing controversy over their influence within the Court. The Associated Press and the *New York Times* deemed Rehnquist's article newsworthy and ran a follow-up, "Sway of Clerks on the Court Cited."[59] Within three months, *U.S. News & World Report* published two more articles about the pros and cons of law clerks' exerting influence on the Court's decision making. William D. Rogers, a former clerk to Justice Reed in the 1952 term, when Rehnquist also clerked, argued that clerks were not decisive in determining the outcome in cases. He insisted that no justice changed a vote due to clerks, and that such influence would be unconstitutional.[60] In response, Rehnquist retreated a bit, but he still maintained that the "political complexion" of the Court's clerks was decidedly on the left.[61]

The storm over the Warren Court continued to grow, along with resistance to *Brown*. In a speech on the Senate floor, conservative Mississippi Democratic senator John C. Stennis quoted Rehnquist's article at length. He suggested that the Court's law clerks, because of their "ever-increasing importance and influence," should face Senate confirmation.[62]

Once again, at Frankfurter's prodding, Bickel published another defense of the Court. Ironically, along with his Yale Law School colleague Robert H. Bork, and Kurland at Chicago, Bickel would later emerge in the 1970s in the forefront of the conservative legal movement critical of the Warren Court.[63] Without naming Rehnquist, Bickel rebutted his and others' criticisms in an article in the *New York Times Magazine*.[64] Privately, however, Bickel actually dismissed Rehnquist as a far-right extremist in his initial draft.[65] He shared his view with Frankfurter, who in earlier correspondence with Bickel made clear his own disapproval of "Bill's loose talk about R.H.J."[66]

Bickel's article underscored the fact that the Court and the legal profession were in transition, and defended that new reality. He argued that (1) clerks were not a "powerful kitchen cabinet" or "ghost writers"; (2) their political views might "enliven the lunch hour" but made "no discernable difference" in the Court's work; and (3) as a group the clerks "no more fit any single political label than will any other eighteen young Americans who are not picked on a political basis."[67]

Not dissuaded by his "old friend," Rehnquist subsequently published a piece in the *Harvard Law Record* (1959), expressing dismay at the Senate Judiciary Committee's failure during its confirmation hearings to question Eisenhower's nominee, Justice Charles Whittaker (1957–1962), about the legitimacy of *Brown*. Once again, Rehnquist profoundly disagreed with that landmark decision: "The Court in *Brown* . . . held in effect that the framers of the Fourteenth Amendment left it to the Court to decide what 'due process' and 'equal protection' meant. Whether or not the framers thought this, it is sufficient for this discussion that the present Court thinks the framers thought it."[68]

Rehnquist's Memo and the Distortion of Jackson's Position in *Brown*

Almost two decades after his clerkship, Rehnquist was an assistant attorney general in charge of the Office of Legal Counsel in the administration of Republican president Richard M. Nixon. In the interim, besides practicing law in Arizona, he closely followed Washington politics, actively campaigned for conservative Republican senator Barry Goldwater during the 1964 presidential election, and opposed enactment of a civil rights law. He also came to know Richard (Dick) Kleindienst, who became deputy attorney general in the Department of Justice under Nixon's attorney general, John Mitchell. Mitchell had been Nixon's campaign manager, law partner, and confidant. During the 1968 presidential election, he promoted Nixon's Southern strategy to win over white Southern votes by promising to appoint "strict constructionists" to the Court and to return "law and order" to the country.[69] Nixon wanted to remold the Court in the image of Frankfurter.

Rehnquist, however, was never in Nixon's inner circle, like Kleindienst and Mitchell. Indeed, he did not meet the president until July 1, 1971, just months before Nixon nominated him to the Court. John Dean, as Nixon's White House counsel, accompanied the president to a meeting run by Rehnquist on the declassification of documents of prior administrations' involvement in Vietnam. This followed the Court's rejection of the administration's attempt to block publication of the so-called Pentagon Papers.[70] Dean recalled Nixon remarking that Rehnquist "dressed like a clown" because of his attire—pink shirt, psychedelic tie, muttonchop sideburns, and heavy black glasses. Nixon, still largely unfamiliar with him, later referred to Rehnquist as "Renchburg."[71]

Rehnquist was nonetheless keenly interested and involved in Nixon's initial, and failed, nominations. As the head of the Department of Justice's Office of Legal Counsel, he oversaw the administration's judicial selection process. Rehnquist maintained a list of potential nominees, vetted possible judicial candidates, and made recommendations to Mitchell. In Dean's words, "Bill Rehnquist had become the personnel director for future justices."[72] During Nixon's first term, Rehnquist oversaw the appointments of Chief Justice Warren E. Burger (1969–1986) and Justice Harry A. Blackmun (1970–1994). He also witnessed the Senate's forced withdrawal of two other nominees—Judges Clement F. Haynsworth Jr.[73] and G. Harrold Carswell[74]—along with several other false starts, including potential female and senatorial nominees, who were deemed unqualified or who withdrew from consideration.[75]

Ironically, considering the missteps with two earlier Nixon nominees, Rehnquist was nominated by Nixon after Lewis F. Powell agreed to accept one of the nominations for the two vacancies—the seats of Justices Black and Harlan—on the Court.[76] Powell had impeccable credentials that would certainly not ignite controversies like those over Haynsworth and Carswell. Powell was a Harvard Law School graduate who became a wealthy lawyer in a large Southern firm; he was also a past president of the American Bar Association. Notably, the ABA, which informally ranks judicial nominees,

A Random Thought on the Segregation Cases

One-hundred fifty years ago this Court held that it was the ultimate judge of the restrictions which the Constitution imposed on the various branches of the national and state government. <u>Marbury</u> v. <u>Madison.</u> This was presumably on the basis that there are standards to be applied other than the personal predilections of the Justices.

As applied to questions of inter-state or state-federal relations, as well as to inter-departmental disputes within the federal government, this doctrine of judicial has worked well. Where theoretically co-ordinate bodies of government are disputing, the Court is well suited to its role as arbiter. This is because these problems involve much less emotionally charged subject matter than do those discussed below. In effect, they determine the skeletal relations of the governments to each other without influencing the substantive business of those governments.

As applied to relations between the individual and the state, the system has worked much less well. The Constitution, of course, deals with indivudal rights, particularly in the First Ten and the Fourteenth Amendments. But as I read the history of this Court, it has seldom been out of hot water when attempting to interpret these individual rights. <u>Fletcher</u> v. <u>Peck</u>, in 1810, represented an attempt by Chief Justice Marshall to extend the protection of the contract clause to infant business. <u>Scott</u> v. <u>Sanford</u> was the result of Taney's effort to protect slaveholders from legislative interference.

After the Civil War, business interest came to dominate the Court, and they in turn ventured into the deep water of protecting certain types of individuals against legislative interference. Championed first by Field, then by Peckham and Brewer, the high water mark of the trend in protecting corporations against legislative influence was probably <u>Lochner</u> v. <u>NY.</u>. To the majority opinion in that case, Holmes replied that the Fourteenth Amendment did not enact Herbert Spencer's Social Statics. Other cases coming later in a similar vein were <u>Adkins</u> v. <u>Children's Hospital</u>, <u>Hammer</u> v. <u>Dagenhart</u>, <u>Tyson</u> v. <u>Banton</u>, <u>Ribnik</u> v. <u>McBride</u>. But eventually the Court called a halt to this reading of its own economic views into the Constitution. Apparently it recognized that where a legislature was dealing with its own citizens, it was not part of the judicial function to thwart public opinion except in extreme cases.

In these cases now before the Court, the Court is, as Davis suggested, being asked to read its own sociological views into the Constitution. Urging a view palpably at variance with precedent and probably with legislative hsitory, appellants seek to convince the Court of the moral wrongness of the treatment they are receiving. I would suggest that this is a question the Court need never reach; for regardless of the Justice's individual views on the merits of segregation, it quite clearly is not one of those extreme cases which commands intervention from one of any conviction. If this Court, because its members individually are "liberal" and dislike segregation, now chooses to strike it down, it differs from the McReynolds court only in the kinds of litigants it favors and the kinds of special claims it protects. To those who would argue that "personal" rights are more sacrosanct than "property" rights, the short answer is that the Constitution makes no such distinction. To the argument made by Marshall that a majority may not deprive a minority of its constitutional right, the answer must be made that while this is sound in theory, in the long run it is the majority who will determine what the constitutional rights of the minority are. One hundred and fifty years of attempts on the part of this Court to protect minority rights of any kind--whether those of business, slaveholders, or Jehovah's Witnesses--have all met the same fate. One by one the cases establishing such rights have been sloughed off, and crept silently to rest. If the present Court is unable to profit by this example, it must be prepared to see its work fade in time, too, as embodying only the sentiments of a transient majority of nine men.

I realize that it is an unpopular and unhumanitarian position, for which I have been excoriated by "liberal" colleagues, but I think <u>Plessy</u> v. <u>Ferguson</u> was right and should be re-affirmed. If the Fourteenth Amendment did not enact Spencer's <u>Social Statics</u>, it just as surely did not enact Myrdahl's <u>American Dilemna</u>.

whr

William H. Rehnquist's memorandum on *Brown v. Board of Education*.

had contributed to the Haynsworth and Carswell defeats in the Senate by the low ratings given both of them, but enthusiastically endorsed Powell. After Powell accepted the nomination, Nixon turned to Rehnquist at the urging of Dean, Kleindienst, and Mitchell. Rehnquist immediately accepted the offer, though he had previously rebuffed a reporter's question about whether he might be nominated, wryly responding, "I'm not from the South, I'm not a woman, and I'm not mediocre."[77]

Unlike Powell, who sailed through the Senate confirmation process and was confirmed by a vote of 89 to 1, Rehnquist faced the headwinds of a storm of criticism. Controversy did not arise over his qualifications; he had graduated at the top of his class at Stanford University Law School and had clerked for Jackson. Rather, it was his hard-line conservativism that led to charges that he was a "segregationist," a "racist," and a "right-wing zealot."[78] Rehnquist also had defended the ill-fated earlier nominations of Haynsworth and Carswell, both conservative Southern judges, in letters published in the *Washington Post*.[79]

After contentious judiciary committee hearings and on the eve of the Senate floor debate over Rehnquist's confirmation in December 1971, *Newsweek* published excerpts from the two-page 1952 memo signed "WHR" (reproduced opposite), entitled "A Random Thought on the Segregation Cases."[80] The bottom line of the WHR memo was unequivocal: *Plessy* and the doctrine of "separate but equal" should be reaffirmed.

Rehnquist's memo had remained unknown. It was among Jackson's papers in the possession of his would-be biographer, Philip Kurland, a well-known conservative critic of the Warren Court at the time. Unlike Frankfurter's papers or those of other justices, Jackson's papers were not donated to the Library of Congress until 1983 and 1984. Even then, they were not processed until 1985—a year before Republican president Ronald Reagan would elevate Rehnquist to the chief justiceship. Kurland, and later his Chicago colleague, Dennis J. Hutchinson, controlled access to the papers with the aim of writing Jackson's biography. Ironically, Kurland, like Bickel earlier in 1955, deemed Rehnquist too extreme, and he brought the 1952 memo to light. Kurland found Rehnquist's explanation "implausible, both because Jackson held more liberal views on race relations and because [Jackson] didn't use his [clerks] for such chores."[81]

Another bombshell dropped a few days later. The *Washington Post* reported that Jackson's longtime secretary, Elsie Douglas, rebuked Rehnquist's assertion that "Jackson would have asked a law clerk to help prepare remarks he would make when the nine justices met to decide whether to overturn the separate-but-equal doctrine." She accused Rehnquist of "smear[ing] the reputation of a great justice."[82] Years later, during the Senate debate over

Rehnquist's 1986 nomination to be chief justice, she reiterated: "It surprises me every time Justice Rehnquist repeats what he said in 1971 that the views he expressed in his 1952 memorandum . . . were those of Justice Jackson rather than his own views. . . . I don't know anyone in the world who was more for equal protection."[83]

Democratic senators and other opponents of Rehnquist immediately seized on the memo as further evidence of his support for segregation and lack of candor. Some Democratic senators—led by Birch Bayh (Ind.), John V. Tunney (Calif.), and Edward Kennedy (Mass.)—renewed their challenges to his veracity in an attempt to reopen the confirmation hearings and thereby delay, if not defeat, his confirmation. By then, a few Republican senators broke ranks, including Senators Edward Brooke (Mass.), the first African American elected to the Senate since Reconstruction, and Jacob Javits (N.Y.)—a prominent, outspoken Jewish liberal Republican.[84]

In spite of the mounting controversy, Rehnquist stood by his claim that the memo reflected Jackson's views, not his own. With the hope of evading defeat, as Haynsworth and Carswell suffered, he sent a letter to the chair of the judiciary committee, Senator James Eastland (D-Miss.), a Southerner opposed to civil rights legislation. Disassociating himself from the memo, Rehnquist maintained it represented Jackson's views:

> A memorandum ["A Random Thought on the Segregation Cases"] in the files of Justice Robert H. Jackson bearing my initials has become the subject of discussion in the Senate debate on my confirmation, and I therefore take the liberty of sending you my recollection of the facts in connection with it. As best I can reconstruct the circumstances after some nineteen years, the memorandum was prepared by me at Justice Jackson's request; it was intended as a rough draft of a statement of *his* views. . . . He expressed concern that the conference should have the benefit of all of the arguments in support of the constitutionality of the "separate but equal" doctrine, as well as those against its constitutionality. . . .
>
> I am satisfied that the memorandum was not designed to be a statement of *my* views on these cases. . . . I am fortified in this conclusion because the bald, simplistic conclusion that *Plessy v. Ferguson* is not an accurate statement of my own views at the time. I believe that the memorandum was prepared by me as a statement of Justice Jackson's tentative views for his own use at conference.[85]

Rehnquist concluded his letter claiming that the memo discussed *Brown* only because of a question Jackson had asked about the binding effect of precedent, and that the justice had not asked for his position on the substantive issue in *Brown*. Finally, for the record, Rehnquist said he fully supported "the legal reasoning and the rights from the standpoint of fundamental fairness of the *Brown* decision."

Rehnquist's letter only fanned the flames. Nixon's Department of Justice and the White House rallied support for the nomination amid the growing opposition in the Democratic-controlled Senate. Attorney General Mitchell remained confident and told Dean: "Hell, he doesn't have the foggiest memory of ever writing [the memo]."[86] Later that same day, Eastland gave a speech on the Senate floor defending Rehnquist. He explained that the letter was not even needed "because the memorandum was certainly what was the law at the time [referring to the 'separate but equal' doctrine], which was 1952." Eastland also claimed that Rehnquist was simply being forthright and fair with the Senate. Although the letter was private correspondence, Eastland proceeded to read it into the public record.[87]

Many found Rehnquist's explanation implausible. Opponents and even some supporters found the letter incredible. Years later, in *The Rehnquist Choice,* John Dean recounted: "To be blunt, I thought he had lied. His explanation was so at odds with the style and contents of his memo to Jackson that it did not pass the smell test. . . . I thought (and still believe) that Rehnquist overreacted to the heat he was getting, and felt he had to reconstruct history to get himself off the hook. To say I was disappointed is an understatement."[88]

Still, the White House and most Republican senators continued their support. Three days after *Newsweek*'s publication of the *Brown* memo, Rehnquist's co-clerk, Donald Cronson, defended him in a telegram from London, where he was a Mobil Oil executive. Cronson's cable was immediately put into the *Congressional Record,*[89] but it only further fueled the fire over confirmation. In offering his support, Cronson inadvertently contradicted Rehnquist's account. Cronson recalled that Jackson asked for a memo on *Brown* and later for a second one "supporting the proposition that *Plessy* was correct." Unlike Rehnquist, however, Cronson claimed that both of them worked on the two memos: "The memorandum supporting Plessy was typed by you, but a great deal of its content was the result of my suggestions. A number of the phrases quoted in Newsweek I can recognize as having been composed by me, and it is probable that the memorandum is more mine than yours."[90] But if so, why hadn't Rehnquist earlier explained that the memo was a collaborative effort? There also remains the indisputable fact that the first memo was signed "DC" and the second one "WHR." In addition, Cronson told the Pulitzer Prize–winning *New York Times* reporter Anthony Lewis that he and Rehnquist "personally thought at the time [1952] that the 1896 decision, *Plessy v. Ferguson*, was wrong."[91]

Cronson's three-page memo, the one signed "DC," was titled "A Few Expressed Prejudices on the Segregation Cases."[92] It stood in sharp contrast with Rehnquist's explanation in other ways as well. Cronson's memo laid out three alternative routes for the Court in *Brown:* (1) overturn *Plessy*; (2) "get around *Plessy* via the back door," affirming its "separate but equal" doctrine as a general rule while holding that, given "the social and psychological factors involved," separate schools cannot be equal; or (3) reaffirm *Plessy*. A fourth possibility offered in the "DC" memo was to affirm the lower courts that found inequality in the four companion cases with *Brown;* and in *Brown* review the lower court's findings upholding segregated schools, but conclude that "there was no physical equality" and remand the case, thereby ducking the issue. However, Cronson doubted that there would be any sentiment on the Court "to duck this again."

Cronson's memo endorsed the second approach, which is basically what the Court eventually did—namely, not overrule *Plessy* per se but instead hold that its doctrine had no place in the field of public education. Contrary to Rehnquist's memo, Cronson also accepted the factual premises offered by Thurgood Marshall and the NAACP Legal Defense Fund: "The enforced separation of the two races stamps the colored race with a badge of inferiority." That meant rejecting Justice Henry Brown's reasoning in *Plessy* that any perceived inequality in segregation was "solely because the colored race chooses to put this construction on it."

Unlike Rehnquist's memo, Cronson's had no doubt "*Plessy* was wrong." Another cert. memo on a petition challenging segregation, in *District of Columbia v. John R. Thompson Co., Inc.* (1953),[93] underscores Cronson's "strong prejudice in favor of curtailing discrimination against colored folks because of their color." *Thompson* was a test case challenging segregated restaurants in the District of Columbia. Besides cafeterias in federal buildings, lunch counters in department stores, and some five-and-dime diners, there were only a few dining places that served blacks. Cronson believed that moral principles should prevail over physical characteristics, like race, in the treatment of people. Yet he was conflicted, as with *Brown,* because Thompson's suit was brought on the basis of two local Reconstruction-era laws enacted in 1872 and 1873 that had never been enforced. Lawyers for Thompson's diner argued that those laws were implicitly repealed by an 1878 federal statute and subsequent legislation that reorganized the district's governance and reasserted congressional control. Cronson thought that Congress, not the Court, had responsibility for desegregating public accommodations, just as it did for the segregated schools in the district. Hence, he made no recommendation on whether to grant review, and instead he somewhat arrogantly concluded, "You are still the justice. And even if you did want to trade jobs with me, I don't think Congress would be very enthusiastic about the switch."

In his memo on *Brown,* Cronson had also ventured that if the clock could be turned back, Justice John Marshall Harlan's dissent in *Plessy* should prevail. That, of course, was impossible. For almost sixty years, *Plessy* had legitimated "not only rules of law, but ways of life." Like Jackson, Cronson worried about the consequences of overruling such a precedent, however incorrect. As he made clear in his cert. memo on the *Thompson* case, he thought—just as Jackson had initially preferred—that Congress should address the segregation problems. His bottom line was for the Court to "confess error in *Plessy,*" remand the case, and, unlike Rehnquist's blunt recommendation to reaffirm *Plessy,* let Congress "straighten out the mess."

Completely contrary to Jackson's draft opinion, Cronson concluded that if Congress refused to address the matter, "then surely this Court should not do so." In sharp contrast, Jackson's drafts leave little doubt that he came to the conclusion, shared by neither Rehnquist nor Cronson, that although it would be preferable to leave the matter to Congress, Congress was unwilling and unlikely to deal with it. For Jackson, the Court thus had a duty to decide. Other institutions had failed to come to terms with segregation, and there was little hope they would do so. Hence, Jackson's draft focuses on the constitutional basis for the Court's ruling against segregated schools.

Cronson's memo on *Brown* was not widely known at the time, but his cable from London many years later highlighted inconsistencies in Rehnquist's assertions. Indiana's Democratic senator Birch Bayh and Massachusetts's Republican senator Edward Brook set forth the inconsistencies and contradictions on the Senate floor,[94] just as scholars would subsequently do.[95] Their attempt to filibuster confirmation nevertheless failed. The Senate Judiciary Committee never cross-examined Rehnquist about his memo. Instead, after a weeklong debate, with most senators eager to leave for Christmas break, Rehnquist was confirmed by a vote of 68 to 26.

In his seminal work, *Simple Justice: The History of* Brown v. Board of Education *and Black America's Struggle for Equality,* Richard Kluger further detailed the inconsistencies and contradictions in Rehnquist's and Cronson's positions in what would become a rather well-known footnote.[96] Kluger concluded that neither Rehnquist's claim about his memo reflecting Jackson's views nor Cronson's assertions were in the least creditable. On the contrary, he was confident that the memos simply stated each one's views.

When reviewing Kluger's 1975 book, *New York Times* reporter Anthony Lewis sought responses from Rehnquist and Cronson to Kluger's four-page footnote that cast doubt on their credibility. Cronson, who had periodically stayed in contact with Rehnquist, prepared "A Short Note on an Unimportant Memorandum," which he first sent to Rehnquist in the hope "that the basically trivial episode of the WHR Memorandum will soon be allowed to attain the obscurity that it deserves."[97]

Cronson's proposed response explained that the "DC" memo recommended reversing *Plessy* and leaving to Congress the job of uprooting segregation. However, he now could not recall why Jackson had asked for the second "WHR" memo. But Cronson did speculate it might have been due to Rehnquist's reputation for staking out conservative positions in what the law clerks dubbed "the Court of Clerks," their lunchtime meetings in the marble temple's cafeteria.[98] Perhaps Jackson had heard from him or other clerks about Rehnquist's defense of *Plessy* during their lunchtime gatherings. Obliquely defending the last line of Rehnquist's memo—"I realize that it is an unpopular and unhumanitarian position, for which I have been excoriated by 'liberal' colleagues, but I think *Plessy v. Ferguson* was right"—Cronson explained in his proposed response to Lewis:

> No one has ever accused William H. Rehnquist of being afraid to defend an unpopular position. His is the sort of mind which dotes on opposition and adversity. It was entirely normal that he should challenge any position held sacred by his fellow law clerks, even if he agreed with that position. Since the principal doctrine upon which all other law clerks were united during October Term 1952 was the proposition that *Plessy v Ferguson* was wrongly decided, Bill Rehnquist defended the contrary position with gusto and cogency. His virtuoso performance in the Court of Clerks on the subject of *Plessy* may have led to composition of the WHR memorandum.

Cronson, as in his 1971 cable, reiterated that the "WHR" memo contained some of his own "purple prose." He specifically identified "the paragraph which asserted that if the Fourteenth Amendment did not enact Herbert Spencer, neither did it enact Myrdal's American Dilemma. But if I was not the principal author of the memorandum, I did make a substantial contribution to it."

Curiously, Cronson now argued Rehnquist's claim that the "WHR" memo reflecting Jackson's views "was a trivial error, and an entirely honest one." In addition, Cronson attached an "Addendum" directly responding to the three questions Kluger raised in the footnote in *Simple Justice*: (1) Why didn't Rehnquist mention to the judiciary committee the first memo was signed "DC"? (2) If Jackson indeed asked for two memos reaching opposite conclusions about *Plessy*, why did Rehnquist claim the second one represented Jackson's position and not his? And (3) if, as Cronson's 1971 London cable asserted, the memos were a collaborative effort, why was one signed "DC" and the other "WHR"?[99]

Cronson offered these explanations to Kluger's questions: (1) Rehnquist failed to mention the first memo because he forgot about it. As for (2) (and contradicting Cronson's own earlier statements), Jackson had not requested two memos reaching opposite results, and "Rehnquist deduced, rather than claimed, that the WHR Memorandum set forth Jackson's views. . . . In fact it was designed to set forth a point of view which was not Jackson's, and which may or may not have been Rehnquist's, but which Jackson might use in conference when cases were discussed." Finally, (3) Rehnquist failed to mention their collaboration because he simply didn't remember.

Given the inconsistencies and contradictions in Cronson's proposed response to Lewis, perhaps not unsurprisingly, Rehnquist suggested to Cronson that he not send Lewis the proposed response, "which he can find a way to tear apart," and presumably reignite the controversy. Moreover, Rehnquist admitted basic inconsistencies in their recollections. But he passed them off as due to Cronson's "more orderly and retentive mind" compared to his own "hazy" memory. In short, Rehnquist concluded, this was "a case where it is best to let sleeping dogs lie."

Surprisingly in some ways, a decade later, Rehnquist granted for the first time an interview with the *New York Times Magazine*.[100] John Jenkins's piece, "The Partisan," was a retrospective on the Court's most conservative justice—then known as "the Lone Ranger" for writing so many solo dissents. His fifty-four solo dissents were more than any of his colleagues in his fifteen years as an associate justice—although Justice Douglas holds the record (208) for solo dissents.[101] Coincidentally, the very next year after the interview, Chief Justice Warren E. Burger (1969–1986) announced his retirement, and Republican president Ronald Reagan nominated Rehnquist to take his place as chief justice and Antonin Scalia to fill the resulting Rehnquist vacant seat.

Inevitably, Jenkins asked Rehnquist about whether he still agreed with the statement in the 1952 "WHR" memo: "To the argument made by Thurgood, not John, Marshall that a majority may not deprive a minority of its constitutional right, the answer must be that while this is sound in theory, in the long run it is the majority who will determine what the constitutional rights of the minority are." Rehnquist said that his views had changed since *Brown,* but he still maintained "there was a perfectly reasonable argument the other way."

Jenkins did not let the matter rest. He asked Jackson's would-be biographer, Dennis J. Hutchinson, about the claim that the memo summarized

Jackson's views. Hutchinson, who supervised the transfer of Jackson's papers to the Library of Congress in 1983 and 1984, had been through "every
box, every detail," and concluded simply that it was an "absurd explanation."
Moreover, Jenkins reported that there were other memos (made publicly
available after Jackson's papers were processed in 1985) further undermin-
ing Rehnquist's claim about the "WHR" memo. They also underscored his
strident conservativism and view of the Court's limited role in defending
the rights of minorities—positions not shared by Jackson. In particular, Jenkins quoted from his memo on *Terry v. Adams* (1953),[102] a "white primary"
case considered at the same time as *Brown.*

For almost three decades, the Court had confronted Southern states' attempts to exclude African Americans from voting in Democratic primary
elections, thus guaranteeing the election of white conservative Democrats.[103] As quoted by Jenkins, Rehnquist's memo in *Terry v. Adams* argued:

> The Constitution does not prevent the majority from banding together, nor
> does it attain success in the effort. It is about time the Court faced the fact
> that the white people in the South don't like the colored people; the Consti-
> tution restrains them from effecting this dislike through state action, but it
> most assuredly did not appoint the Court as a sociological watchdog to rear
> every time private discrimination raises its admittedly ugly head.

Jenkins, though, neglected to note Rehnquist's confession in his memo that
he had "a mental block against the case" because other clerks wanted to
"show those damn southerners," whereas he took "a dim view of this pathological search for discrimination."[104]

In line with Rehnquist's memo, Jackson voted against finding a Fourteenth Amendment violation at the first conference discussion of *Terry v. Adams,* then drafted a nine-page dissent. But Jackson subsequently changed his
mind and prepared a concurring opinion in which he concluded that black
voters were discriminated against in violation of the Fifteenth Amendment,
again declining to follow Rehnquist's recommendation. In the end, Jackson
withheld the concurrence, as he did in *Brown,* and joined Justice Tom Clark's
concurring opinion instead.[105]

The following year, during Rehnquist's 1986 confirmation hearings to be
chief justice, the controversy over his memo on *Brown* inevitably resurfaced.
So too did Kluger's footnote in *Simple Justice* that cast doubt on Rehnquist's
and Cronson's truthfulness. Accusations also arose that in the 1960s Rehnquist had harassed minority voters in polling lines and opposed passage of a
local civil rights law. At these hearings, his memo on *Brown* was introduced
into the record and he had to testify about his use of "I" in the memo, about

his position on *Plessy* at the time, and about whether the memo represented Jackson's views, among other discrepancies and accusations.

During the 1986 confirmation hearings, Senator Kennedy led the opposition, calling Rehnquist "too extreme on freedom of speech, too extreme on separation of church and state, too extreme to be Chief Justice." That triggered Utah's Republican senator Orrin Hatch to counter that the judiciary committee's hearings threatened to become a "Rehnquisition."

True to his Swedish background, Rehnquist stood firm. He again denied that the memo reflected his views and continued to maintain that it represented those of Jackson. When asked by Senator Kennedy about the "WHR" memo on *Brown* and who "the 'I's refer to? Do the 'I's refer to you Mr. Rehnquist?" Rehnquist replied, "I, I do not think they do." To which Kennedy repeated: "You maintain that the 'I's refer to Justice Jackson?" "Yes," he again responded, it was "obviously something for him to say [in conference]."[106]

When questioned by Senator Joseph R. Biden (D-Del.) about whether Cronson was correct in claiming that Rehnquist strongly defended *Plessy* during the law clerks' luncheons, he initially said, "No, I do not think he is." But he later backtracked, stating: "Again, it is hard to remember back, but I think it probably seemed to me at the time that some of the [other clerks] simply were not facing the arguments on the other side, and I thought they ought to be faced."[107] Senator Howard M. Metzenbaum (D-Ohio) subsequently outlined a number of seemingly irreconcilable statements in Rehnquist's testimony about the memo and whether the use of "I" indicated his (not Jackson's) position that *Plessy* should be reaffirmed. Once again, evading a direct response, Rehnquist said: "I would suspect that a logical interpretation [of 'I' in the memo] is I perhaps imagined this is the way Justices spoke in conference."[108] And so it went.

Democratic senators confronted an uphill battle against the elevation of a sitting member of the Court to be chief justice, especially in a Republican-controlled Senate. The most Democrats accomplished was a reassertion of the Senate Judiciary Committee's power to consider the judicial philosophy of nominees, no less than presidents do in selecting them. Ultimately Rehnquist was confirmed by a vote of 65 to 33. Southern Democrats voted with Republicans, and only two Republicans joined the thirty-one Democrats voting against confirmation.

In retrospect, the controversy over Rehnquist's memo and Jackson's views on *Brown* never reached a resolution. It even divided those who subsequently studied the documents and records. Numerous legal scholars, historians, political scientists, and other Court watchers dissected, analyzed, and speculated on the veracity of Rehnquist's claims and his testimony, and there were a few who compared Rehnquist's statements with Jackson's unpublished opinion. The overwhelming number of those who investigated doubted Rehnquist's credibility. Some, like John Dean, flatly concluded he lied.[109] Still, a few more charitably accepted that Rehnquist's memo could possibly have been in line with Jackson's thinking.

Scholars such as New York University professor Bernard Schwartz concluded that it is simply untenable to contend that Jackson ever supported upholding *Plessy*.[110] Their conclusions were consistent with those of Kurland and Hutchinson, the custodians of Jackson's papers, as well as others who compared the documents and historical record.[111] A preponderance of the evidence established, just as Kluger concluded in *Simple Justice*, "that the memorandum in question—the one that threatened to deprive William Rehnquist of his place on the Supreme Court—was an accurate statement of his own views on segregation, not those of Robert Jackson, who, by contrast, was a staunch libertarian and humanist."[112]

There were, to be sure, a few who challenged that view. Harvard Law School professor Mark Tushnet, for one, did so, although he did not do so primarily on the basis of the truthfulness of Rehnquist's claims. Instead, he argued that Jackson was "ambivalent" and not as libertarian or humanistic as portrayed.[113] Still others contended, no less implausibly, that Rehnquist's memos on *Brown* and *Terry v. Adams* largely anticipated Jackson's views, instead of promoting his own conservative stance on minority rights and the role of the Court.[114]

One largely neglected aspect of the debate over Rehnquist's memo involves when it was written. That issue is important because it raises a further question: whether the memo in fact had any influence on Jackson. University of Wisconsin Law School professor Brad Snyder persuasively argued that Rehnquist's memo was almost certainly written shortly after hearing the first round of oral arguments, on December 9–11, 1952, after the historic clash between John W. Davis, representing South Carolina and a preeminent Supreme Court litigator,[115] and Thurgood Marshall.[116] The first couple of paragraphs of the memo echo the argument made by Davis that the matter should not be decided by the justices' personal preferences and should be left to Congress. In the penultimate sentence of his memo, Rehnquist asserted, "The court is, as Davis suggested, being asked to read its own sociological views in the Constitution." That is a view Rehnquist shared and correctly assumed concerned Jackson. Later, during the oral argument, Davis also made reference to Gunnar Myrdal's 1944 study of the causes and consequences of segregation, *An American Dilemma*. During rebuttal time, Thurgood Marshall asked the justices to take judicial notice of Myrdal's study, which the Court did cite in footnote 11 of *Brown*. The last line of the memo certainly reflects that exchange: "If the Fourteenth Amendment did not enact Spencer's *Social Statics* [*sic*], it just as surely did not enact Myrdal's *American Dilemma*."

If, as appears probable, Rehnquist's memo was written shortly after he heard the first round of oral arguments, it was at most simply in line with some of the concerns that Jackson had at the time. Rehnquist's memo by no means, however, reflected or influenced Jackson's thinking regarding any possibility of upholding *Plessy*. To be sure, Jackson preferred for Congress to act on segregation. Indeed, Jackson was preoccupied, as evident in several initial drafts of his unpublished opinion, with how to craft a constitutional justification for the Court's rendering such a "political decision," along with how to deal with the inevitable problems of achieving compliance with such a massive desegregation ruling.

In other words, Jackson's concerns were different from those expressed in both Rehnquist's and Cronson's memos. As Jackson put it in the very first draft, "we must act because our representative system has failed." Yes, he preferred congressional rather than judicial action, but not because of "a desire to pass responsibility." He was more concerned about the limitations of a judicial remedy as opposed to congressional legislation.[117]

More crucially missed or neglected in the Senate hearings and the subsequent analyses was the fact that almost a year after Rehnquist's memo and two days before rearguments in *Brown* on December 7, 1953, Jackson prepared the first draft of his unpublished opinion. Notably, the draft was also written as though the decision had already been made, completely contrary to what one might presume from the substance and tone of Rehnquist's memo. At the outset of the draft opinion, Jackson laid out his principal concerns: "My real difficulty is not with the conclusion which is congenial to my own background and policy preconceptions. My difficulty is to justify it upon any sound juridical basis, other than the will of the temporary occupants of the Bench." Moreover, at several points, Jackson indicated that the outcome was a foregone conclusion. Section 2 of the draft, for example, began, "The juridical basis for holding that a Constitution which for neigh a century has tolerated segregation, *this morning forbids it,* [emphasis added] is more than usually dubious. The basis of our decision as to the states is, of course, the equal protection clause and due process clause of the Fourteenth Amendment."

In sum, without any doubt, in 1971 and 1986 Rehnquist at the very least misled and misrepresented whose views his memo represented, if not outright lied.

Jackson did not circulate the draft opinion to other justices; nor did he share it with a law clerk until after the sixth (and last) revision was completed on March 15, 1954.[118] He then asked E. Barrett Prettyman Jr. to read and comment on it, apparently in anticipation of another revision. That was just two weeks before Jackson suffered a heart attack on March 30 and was hospitalized until May 17, 1954. On May 7, Chief Justice Warren circulated drafts of the Court's opinions in *Brown* and *Bolling*. The next day, Warren took them with him to the hospital to discuss with Jackson. Afterward, Jackson asked Prettyman to read Warren's drafts before they went over them together.

Jackson had a closer working relationship and longer association with Prettyman as a law clerk than he had with either Rehnquist or Cronson. When Jackson went to Washington, D.C., in 1934, he replaced Prettyman's father as general counsel for the Internal Revenue Service. Although, as Frankfurter observed, that was rough for the senior Prettyman, the two became friends.[119] Two decades later, the senior Prettyman, at the time a judge on the Court of Appeals for the District of Columbia Circuit, sent Jackson a speech on lawyering by his son, who had delivered it as a delegate from the University of Virginia Law School at the American Law Student Association Convention.[120] Subsequently, Prettyman Jr. invited Jackson to give a talk at the UVA law school; after graduating, he wrote Jackson about the possibility of a clerkship. Jackson agreed to take him on but told him that he would be the sole clerk, because he would "never have two law clerks again."[121] Prettyman then proved so agreeable that after Jackson's death,[122] he clerked for Justices Frankfurter and then Harlan, who had filled Jackson's seat. Prettyman thus became the only law clerk to have worked for three different members of the Court.

As for Warren's draft, Prettyman agreed with Jackson that it was in the ballpark. In a note attached to the opinion, Warren emphasized that it was "short, readable by the lay public, non-rhetorical, unemotional and, above all, non-accusatory."[123] Although they felt reassured, Jackson and Prettyman still wanted more legal analysis in the opinion. Jackson also thought that Warren's draft was too equivocal about the intent of the framers of the Fourteenth Amendment. He had concluded that, in all honesty, the framers expected segregation to continue. This was clear from the continued funding for segregated schools in the District of Columbia. But that did not deeply disturb Jackson. What mattered most to him was how and why the Fourteenth Amendment applied to the new realities of a country that were very different from those in the past and which were continuing to change dramatically. The Constitution had not changed, but the country had. For Jackson, that justified the ruling.

After their discussion of Warren's draft, Jackson asked Prettyman to draft a paragraph, based on his earlier memo on Jackson's ultimately unpublished opinion, for use when he again talked with the chief justice. When Warren returned the same afternoon, however, Jackson did not show him the proposed paragraph. Rather, he simply told him about the nature of its contents. Warren declined to go along with virtually all of Jackson's suggestions, but he did incorporate one sentence concerning the advances of African Americans: "Today, in contrast, many Negroes have achieved outstanding success in the arts and sciences, as well as in the business and professional world."[124]

A little over two months after Jackson's death, Prettyman recorded the events in a memo he kept for himself. In it, he agreed that the Court had made the right decision. Warren's draft covered and was limited to only "segregation *in public schools*," whereas Jackson's justification for the decision "could be applied to segregation in general." The chief justice, in Prettyman's view, correctly persuaded Jackson that "the Court should not even intimate that segregation would fall in other areas."[125]

As for Jackson's draft opinion, Prettyman told him that it began too negatively "with fears and doubts." Instead, it should begin with a "clear and affirmative statement" of the unconstitutionality of segregated schools. At one point, Prettyman bluntly underscored, "In all frankness: if you are going to reach the decision you do, you should not write as if you were ashamed to reach it."[126]

In the eight-page memo to Jackson, Prettyman suggested a complete reorganization of the draft. It should begin, not end, in the last section, with the "meat of the opinion," which concluded that there was "no longer a legal basis for separate but equal facilities." That should then be followed by section 2, showing that the history of the Fourteenth Amendment was inconclusive. But in Prettyman's view, that still did not warrant the conclusion that segregation had always been unconstitutional, nor fully explain what the decision rested on. After that, Prettyman suggested, the discussion of past judges' understanding of the Fourteenth Amendment should be moved up. Jackson's draft opinion, then, should end with the last few paragraphs dealing briefly with the Court's decree and achieving compliance.[127]

Substantively, Prettyman also disagreed with Jackson's argument that Congress could and should deal with segregation in the states. Until *Brown,* the Court had not held that segregation was invalid under the Fourteenth Amendment. On the contrary, it had held otherwise. Hence, it was unreasonable to expect that Congress—exercising "its source of power" in section 5, the enforcement clause of the Fourteenth Amendment—would abolish segregation in the states. He also took exception to the idea of Congress creating a federal agency to oversee compliance with desegregation. In his view, achieving compliance with *Brown*'s mandate should be left to local school districts, subject to supervision by the lower federal courts.

Finally, Prettyman most strongly objected to Jackson's intimating that the basis and underlying reasoning for the result implies "the end to segregation in all its forms—in housing, recreation, etc." That would hit the South with too strong of a punch. "Why not," Prettyman recommended, "let them think the battle has been lost as to schools and is only just beginning on housing, etc."[128]

Although once contemplating another revision, Jackson instead simply abandoned any idea of publishing the opinion for a number of reasons.[129] Richard Kluger in *Simple Justice* speculated that "he would have been likely to activate his concurrence memorandum only if Warren's opinion seemed to him a piece of irresponsible butchery."[130] There is no denying the fact that Warren's draft opinion was not as bad as Jackson once feared was a factor. Jackson also agreed with the other justices on the importance of a unanimous decision, unencumbered by separate individual opinions, which might detract from and undermine the ruling. In addition, Prettyman's extensive critique convinced him that another major revision was out of the question. It would take too much time, the end of the term was approaching, and he was still weak from recovering from the heart attack.

On May 17, 1954, Jackson left the hospital in order to make a full bench when Chief Justice Warren announced the Court's unanimous decision. Almost six months later, after a second heart attack, he died on October 9, 1954. Jackson thus did not participate in deciding what had greatly concerned him—namely, how to formulate the remedial decree in *Brown II*.[131]

CHAPTER FOUR

Crossing the Rubicon

Alone in his chamber on the second floor of the Court, Jackson was not ambivalent when working on drafts of his concurrence for *Brown*.[1] For a year after hearing the first round of oral arguments, he brooded about the segregation cases before beginning the first draft, written almost half a year before the Court's decision came down. During that time, he continually conversed with himself about anxieties over constitutional justifications for the ruling, the limits of judicial power in American politics, and, as he correctly foresaw, the problem of remedies and the inexorable conflicts that could undermine compliance.[2] He had been ambivalent about the internment of Japanese Americans when dissenting in *Korematsu v. United States* (1944).[3] His fifth draft in *Brown* highlighted that connection in noting that *Korematsu* had upheld the classification of citizens according to their "racial ancestry," in deference to Congress and the president.

The Court was asked to do the same in *Brown* as in *Korematsu*. But the historical circumstances were vastly different and the stakes much higher. The states were defending racial classifications, there was inertia in Congress, and there was little promise of the president addressing the matter of segregation. Admittedly, the same year that Jackson went to the Court in 1941, Roosevelt created the Fair Employment Practice Commission and banned governmental subcontracting to businesses discriminating against blacks and other minorities. Roosevelt considered going farther, but it remained for President Harry S. Truman to issue executive orders in 1948 that led to the start of racially integrating the military and the federal government. Those were the first significant governmental efforts toward desegregation since Reconstruction.

Ten years after the decision in *Korematsu*, Jackson, having abandoned initial hopes that Congress might deal with the problem of segregation, struggled with the history and cultural heritage of white supremacy—underlying segregated schools and public accommodations, as well as laws banning interracial marriages, or antimiscegenation—derived from combining Latin *miscere*, "to mix," and *genus*, "race." They were sustained in order to prevent "contacts which threaten dilution of blood or dissipation of faith." The "instinct for self-preservation," according to Jackson, accounted for segregation in the North. But in the South, there additionally remained long after the Civil War, often referred to as "the great American white conflict" or "war of northern aggression," deep resentment of loss to the North and "the humiliation of carpet bagging" during Reconstruction.[4] There was also a way of life that the Court itself had sanctioned for well over half a century.

In *Brown,* Jackson crossed the Rubicon into a world he believed would be ridden with strife, even if not fully comprehending the extent of the political ramifications and repercussions of the Court's decision.

"Between Two Worlds"

"Since the close of the Civil war, the United States has been 'hesitating between two worlds—one dead, the other powerless to be born.'" This opening line, paraphrasing Arnold's "Stanzas from the Grande Chartreuse," appeared in all of Jackson's drafts. Arnold was known for austere and occasionally pompous prose. Jackson was known for his literary flair and command of literature; he was always a transcendentalist.[5]

For Jackson, the racial problem could not be resolved until we confronted "our hypocrisies." Neither the North nor the South was willing to do so. Segregation, as he put it in the fourth draft, "outlived whatever original justification it may have had and is no longer wise or fair public policy." That conclusion comported with his background and political views. Moreover, he deemed economic and political developments to mark segregation "for a certain and early, if gradual extinction." Keenly aware of the limitations of the law's capacity to transform prevailing mores, Jackson emphasized, "Economic and social forces seem to mark discrimination for extinction even faster than legal measures." He thought, as did other justices, including Black and Reed, that "within a generation segregation will be outlawed." He also acknowledged, however, that "Constitutions are easier amended than social customs."

For Jackson, *Brown* was clearly a political decision. Frankfurter resisted that reality and hence strove to put off deciding the segregation cases as well as the challenges to state antimiscegenation laws and other controversies. But for Jackson, the political was personal, though in a different way, and above Frankfurter's emotional appeals. All of his drafts mentioned that as a young man growing up in upstate New York, there were few blacks in public schools, and little thought given to segregation. In his second revised draft, completed after hearing the second round of oral arguments and Chief Justice Warren having led the conference discussion of *Brown,* Jackson admitted "to little personal experience or firsthand knowledge by which to test many of the arguments advanced in these cases." Judging himself in a moment of near self-doubt, he confessed difficulties in fully understanding "the emotional and traditional background of the present problem."

Unlike Frankfurter's deeply personal dissent in *West Virginia State Board of*

Education v. Barnette (1943),[6] Jackson's draft opinion avoided such personalization. On the contrary, each draft became less personal in working to reconcile law and politics, and to convince himself of a constitutional justification for the decision. To be sure, Jackson's commitment to impersonal and impartial judging appears at times in conflict with the unique flair of many of his opinions. But here, the personal references and reflections served to reinforce what he saw as the common sense of the matter.

Well aware the Court's decision would be regarded by many in the South as "unjustifiable," Jackson believed that he neither could nor must address that charge. Likewise, he conceded "no knowledge to judge" whether the Court's ruling would "diminish or increase racial tensions." In the penultimate fifth draft, in lines later dropped in the final draft, Jackson confessed his belief "that if the use of judicial power were also needlessly ruthless and inconsiderate of the conditions which have brought about and continued this custom it may defeat the purposes of the decision." On that point all of the justices agreed, especially Justices Black, Reed, and Clark. It was also a point Frankfurter fervently pushed.

A principled yet pragmatic balancer, Jackson weighed the conflicting claims on both sides. In *Brown,* he continually pondered the competing claims of those subject to segregation against those who would, by "a recasting of society by judicial fiat," be forced from a way of life they understood as constitutionally permissible.

At about the same time he was working on the unpublished opinion, he was also preparing his Godkin lectures, in which he further elaborated his conviction about the inappropriateness of courts seizing "the initiative in shaping the policy of law, either by constitutional interpretation, or statutory construction." He similarly regretted that a "cult of libertarian judicial activists" was assailing the Court for renouncing too much power, just as earlier New Deal "liberals," like himself, had been critical of the pre-1937 Court for "*assuming* too much power" (emphasis added). Such libertarian criticism misleadingly encouraged, in his view, "a belief that the judges may be left to correct the result of public indifference to liberty."[7] Still, as Jackson's drafts make clear, such a correction was precisely what the Court was asked to do in *Brown.* The Court had to deal with the problem of segregated schools as a result of the public's support or indifference to them, congressional inertia, and the institutional failures of representative government.

Furthermore, some form of separation, Jackson thought, was universal, "instinctive with every race, faith, state or culture," and resulted in legal and social measures "to protect and perpetuate those qualities, real or fancied, which it especially values in itself." The fifth draft emphasized that "we should also weigh the psychological effect on those who are coerced out of it. While the pro-segregation emotion may seem to us less rational than the anti-segregation emotion, we can hardly deny the sincerity and passion of those who think that their blood, birth and lineage are something worthy of protection by separatism." For that reason, Jackson was convinced racial problems in the South involved more than "mere racial prejudice." They were bound up with a socially complicated "white war and white politics."

The first section of the fifth draft concluded rather pessimistically. He worried that the questions of constitutional interpretation and of the limits of judicial power presented by the segregation cases were "as far-reaching as any that have been before the Court since its establishment." Eliminated from that draft was his previous emphasis on the concern that, because they bore directly on the scope and form of a court-ordered remedy, "the Court must face the questions of method and standards of constitutional interpretation."

Contemplating "White Supremacy" and "Majestic Generalities"

The second section of the sixth and last draft, "Does Existing Law Condemn Segregation?," turned to the role of the Court in interpreting the Constitution and overturning precedents as long-standing as *Plessy v. Ferguson*. It was heavily revised and retitled several times. It was "Constitutional Basis" in the first draft, "Basis in Existing Law for Decision" in the second and fourth drafts, and "Existing Law Does Not Condemn Segregation" in the fifth.

The first draft of that section, written on December 7, 1953, just before rearguments in *Brown,* posed a fundamental question of constitutional interpretation: What was the "basis for holding that a Constitution which for neigh a century has tolerated segregation, *this morning forbids it* (emphasis added), is more than usually dubious."

The Fourteenth Amendment's due process and equal protection clauses were the bases for the Court's decision in *Brown* to strike down segregated schools in the states, and the Fifth Amendment's due process clause the basis in the companion case, *Bolling v. Sharpe,* for the District of Columbia. Yet neither of those amendments says anything about either education or segregation.

In every one of the drafts, Jackson pondered how lawyers and the public could or would be persuaded by the Court's reasoning and ruling. What would persuade them to accept that segregated schools, understood as constitutionally permissible since 1791 in the District of Columbia and in the states since the ratification of the Fourteenth Amendment in 1868, were now constitutionally impermissible? How could such a deeply rooted, socially settled, and judicially sanctioned practice now violate the Constitution?

Jackson then turned to consideration of what he called "the original will" of the framers of the Fourteenth Amendment. In doing so, he almost unwittingly anticipated the major ensuing legal and political debate, now decades old, over the "original intent" or "original public understanding" of constitutional provisions.[8] He also went to the heart of constitutional interpretation in thinking about the level of generality that should be given to the application of provisions like due process and equal protection, regardless of their particular historical context.

From the first to last draft, Jackson meditated on the application of the "majestic and sweeping generalities" of the Fourteenth Amendment. Early drafts contained more extensive discussions, much of which, alas, was eliminated, modified, or shifted to later sections. The second draft, for instance, expressly embraced the well-known observation made by Justice Benjamin N. Cardozo (1932–1938)[9] that those constitutional generalities "have a content and significance that vary from age to age."

The fourth draft further explained, "Certainly no one familiar with his [Cardozo's] teachings would think this meant, what some people advocate, that we declare new constitutional law with the freedom of a constitutional convention sitting continuously and with no necessity for submitting its innovations for approval of Congress, ratification by the states or approval of the people." That line was virtually identical to his charge, over a decade earlier in *The Struggle for Judicial Supremacy*, that the pre-1937 Court "sat almost as a continuous constitutional convention."[10] Undeniably for Jackson, the problems *Brown* posed were "refracted through the experience of the Roosevelt struggle against the pre–New Deal Court."[11]

In this regard, he found agreement with his fellow New Dealer but frequent foe on the bench, Justice Black. In almost the same words, Black later warned that abandoning or distorting constitutional text would turn the Court into a "continuously functioning constitutional convention." Black dissented in *Katz v. United States* (1967),[12] where the Court held that the Fourth Amendment's prohibition on "unreasonable searches and seizures" and warrant requirements applied to wiretapping. This judicial champion of "absolutism" or "literalism" fiercely and persistently fought against the specific words of the constitutional text losing their (in his view) meaning. In *Katz,* he emphatically stated: "I simply cannot in good conscience give meaning to words which they have never before been thought to have. . . . I will not distort the words of the Amendment in order to 'keep the Constitution up to date' or 'to bring it into harmony with the times.'" Yet both he and Jackson were firm about the outcome in *Brown* and saw no other choice.

How to apply the "majestic generalities" of the Fourteenth Amendment, Jackson thought, brought us "squarely to the question whether we shall interpret these generalities as they were understood by the age that framed and adopted them or by the age that now reads them." That critical question presented, as the fourth draft emphasized, "a controversy as old as the Republic"—whether and how the Court should apply constitutional generalities.

After searching for the "original public will" of the Fourteenth Amendment, Jackson concluded, in the fourth and final drafts, that "all that I can fairly get from the legislative debates is that it was a passionate, confused, and deplorable era." Indeed, counsel on each side in *Brown,* in briefs and oral arguments, presented seemingly compelling evidence supporting their competing positions about the "original intent" and scope of the Fourteenth Amendment. Also, like Frankfurter,[13] Jackson often corresponded with Stanford University Law School's legal historian, Charles Fairman. Both justices off the bench sought further insight or confirmation about the origins and scope of the amendment, particularly with respect to the application or nationalization of the guarantees of the Bill of Rights to the states.[14]

The history of the Fourteenth Amendment, according to Jackson, appeared conflicting, subject to revisionism, and inconclusive. Moreover, in his view, history did not always provide a definitive answer to the question at hand. Often that was true simply because the question had not been considered or fully addressed. Jackson concluded that there was no conclusive evidence that those who drafted and ratified the Civil War Amendments ever "reached the point of thinking about either segregation or education of the Negro as a current problem." Furthermore, it was "harder still to find that the Amendments were designed to be a solution." In addition, Jackson was troubled about the potential implication of the ruling in *Brown* that the generalities of the Fourteenth Amendment could "be read to virtually replace our federation with a unitary form of government." The stakes were high for the Court and the country. About that he harbored no doubts.

From attempting to divine the original intent of the Fourteenth Amendment and its application, Jackson turned "from words to deeds as evidence of purpose" for determining "the original public understanding" of the amendment. In this respect, Jackson differed from Justice Oliver Wendell Holmes, who tended to look to the broad currents of history. As Holmes once observed, "The case before us must be considered in the light of our whole experience and not merely in that of what was said a hundred years ago."[15]

Like Frankfurter, Jackson admired Holmes. But in this section of the draft opinion, Jackson zeroed in on the limited contours of the immediate historical context of the Fourteenth Amendment. He considered the application of the amendment's due process and equal protection guarantees only at a level of generality set by the practices at the time of the amendment's adoption. He did not do so in a broader sense of a constitutional principle of equality. Hence, once again, Jackson concluded that there was no historical basis for the eventual ruling in *Brown*. Indeed, the historical evidence pointed in the opposite direction.

Looking at the historical record of the Thirty-Ninth Congress's passage of the Fourteenth Amendment, nothing indicated to Jackson that segregated schools were even thought to be prohibited. Furthermore, he emphasized that the Thirty-Ninth Congress and every Congress afterwards funded segregated schools in the District of Columbia. He acknowledged that certainly there were some protests. But overall the history of congressional legislation, like that of the adoption of the Fourteenth and Fifteenth amendments, undeniably failed to provide any indication that racially segregated schools were unconstitutional.[16] Again, that was underscored by Congress's continually sustaining those schools in the nation's capital, along with ignoring them in the states.

No less significantly, when Congress readmitted elected representatives from the Confederate states after the Civil War, upon their acceptance of the provisions of the Fourteenth Amendment, there was no hint that support for segregated schools barred those representatives from returning to Congress or their states from rejoining the Union.

Similarly, turning from Congress to state practices at the time of the ratification of the Fourteenth Amendment, Jackson believed it was "equally impossible to reconcile with any understanding that the Amendment would prohibit segregation in schools." Much like Justice Antonin Scalia often would do when the framers' intent was unclear or "gray,"[17] Jackson counted on state laws to determine the tradition or historical understanding of what was deemed constitutionally permissible. He noted that five states that had segregated schools did abandon them after the ratification of the Fourteenth Amendment, while four with such schools refused to ratify the amendment. Nine Northern and two border states continued or later established racially segregated schools after the amendment was ratified. Moreover, all eight states that had belonged to the Confederacy maintained segregated schools. Hence, at the time of *Brown,* seventeen states permitted or legally mandated racial segregation in public schools.

There was simply no denying a lack of consensus among the states, any more than in Congress, about the Fourteenth Amendment's not prohibiting segregated schools. That conclusion was reinforced by the practices of state administrators, courts, and legislatures in both the North and the South.

Such long-standing customs and practices Jackson deemed "a powerful law-maker." They were rooted "in the habit and usage of people in their local communities."

Accordingly, however convenient to conclude otherwise, Jackson frankly conceded that the conventional materials and methods of constitutional interpretation unquestionably failed to provide a firm basis for holding that racially segregated schools ran afoul of either the due process clause or the equal protection clause in the Fifth and Fourteenth amendments.

"A Living Constitution"

"Does the Amendment Contemplate Changed Conditions?," the third section of the fifth and the final drafts, became somewhat more optimistic. From the confines of the limited historical context surrounding the Fourteenth Amendment's adoption, Jackson contemplated the less historically limited concepts embodied in its guarantees. By reading the amendment literally, he observed that it "does not attempt to say the last word on the concrete application of its pregnant generalities." In turning to an analysis of the text, he once again presciently anticipated subsequent debates over "strict constructionism." That still-resonating legal and political debate followed Republican president Nixon's promises to appoint only "strict constructionists" in an effort to purportedly remake the Court into Frankfurter's vision of "judicial self-restraint."[18] Critics, of course, countered that "strict constructionism" in constitutional interpretation was misguided, misleading, impossible, unrealistic, untruthful, unwise, and manipulable.[19]

In turning to a textual analysis, though, Jackson did not adopt "strict constructionism" per se. Rather, he embraced the idea of "a living Constitution." Citing a list of prior rulings in support, he candidly acknowledged: "Of course the Constitution must be a living instrument and can not be read as if written in a dead language. It is neither novel nor radical doctrine that statutes once constitutional may become invalid by changing conditions and those good in one state of facts may be bad under another."

Another major debate over methods of constitutional interpretation was thus foreshadowed. Justice William J. Brennan, for one, countered advocates of "strict constructionism" and a "jurisprudence of original intent." Shortly before the celebration in 1987 of the bicentennial of the Constitution, he pointed out:

> The Constitution is fundamentally a public text—the monumental charter of a government and a people. . . . We look to the history of the time of the framing and to the intervening history of interpretation. But the ultimate question must be: what do the words of the text mean in our time? For the

genius of the Constitution rests not in any static meaning it might have had in a world dead and gone, but in the adaptability of its great principles to cope with current problems and current needs.[20]

At the outset, however, Jackson thought that it was the role of Congress to interpret the Fourteenth Amendment and deal with the problems of segregation. Nor was he alone in taking that view. At the first conference discussion of *Brown* after hearing the initial oral arguments in December 1952, Justice Black had told the others, "At first blush I would have said it was up to Congress, but if we declare confiscation and other laws unconstitutional then we can [with] segregation."[21] Jackson agreed but was much more cautious and hesitant.

The "majestic" or "pregnant generalities" of the Fourteenth Amendment, as Jackson initially viewed them, were explicitly for Congress to interpret and apply. Notably, the enforcement clause of the amendment, section 5, specifically provides: "The Congress shall have the power to enforce, by appropriate legislation, the provisions of this Article." That provided a textual basis for Congress to "give effect from time to time to the changes of conditions and public opinion." Ninety years after the amendment's adoption, in his 1958 Oliver Wendell Holmes lectures at Harvard Law School, Judge Learned Hand similarly took Jackson's initial position, though he did so when sharply criticizing the reasoning and ruling in *Brown*.[22]

Jackson furthermore was confident that the post-1937 Court would uphold congressional authority and action to outlaw segregation, under either the Fourteenth Amendment or the interstate commerce clause of Article I. Indeed, the Warren Court did just that a decade later when it upheld the Civil Rights Act of 1964.[23]

References to the text of section 5 in the Fourteenth Amendment, along with the limitations of the power of courts compared to that of Congress, were prominent throughout several of Jackson's drafts, including the final one. It was simply up to Congress and state legislatures to deal with such a momentous matter as desegregating schools and the "far-reaching implications" of doing so.

Nonetheless, as the second draft made plain, Jackson never doubted that the Fourteenth Amendment "does not attempt to speak the last word on the subjects with which it deals in such generalities." Although the amendment explicitly empowers Congress, not the Supreme Court, to deal with the matter, the undeniable fact remained that Congress had utterly failed, and almost certainly would not do so. "We must assume," he explained, "Congress is not opposed to segregation and does not consider it an obstacle to the achievement of the purposes of the Fourteenth Amendment."

The second draft once again underscored that Congress sustained segregated schools in the nation's capital and "made no effort to outlaw it" in the states. In addition, Jackson pointed out that Southern representatives and senators wielded enough power to prevent any such congressional action. He fully understood the implications: "But that is to say that the Court should intervene to promulgate as a law that which our Constitutional representative system will not enact." The problem was deeper still. The country suffered from a "schizophrenic division" in electing presidents, like Roosevelt, opposed to segregation but with limited authority to address the problem, while repeatedly reelecting members of Congress who favored—or at least tolerated—the enforced separation of the races.

In short, Jackson concluded, "It means nothing less than we must act because our representative system has failed."

Along with major cutting and pasting on February 15, 1954, the fourth draft extensively discussed Jackson's fears about the Court's opinion not appearing to have the force of law. More specifically, he was concerned that the decision might focus too much on the arguments made by Thurgood Marshall and the NAACP Legal Defense Fund, relying on social science studies on the effects of segregation. Some of these were indeed cited in *Brown*'s (in)famous footnote 11.

At the justices' conference discussion on December 13, 1952, two days after hearing the first round of oral arguments in *Brown*, according to Justice Clark's notes, Jackson dismissively said that "[Thurgood] Marshall's briefs starts + ends [*sic*] with sociology."[24] Jackson never yielded from that position, as is evident in every revision of the unpublished opinion.

Acknowledging "a good many considerations are urged upon us to decree an end to segregation regardless of what the [Fourteenth and Fifteenth] Amendments originally meant," Jackson nonetheless discounted as inappropriate such "extra-legal criteria from sociological, psychological and political sciences." He strongly resisted the "sociological jurisprudence" advanced decades earlier by Roscoe Pound, the former dean of Harvard Law School.[25] To Jackson, the idea that judges should become "social engineers" was anathema, an abandonment of the judicial function, and antithetical to the role of judges and the Court in a system of separate political branches.

Nor did Jackson need social scientific studies to persuade him or, as he viewed it, to provide a basis for the ruling in *Brown*. Segregation, as he further explained in a draft, "is said to be based on a philosophy of inherent inequality of races, and . . . it creates in young Negro children an inferiority complex." But those very psychosociological claims were contested and remained in dispute. Nonetheless, Jackson did not deny that segregation had psychological and sociological consequences. Recalling his youth in upstate New York and school life without segregation, he again made plain that "the Negro still was greatly disadvantaged and must have felt its sting." Still, Jackson thought he had "little competence to judge" the validity of such social scientific evidence, and moreover he remained convinced that it would be an inappropriate basis for the Court's decision.

Jackson's lengthy discussion of opposition to a ruling based on social science studies was curiously (and unfortunately) dropped in the final version of the draft. He had emphasized that even if "all the woes of colored children would be solved by forcing them into white company," such "elusive psychological and subjective factors" should not be imported into the Fourteenth Amendment's guarantee of equal protection under the law. Such psychosociological findings were "not determinable with satisfactory objectivity or measurable with reasonable certainty." He feared that the Court's opinion would prove too sociological and not legally persuasive, especially because the decision "would still be capricious enough," even if the Court adhered solely to the "objective criteria of the judicial process" and adversary process.

"The real question" for Jackson was strictly "whether the Constitution permits any classification or separation of Negro and White merely on the basis of color or racial descent." If it did not, he thought, then all of the psychosociological studies and "policy arguments are superfluous and, if so, they are for consideration of the legislatures not the courts."

Jackson's position foreshadowed the controversy that erupted over footnote 11 in *Brown.* James Reston in the *New York Times,* though supporting the decision, blasted the Court's opinion as "A Sociological Decision" that "read more like an expert paper on sociology than a Supreme Court opinion."[26] J. Harvie Wilkinson, a former clerk to Justice Lewis F. Powell Jr. and judge on the Court of Appeals for the Fourth Circuit, later observed that footnote 11 was one of "the most inflammatory English ever in fine print."[27]

Footnote 11 cited seven works by psychologists and sociologists. In particular, it noted the works of Kenneth B. Clark's *Effect of Prejudice and Discrimination on Personality Development,* prepared for a 1950 Midcentury White House Conference on Children and Youth, and Gunnar Myrdal's *An American Dilemma: The Negro Problem and Modern Democracy.*

Kenneth Clark was a black assistant professor of psychology at the City College of New York, who later became the first black president of the American Psychological Association. He had been hired by the NAACP Legal Defense Fund to conduct studies of the effects of segregation on school-children. In what would be known, and hotly contested and derided, as the "doll study," he showed black and white dolls to black children and asked which they preferred. The children, despite being black themselves, tended to pick the white doll. Clark concluded that the experiment demonstrated the demeaning effects of segregated schools on black schoolchildren, marking them with a sense of inferiority. His study was challenged as methodologically flawed and its conclusions as unsupported, both when he testified at trials in companion cases to *Brown* and then later in law reviews and social science journals.[28]

No less controversial was Myrdal's *American Dilemma.* Together with a team of researchers, Myrdal, a Swedish sociologist and socialist, produced the first major empirical study of race relations in the United States. The 1944 book became the premier study, both acclaimed and denounced for its indictment of racism, segregation, and history of white supremacy in America.

The Court in *Brown* cited their study in support of its decision. As the Court explained in footnote 11: "Whatever may have been the extent of psychological knowledge at the time of *Plessy v. Ferguson,* this finding [that racial segregation harms black children] is amply supported by modern authority." Chief Justice Warren's law clerk, Earl E. Pollock, later explained that the only reason why this line was inserted was to rebut "the cheap psychology of *Plessy* that said inferiority was only in the minds of the Negro." Warren thought that assertion was "preposterous," even though it was repeated and debated in all of the briefs.[29] Yet the fact remained that Kenneth Clark and other psychologists were recruited by the NAACP Legal Defense Fund precisely in order to conduct studies that would discredit *Plessy*'s psychological presupposition.

Placed in historical perspective, the Court had done somersaults with the psychological premises on which it supported its rulings, including *Dred Scott v. Sanford* (1957),[30] *Plessy v. Ferguson* (1896), and then *Brown.* In *Dred Scott,* Chief Justice Roger B. Taney (1836–1864), when ruling that Dred Scott lacked standing to sue because he was black and hence was not a citizen, based the Court's decision on a strict construction of the Constitution and its history. At the time of the framing of the Constitution, Taney reasoned, blacks were deemed "a subordinate and inferior class of beings, who had been subjugated by the dominate race." That underlying psychological predicate was flipped almost forty years later in *Plessy.* Writing for the Court in *Plessy,* Justice Henry Brown upheld the doctrine of "separate but equal." If "the enforced separation of the two races stamps the colored race with a badge of inferiority," Brown maintained, it was "solely because the colored race chooses to put that construction upon it." Then, almost sixty years later, in *Brown,* the Court flipped again and rejected the psychological predicate and language in *Plessy* as applicable to public schools.

In *Brown,* only two justices, Black and Clark, expressed concerns to Chief Justice Warren about footnote 11. Notably, Jackson did not express concerns, in spite of his thinking that such studies were an inappropriate basis for the Court's ruling. Justice Tom Clark later told Richard Kluger, "I questioned the Chief's going with Myrdal in the opinion. I told him—and Hugo Black did, too—that it wouldn't go down well in the South. And he didn't need it."[31] Clark also asked Warren to insert the initial "K" before the last name of psychologist Clark, unlike other last names cited in the footnote. He did not want any confusion that the footnote was referring to Kenneth B. Clark, not him.

Jackson and his law clerk, Rehnquist, were not alone in deeming such psychological sources inappropriate and unnecessary.[32] William Coleman, who in 1948 became the first black clerk at the Court, had initially doubted the social science arguments would prove persuasive. On the basis of his clerkship with Frankfurter, he was also dubious about Kenneth Clark's methodology and conclusions. "Jesus Christ," he told Kluger, "those damned dolls! I thought it was a joke."[33] Likewise, Alexander Bickel thought it was a mistake to cite Clark's experimental studies. He worried about "the vulnerability of the doll tests," and he worried more generally about even invoking social science at all. It might have been better for the Court's opinion, he suggested, to "have said straightforwardly that *Plessy* was based on a self-invented philosophy." As Bickel observed, however, Chief Justice Warren and the other justices wanted a "small target."[34] They did not want to pick an even bigger fight.

Looking back years later, Warren rationalized footnote 11 as simply a way of spotlighting that the Court's ruling "was the antithesis of what was said in *Plessy.*" He viewed it as an innocuous way of acknowledging contemporary social science support, not as the substantive basis for the *Brown* decision. "It was only a note, after all."[35]

Footnote 11 nevertheless proved extraordinarily controversial. It was hotly debated not only among academics but also more broadly as a political matter. Among many others, former member of the Court (and at the time South Carolina's governor) James Byrnes lashed out against the Court for usurping the powers of Congress and the states. When doing so, he sharply criticized the citation of the works of psychologists and sociologists. Byrnes emphasized that the Court, when dealing with group libel and racially inflammatory speech just two years earlier in *Beauharnais v. Illinois* (1952),[36] had said, "It is not within our competence to confirm or deny claims of social scientists as to the dependence of the individual on the position of his racial or religious group in the community." As Jackson's unpublished opinion shows, he thought so too.

Byrnes had caught the Court in a contradiction or inconsistency regarding the use of social science in *Beauharnais* and *Brown*'s footnote 11. But he went further. He specifically expressed outrage over the citation to Myrdal's *American Dilemma*. Millions of people, he claimed, knew that Myrdal's conclusions about segregation were false.

Ironically, Byrnes's argument only confirmed Myrdal's bottom line. For, in defending segregation, Byrnes contended that breaking up segregated schools and other social barriers between the races would "ultimately bring about the intermarriage of the races." At the time, twenty-three states prohibited miscegenation. As Byrnes saw it, that demonstrated a widespread "fear of mongrelization of the [white] race. To prevent this, the white people of the South are willing to make every sacrifice."[37]

Unlike Byrnes and other critics of the Warren Court, Jackson did not view *Brown* as usurping the powers of either Congress or the states, even though he remained wary of the Court's overreaching. Instead, for Jackson, it was precisely due to the failure of other political institutions, particularly Congress, to respond to the problems of segregation that forced the Court's hand.

The Court, he knew, nonetheless did not always get it right—which was another reason for caution. Fresh in Jackson's mind was a recent ruling in *Ray v. Blair*,[38] handed down in April 1952. The majority upheld a rule of Alabama's Democratic Executive Committee requiring delegates to the Electoral College to pledge, in its state primaries, to support nominees of its state's national conventions on presidential elections. Writing for the Court in that case, Justice Reed reversed the state supreme court's decision that the rule violated the Twelfth Amendment's process for the Electoral College's selection of the president.

Jackson, in dissent, joined by Justice Douglas, agreed with the analysis of Alabama's state supreme court about the "original intent" of the Twelfth Amendment and the practices at the time of the founding, before the emergence of modern political parties. Citing the *Federalist Papers No. 68*, Jackson pointed to the original understanding of the amendment, implicit in its text, that delegates to the Electoral College were "free agents." They were not intended to be "party lackeys and intellectual nonentities" who came along with the rise of political parties. In his words, "In effect, before one can become an elector for Alabama, its law requires he must pawn his ballot to a candidate not yet named, by a convention not yet held, of delegates not yet chosen." Nonetheless, the Court's majority simply sanctioned a mechanism for the Democratic Party in the South to control elections, as the Democratic Party tried to do in the "white primary" cases.[39] Such rules maintained racial discrimination in the electoral process and institutional dysfunctionalism. The Electoral College, Jackson said, "suffered atrophy almost indistinguishable from *rigor mortis*." The direct election of the president, he suggested, would be preferable to political parties' manipulations that undermine truly representative government.

In all six drafts, Jackson repeatedly stressed that courts may only resolve conflicts between particular litigants, and that they only have the limited power of contempt to enforce their decisions. Like Black, Frankfurter, and others, he had initially resisted expressly acknowledging that *Brown* and companion cases were class-action lawsuits. He did so for a number of reasons.

His first draft contained a lengthy discussion of why congressional action was preferable to the Court intervening in this and other matters in which "it lacks special competence, let alone machinery of implementation."[40] As he further elaborated in the Godkin lectures, Article III of the Constitution limits the Court's power to deciding only actual "cases or controversies." The methods of the judicial process, furthermore, "make it unfit for solving some kinds of problems which elements of our society have from time to time expected the Supreme Court to settle." Unlike Congress's legislative powers, a "judicial decree, however, broadly worded," technically only binds a particular litigation. "As to others, it is merely a weather vane showing which way the wind is blowing."[41]

Along the same lines as the Godkin lectures about the limitations of the Court's power and of the judicial process, the first draft emphasized that a judicial decree "against one school district or one set of school officials does not bind any other district so as to subject them to contempt proceedings." That made it "costly," "time consuming," and "impossible for a disadvantaged people to accomplish on any broad scale." Additionally, he noted that the "separate but equal" doctrine had "encountered little resistance and was easy to enforce in comparison to the edict [that would be announced in *Brown*] that segregation is totally abolished."

In contrast to a judicial remedy, he suggested that Congress could abolish segregated schools and then establish an administrative agency to oversee the implementation of desegregation. That "could lift the heavy burden of private litigation from disadvantaged people" and "secure enforcement of the policy." In concluding this section, he added, "Where a private right is common to many persons of a class and the invasions of that right are numerous and complicated, it always has been found impossible to get general and effective enforcement by the case by case method of litigation. Those rights have to be made public concern and dealt with by mass methods, not by the slow evolution of decisional law."

In January 1954, three days after completing the third draft, the justices, at his suggestion, voted in conference to carry *Brown* over to the next term for rearguments on the question of remedies. Almost a month later, in mid-February 1954, Jackson revised the draft for the fourth time. This one abandoned any hope for congressional action. As Frankfurter later recounted in a letter to Judge Learned Hand: "The fact of the matter is that Bob Jackson tried his hand at a justification for leaving the matter to Sec. 5 of Art. XIV, 'Congress shall have powers to enforce, etc.' and finally gave up."[42]

In the end, when announcing that the segregation cases would be restored to the docket for rearguments on the questions about the formulation of a remedial decree, the Court's opinion in *Brown* acknowledged what all the justices knew all too well. *Brown* and its companion cases were class-action lawsuits. In his memoirs, Chief Justice Warren emphasized that *Brown* had only held that segregated schools were unconstitutional. The Court's decision left many other questions unanswered, including whether lawsuits against segregated schools could be brought "as *class* actions for all who were similarly situated or should persons actually joining in the action be entitled to relief only for themselves? What court should determine the decree in each case?"[43] For those reasons, just as Jackson had suggested, the segregation cases were carried over for reargument on the question of remedies in *Brown II.* In announcing that, however, the Court expressly stated, "Because these are class actions, because of the wide applicability of this decision, and because of the great variety of local conditions, the formulation of decrees in these cases presents problems of considerable complexity. . . . We have now announced that such segregation is a denial of the equal protection of the laws. . . . The parties are requested to present further argument on the nature of the remedial decree that should be ordered."

Jackson fully comprehended that *Brown* would embark the Court "upon a widespread reform of social customs and habits of countless communities."

Justice Jackson in his chambers in the Supreme Court. Robert H. Jackson Center

Indeed, he agonized over that with each revision of the unpublished opinion. It always remained deeply troubling. In one of the Godkin lectures, he further explained, "My philosophy has been and continues to be that . . . [the Court] cannot and should not try to seize the initiative in shaping the policy of law." Thinking about and comparing the pre- and post-1937 Court, he concluded that "there is a limit beyond which the Court incurs the charge of trying to supersede the law-making branches." When the Court goes too far and crosses that line, it has been accused of becoming a "super legislature," "legislating from the bench," and publicly rebuked. No less disturbing for Jackson was that he could not think of any modern instance when courts "saved a whole people from the great currents of intolerance, passion, usurpation, and tyranny."[44]

Like renowned federal appellate court judge Learned Hand and other New Deal liberal judges, Jackson was keenly aware of the questionable propriety and resulting problems of second-guessing the reasonableness of legislation, as the pre-1937 Court had done. A decade earlier, Hand had famously observed, "I often wonder whether we do not rest our hopes too much upon constitutions, upon laws, and upon courts. These are false hopes.

. . . Liberty lies in the hearts of men and women; when it dies there, no constitution, no law, no court can even do much to help it."[45]

Similarly, Jackson worried that many people would—and they later did—consider *Brown* a "disaster by decree."[46] As he pointed out in his last draft, "The futility of effective reform of our society by judicial decree is demonstrated by the history of this matter." Earlier decisions, in *Sweatt v. Painter* (1950), *McLaurin v. Oklahoma State Regents* (1950), and *Henderson v. United States* (1950),[47] on enforcing the equality part of the "separate but equal" doctrine, "remained a dead letter in a large part of the country." Given such recent history, together with the experience of the 1937 "constitutional crisis" over the Court and the Constitution, Jackson had every reason to think that declaring segregated schools unconstitutional would not prove "any more self-executing or any more effectively executed."

Still, the promise of "separate but equal" was a false promise of hope. As Jackson noted in the first draft, "One needs only to be a casual traveler in many parts of the country to see for himself" the inequity of the doctrine. His observation was based not on social science findings but on the experience of growing up in an exclusively white rural community in upstate New York and then much later confronting segregation after moving to Washington, D.C. Undoubtedly Chief Justice Warren's retelling of his own experience with segregation after moving East may have reaffirmed Jackson's view. Shortly after joining the Court, Warren visited Civil War sites in Virginia, driven by his black chauffeur. At the end of the first day of the planned trip, Warren checked into a hotel, assuming his driver would do the same. The next morning, he found the driver sleeping in the back of the car, and he learned that there were no rooms available for a black man in segregated Virginia. Warren was embarrassed and ashamed, and he immediately asked to be driven back to the District of Columbia.[48]

Such experiences, regardless of the social science evidence presented in briefs and oral arguments in *Brown,* were enough for Jackson to simply take "judicial notice" of the fact that "the separate but equal doctrine remained a dead letter as to its equality aspect." Moreover, Truman's 1947 presidential commission on higher education had already concluded in no uncertain terms: "The separate and equal principle has nowhere been fully honored, educational facilities for Negroes in segregated areas are inferior to those provided for whites. Whether one considers enrollment, over-all costs per student, teachers' salaries, transportation facilities, availability of secondary schools, or opportunities for undergraduate or graduate study, the consequences of segregation are always the same, and always adverse to the Negro citizen."[49] Jackson put it even more bluntly: "We need not, on a matter of nation-wide common knowledge, be so dumb as to pretend an absence of knowledge."

While the justices were considering *Brown,* they were also beginning to confront, and to avoid addressing, challenges to state antimiscegenation laws,[50] as well as other racially charged due process and death penalty appeals.[51] The Court ducked these questions by denying review or by summarily handing down summary per curiam opinions remanding the case to state and lower federal courts.

The problems that the coming challenges to antimiscegenation laws posed were as acute, if not more so, as those that challenged segregated schools. But the two were fundamentally intertwined. Both challenges sought to overturn long-standing precedents that went to the core of white supremacy and its opposition to any mixing of races, whether in schools, public accommodations, or marriage. The Court had indeed upheld and approved of Alabama's antimiscegenation in *Pace v. Alabama* (1883).[52]

In *Pace,* the Court applied the same reasoning and factual premises that a little over a decade later in *Plessy* would entrench the doctrine of "separate but equal." Justice Stephen Field (1863–1897) reasoned in *Pace* that because the antimiscegenation law applied equally to whites and nonwhites, it did not run afoul of the Fourteenth Amendment. All of the justices agreed, including Justice John M. Harlan, who would later dissent in *Plessy,* (in)famously asserting that "the Constitution is colorblind."

Almost seventy years after *Pace,* and shortly after that Court had decided *Brown I* but was still wrestling with the matter of a remedial decree that it would announce in *Brown II* (1955), another challenge to Alabama's antimiscegenation law arrived. In that case, *Jackson v. Alabama* (1954),[53] the Court simply denied review, without an opinion or dissent.

Frankfurter, though hardly alone in this regard, pressed on technical jurisdictional grounds to avoid challenges to state antimiscegenation laws. He professed worries about the "deep feeling" Southerners had for such laws. Declaring them unconstitutional, he feared, would probably divide the justices and provoke further confrontations with state supreme courts in the South. Opposition to the ruling in *Brown* would almost certainly intensify. The Court, Frankfurter warned, would be thrust "into the vortex of the present disquietude" in the country over race relations.[54]

The Court refused to grant review in yet another challenge to a state antimiscegenation law between *Brown I* and *Brown II.* The case, *Naim v. Naim,* involved a Chinese man whose marriage to a white woman was annulled by a Virginia court on the grounds that their marriage violated the state's antimiscegenation law. On appeal, the Court remanded the case back to the state courts for reconsideration in light of the fact that the couple were married in North Carolina, where marriages between Asians and whites were legally permissible. The Virginia Supreme Court of Appeals, however, rebuked the order. It held that the trial record was adequate and that according to state law, the Naims were divorced. On a second appeal to the Supreme Court, Frankfurter crafted a per curiam opinion dismissing the case on the technicality that the state court's refusal to act left "the case devoid of a properly presented federal question."

As he had previously done in *Jackson v. Alabama,* Frankfurter successfully persuaded the justices to employ technical jurisdictional grounds to avoid the issue. He did admit, however, "a conflict between moral and technical legal considerations."[55] Chief Justice Warren and Justice Black had in fact strongly opposed Frankfurter's manipulation of legal technicalities. They considered dissenting from the denial of review in *Naim*[56] but decided against doing so. Nevertheless, Warren became further disenchanted with and distrustful of Frankfurter, and remained so.

State supreme courts in the South were already defiant, refusing to follow other rulings against racial discrimination. When the Virginia Supreme Court of Appeals reaffirmed the trial court's application upholding of its state antimiscegenation statute in *Naim v. Naim,*[57] it effectively nullified the Court's order.[58] As the *Richmond New Leader* reported in a front-page headline, "Virginia Rejects Order of U.S. Supreme Court."[59] That state court ruling reinforced the denunciation of the Warren Court in the 1956 congressional "Southern Manifesto."[60] Beyond that, the Conference of Chief Justices of the states would before too long issue a unanimous report charging the Warren Court with usurping state powers.[61]

In correspondence with Judge Learned Hand, Frankfurter acknowledged that challenges to antimiscegenation laws were "vividly in the offing." He candidly revealed that "we twice—shunted [them] away and I pray we may be able to do it again, without being too brazenly evasive." For Frankfurter, the antimiscegenation cases presented a burden the Court could and should not bear in applying the Fourteenth Amendment's guarantee of equal protection. Those antimiscegenation cases presented another "political thicket" that the Court should not enter, just as, in his view, the Court should avoid the issue of malapportioned state legislatures.[62] Indeed, he told Judge Hand that, unlike Justice Cardozo, he thought the Fourteenth Amendment "was too vague, too much open to subjective interpretation for judicial enforcement." Hence, challenges under that amendment should be viewed as raising "political questions" unsuited for the Court's consideration.[63]

As with the issue of malapportioned state legislatures, Frankfurter vowed to work hard "to put off a decision on miscegenation as long as I can—just as Bob Jackson & I worked astutely & persistently in putting off a head-on decision on segregation [in *Brown*]."[64] Or, as Justice Douglas put it, "One bombshell at a time is enough,"[65] even though he and Justice Black would not have invoked jurisdictional technicalities to avoid or delay dealing with the challenges to antimiscegenation laws.

Judge Hand, however, tried to remain faithful to the ideal of "the rule of law." He could not see how it was possible in light of *Brown* to avoid holding antimiscegenation laws unconstitutional.[66] Frankfurter sent him a copy of Bickel's *Harvard Law Review* article on "The Original Understanding and the Segregation Decision." Bickel, while clerking for Frankfurter, wrote a memorandum on the history of the Fourteenth Amendment based on a study of the *Congressional Globe*'s records at the time the amendment was adopted. He found the historical record on the adoption of the amendment "inconclusive," but he concluded that it was "not intended to confer any right of intermarriage, the right to sit on juries, or the right to vote."[67] On the other hand, Bickel believed the historical record provided a basis for growth in the interpretation and application of the Fourteenth Amendment, and thus supported the decision in *Brown*. Frankfurter circulated Bickel's memorandum to the other justices in order to reinforce the view that the Fourteenth Amendment's history was "inconclusive in the sense that the Congress as an enacting body neither manifested that the amendment outlawed segregation to that end, nor that it manifested the opposite." Ultimately, the Court's opinion in *Brown* likewise deemed the history of the Fourteenth Amendment to be "inconclusive."[68]

Judge Hand nonetheless remained unconvinced that Bickel's study or the Court's opinion in *Brown* changed anything. He didn't see how "you lads can duck" the antimiscegenation matter.[69] Nor was he alone.[70] Hand could not escape thinking that *Brown* had laid down "an imperative command" that "race must not be considered as a determining factor, regardless of the 'values' at stake."

Responding to Hand, Frankfurter dismissed the idea that the freedom to marry was an "inherent right." He went to a logical extreme, much like Justice Scalia would do decades later when dissenting from the Court's striking down state laws criminalizing homosexual sodomy and when invalidating state bans on same-sex marriage.[71] "What about restraints," Frankfurter countered, "on marriages by cousins & uncles & the like?" In closing the letter to Hand, he stressed that Chief Justice Warren's opinion in *Brown* was "wholly justified in speaking of 'the inconclusive nature of the Amendment's history.'"[72]

Significantly, as Stanford University Law School professor Gerald Gunther—another former Frankfurter clerk and the author of the definitive Hand biography—pointed out, Frankfurter successfully disabused Hand of the view that *Brown* announced an absolute ban on racial discrimination, including laws that prohibited interracial marriages.[73] As a result of Frankfurter's persistence, Hand was even more distrustful of courts becoming "Platonic Guardians." In his 1958 Oliver Wendell Holmes lectures on the Bill of Rights,[74] about which he brooded for a decade and considered his "goddam lectures,"[75] Hand surprisingly and controversially sharply criticized *Brown*. He chastised the Court not only for failing to expressly overturn *Plessy* but also for its coup de main—its swift back-of-the-hand blow to the doctrine of "separate but equal" without providing any coherent reasoning or principle for the decision.[76] In short, Hand, a leading liberal jurist at the time, accused the Court of usurping legislative powers, just as Byrnes and other conservative critics of *Brown* were doing.[77]

As usual, Frankfurter sought the last word. Writing again to Hand, he reaffirmed that *Brown* did not lay down an absolute rule against racial discrimination. "Is it an absolute on 'equal protection' to have concluded," he insisted, quoting again from the Court's opinion in *Brown,* "that in the field of public education the doctrine of 'separate but equal' has no place."[78] Five months later, in another letter to Hand, Frankfurter reiterated that he could not see "why as a matter of intellectual honesty in starting with the *Segregation Cases* the invalidity of the miscegenation laws follows."[79] *Brown* and the Fourteenth Amendment, for Frankfurter, were a curse on the courts—nothing more or less.

Of course, Frankfurter had defenders. These included his former law clerk, Alexander Bickel. Bickel subsequently argued rhetorically:

> Would it have been wise, at a time when the Court had just pronounced its new integration principle, when it was subject to scurrilous attack by men who predicted that integration of the schools would lead directly to the "mongrelization of the race" and that this was the result the Court had really willed, would it have been wise, just then, in the first case of its sort on an issue that the Negro community as a whole can hardly be said to be pressing hard at the moment, to declare that the states may not prohibit racial intermarriage?[80]

Others, however, agreed with Judge Hand in criticizing the Court's entire approach to the segregation and antimiscegenation cases. Herbert Wechsler, Columbia University Law School professor and former clerk to Justice Harlan F. Stone, was one of them. Though attempting to rebut Judge

Hand's criticisms of the Court's opinion in *Brown*, Wechsler, while searching for a principled constitutional justification for the decision,[81] nonetheless agreed with Hand that the Court's handling of *Naim v. Naim* was "wholly without basis in law."[82]

Judge Hand and Wechsler, of course, were correct that the logical implications of the underlying principle of equal protection precluded any racial discrimination. Frankfurter and Bickel keenly understood how limited the ruling in *Brown* actually was at the time, and what it did and did not decide.

Both Frankfurter and Hand were pessimistic, but in different ways. Hand's pessimism stemmed from despair over his faith in "the rule of law" and devotion to interpreting "inscrutable principles." In contrast, Frankfurter was consumed with the Court's overreaching and the political ramifications of its rulings. In other words, there was a clash between principles of constitutional law and judicial politics. Hand was a hedgehog, who was preoccupied with a self-doubting search for "the rule of law,"[83] while Frankfurter was a fox, who always had an eye open to guarding against new challenges that might draw the Court into larger political controversies and that hence had to be fought off.[84]

Jackson was all too aware of the problems that concerned Frankfurter and Judge Hand, which were raised by challenges to antimiscegenation laws. Of greater concern to him, though, and more practical than theoretical, were the decades of raging political battles that he envisioned, with litigation from school district to school district, and with the lower federal courts bearing the burden, which they eventually did.[85] Without congressional and presidential support, Jackson correctly thought that the Court would be brought "into contempt and the judicial process into discredit," just as in the pre-1937 era. He confidently predicted, as later historians, legal scholars, and political scientists would argue, that the Court might well prove a "hollow hope" for those seeking such major social change.[86] Along with Justice Reed and some others on the Court, he believed—albeit wrongly, as it turned out—that it would take "two generations of litigation" to eliminate segregation.[87]

Jackson's final draft concluded this section by recognizing "that our decision does not end but begins the struggle over segregation." The process of desegregation, he knew, would be long and difficult. Accordingly, the Court's remedial decree had to be flexible in accommodating differences among diverse school districts and communities. As Jackson also pointed out, the Department of Justice had conceded that immediate enforcement of any judicial decree "condemning segregation [was] impossible." The difficulties of compliance loomed too large. They involved the probable reorganization of some school districts, the building of new facilities, the changing teacher and student assignments, along with many other anticipated and unanticipated consequences. These would in turn raise countless financial and political problems for local communities, quite apart from the expected opposition in many parts of the country to the Court's ordering an end to a way of life.

"A gigantic administrative job has to be undertaken" in order to achieve integrated school systems, Jackson predicted. At the same time, he repeatedly returned to thinking about the inexorable burdens that would have to be borne by lower federal court judges in overseeing the implementation of *Brown*'s mandate. They would be subjected—as they indeed were—"to local pressures" and left without clear "standards to justify their decisions to their neighbors, whose opinions they must resist."[88] Chief Justice Warren himself later acknowledged, "We left those judges the job of implementing [*Brown*] in a region where three centuries of slavery and invidious segregation had case-hardened a way of life that permitted no deviations from the theory of white supremacy."[89]

Such inevitable consequences for the courts and the country were nonetheless ultimately due to the failures of Congress and representative government to address segregation. Still, even when push came to shove, Jackson confessed that such failures were "not a sound basis for judicial action."

RACE, SEX, EDUCATION, AND CONSTITUTIONAL CHANGE

The closing section of the last draft, "The Limits and Basis of Judicial Action," was perhaps the most optimistic and important of all. There, Jackson at last dealt fully with the constitutional justification for the Court's ruling, and ended with his overriding concern about the formulation of a remedial decree. The section incorporated parts of earlier versions, but its title reflected notable evolution, from those in the first draft's opening two sections, "The Inadequacy of Judicial Power" and "Legislative Remedy," to that in the third draft's section 7, "The Decree," to the penultimate fifth draft's section 4, "Judicial No Medium of Social Transition."

Somewhat surprisingly, the section begins almost apologetically. Jackson conceded that Congress and the country should be excused for not coming to terms with segregation. Moreover, confusion about and conflict over *Brown* was to be expected and excused. It bore keeping in mind that the Court had sanctioned and legitimated the doctrine of "separate but equal" for generations. As Jackson observed, though in a slightly different form than in the previous fifth revision, "It is not unlikely that a considerable part of the inertia of Congress and of the country has been due to the belief that the existing system is Constitutional." For well over a century, the Court had aided, abided, and reinforced racial prejudices.

Nor did Jackson cast blame on past justices and judges. They may have made mistakes "long ago" in interpreting the Fourteenth Amendment. But he recognized some flexibility in the interpretation of the amendment. He explicitly did so in the fifth draft—the longest of the revisions, completed on March 1, 1954, the same day the Senate finally confirmed Warren as chief justice after his recess appointment. Jackson observed, "If the Court was right to declare that the Amendment was self-executing to the extent of requiring equal if separate facilities, there is the same power and duty to say whether, under present conditions, that doctrine still is valid."

Jackson noted that previous courts had presumed blacks were inferior, as the Taney Court had done in *Dred Scott*, and relied on "precedents from slave days" or "sometimes their own experiences." Hence, they based their decisions on what "was not a legal so much as a factual assumption." Again, rather deferentially and nonaccusatorially, Jackson confessed that "whether these early judges were right or wrong in their times I do not know."

"The real question to me," he explained in the fifth draft, was whether "segregation can today be sustained," even assuming the same factual premises of earlier judges who upheld racial classification. He further spelled out his thinking in that draft: "Whatever may have been true at an earlier period, the mere fact that one is colored does not today create a reasonable presumption that he is inferior, retarded, or a special problem in education."

In both the fifth and final drafts of his unpublished opinion, Jackson then mentioned the significant progress African Americans had made in spite of the conditions and hardships of segregation. Separate, segregated schools undeniably had "been, up to now, wholly to the Negro's disadvantage." Since the 1860s and throughout the late nineteenth and early twentieth centuries, their advancements were nevertheless "spectacular and . . . one of the swiftest and most dramatic advances in the annals of man." Just as Warren would note in the Court's opinion in *Brown,* Jackson emphasized that at the time of the adoption of the Fourteenth Amendment, "the Negro population as a whole was a different people than today."

It was obvious to Jackson that "earlier assumptions based on race alone" no longer held. Indeed, the "mere possession of colored blood, in whole or in part, no longer affords a reasonable basis for a classification for education purposes," and "each individual must be rated on his own merits."

At about this point in an earlier draft, Jackson had confidently and clearly stated his bottom line for a constitutional justification of the Court's decision: "I think that the change which warrants *our decision* is not a change in the Constitution but in the Negro population" (emphasis added). That sentence was unfortunately omitted from the last draft, which was completed on March 15, 1954, just two weeks before Jackson suffered a heart attack. He did, however, include that line in the fourth draft, finished a month before, on February 15, 1954, and almost three months before the decision in *Brown* was announced.

That sentence candidly and concisely revealed the basis for the explanation Jackson gave in the final draft: that it was "neither novel nor radical doctrine" to invalidate statutes once deemed constitutional "by reason of changing conditions." In other words, the Constitution was not a "dead letter" but a "living document." As he had emphasized in prior drafts, constitutional interpretation may not be held hostage, in a straightjacket, bound by earlier factual presumptions or premises long out-of-date, irrelevant, or discarded.

Rather what was decisive in constitutional interpretation were the factual premises, predicates, or presuppositions—the "realist premises"[90] or social facts—on which the interpretation of the Constitution and the Court's rulings had and should have rested. As he stressed in several drafts, the factual premises underpinning *Dred Scott* and *Plessy* were outdated and discredited by the social and economic developments of African Americans. Likewise, Chief Justice Warren's opinion for the Court acknowledged the societal changes that had taken place since *Plessy* when holding, in *Brown,* that the "separate but equal" doctrine no longer applied in the area of public education. Although, as earlier discussed, footnote 11 was controversial, it was inserted and cited social science studies of the effects of segregation on schoolchildren published in leading journals, such as the *International Journal of Opinion and Attitude Research* and the *Journal of Psychology,* besides Myrdal's *American Dilemma.*

Neither Jackson's reasoning in the unpublished opinion nor that in the Court's final opinion was unique in at least one respect. The Court often bases its constitutional interpretation and its decisions on whether to overturn precedents on recognizing different factual premises.[91] In *Planned Parenthood of Southeastern Pennsylvania v. Casey* (1992),[92] for a notable example, a bare majority declined, on just such a basis, to expressly overturn the landmark ruling on abortion in *Roe v. Wade.*[93]

In *Casey,* a plurality of the justices—Sandra Day O'Connor (1981–2006), Anthony Kennedy (1986–), and David Souter (1990–2009)—voted to uphold "the essential holding of *Roe.*" They were joined in part by Justices Stevens and Blackmun. In the section of the Court's opinion dealing with stare decisis and whether *Roe* should be overruled, according to Justice Souter, who wrote and delivered that portion of the opinion, who identified only two other comparable controversies. One was *Lochner v. New York* (1905),[94] with its "liberty of contract" doctrine, in which the Court overturned *West Coast Hotel Co. v. Parrish*,[95] during the fight over the New Deal and "constitutional crisis" of 1937. The second was *Plessy*, which Souter mistakenly observed or overstated as having been reversed in *Brown*. The precedents the Court established in *Lochner* and *Plessy* were properly abandoned, Souter reasoned, "on the basis of facts, or an understanding of facts, changed from those which furnished the claimed justifications for earlier constitutional revolutions. The overruling decisions were comprehensible to the Nation, and defensible, as the Court's responses to changed circumstances." Quoting from Jackson's *Struggle for Judicial Supremacy*, Souter found support in the observation, "The older world of *laissez-faire* was recognized everywhere outside the Court to be dead."[96] By contrast, Souter explained adhering to precedent in *Casey* was justified because "no change in *Roe*'s factual underpinning has left its central holding obsolete."

To be sure, the two dissenting opinions in *Casey*, one by Chief Justice Rehnquist and the other by Justice Scalia, both of which were joined by Justices Byron White (1962–1993) and Clarence Thomas (1991–), sharply disagreed with those analogies, analyses, and factual premises. Nonetheless, Souter maintained that reversing prior rulings was defensible when the underlying social facts or factual presuppositions "have so changed, or come to be seen so differently, as to have robbed the old rule of significant application or justification."[97]

Justice Kennedy used similar reasoning in *Lawrence v. Texas* (2003).[98] In his opinion for the Court overruling *Bowers v. Hardwick* (1986),[99] which had upheld state laws criminalizing certain homosexual acts, he relied on changing factual premises. So too in *Obergefell v. Hodges* (2015),[100] in which the Court struck down state bans on same-sex marriages, Kennedy justified the ruling on changes "in the Nation's experiences with the rights of gays and lesbians," including "substantial cultural and political developments." He also cited changes in the American Psychiatric Association's position on homosexuality, as well as shifts in medical and societal factual presumptions about homosexuality.

Jackson identified the two major factual premises that supported the ruling in *Brown* and providing its determinative constitutional justification. First was the assimilation of whites and blacks as never before and in the foreseeable future.[101] Second was the change in public education, which was no longer held to be a privilege but rather a duty and a right "enforced by compulsory education laws."

"Blush or shudder, as many will, mixture of blood has been making inroads on segregation faster than change in the law. No clear line of separation between the races has been observed. More and more a large population with as much claim to white as to colored baffles any justice in classification for segregation." Jackson thus explicitly laid bare the incoherence of antimiscegenation laws. He also pointed to the wide discrepancies in their application. He knew, of course, that Homer Plessy, who challenged Louisiana's antimiscegenation law, was a French-speaking Creole and an octoroon—only one-eighth of African descent from his great-grandfather. By the 1940s, thirty states banned interracial marriages. Of those, six barred the marriage of couples in which one partner had "one-eighth Negro blood."[102] Most laws banning interracial marriages, however, were based on simple classifications of various "races," including Mongolians, Chinese, Japanese, Asiatic Indians, American Indians, and mulattoes.[103] But these laws were not uniform in their classifications or in specifying percentages of racial ancestry.

Jackson was a great stylist, no doubt about it. With his usual flair for words, his frank, straightforward observation identified the deepest worry of a number of the justices. They were not only troubled by the scope of such a momentous decision on desegregation, the issues of constitutional interpretation, and the inexorable and myriad administrative problems of dismantling dual school systems but also by the anticipated political backlash. There was an enormous difference between ordering the admission of one or two black students into graduate or law school, as in *Sweatt* and *McLaurin,* and mandating the elimination of all racially segregated public schools. The sheer magnitude of the number of communities, school districts, and students affected was daunting enough. But the prospects for attaining compliance with the Court's desegregation mandate for primary and secondary schools raised another major concern. Among others, Justice Clark, in a memorandum on *Sweatt* and *McLaurin,* warned about the repercussions of extending those rulings to primary and secondary schools. He did so despite admitting the illogic of drawing a distinction between racial separation in graduate education and that in elementary or high schools. He also acknowledged that drawing that distinction might have an impact on young schoolchildren.[104] But there was still more.

Jackson raised a related but crucial consideration—namely, inviting more mixing of races and sexes in the lower levels of public schools. Several justices expressly worried about that in conference discussions, memos, and elsewhere. It was not only Reed and Frankfurter who shared such concerns about "the mixing of races."[105] At the December 13, 1953, conference, for instance, according to Justice Douglas's records, after Chief Justice Vinson summarized the segregation cases, senior associate Justice Hugo Black kicked off the discussion by stating that the "reason for segregation is the opinion the colored people are inferior." He continued, "Southerners say it is to prevent the mixture of the races."[106]

So too, at that conference, Justice Clark, who was from Texas, emphasized that in his state, "the problem is as acute as anywhere." Texas, he explained, "also has the Mexican problem—Mexican boy of 15 is in a class with a negro girl of 12. Some negro girls get into trouble." For that reason, Clark was among those justices who, for various other reasons, favored delaying any decision.[107]

Such concerns were by no means confined to the Court. Chief Justice Warren later recalled being at a White House dinner while *Brown* was under consideration. He was seated next to President Eisenhower and within speaking range of John W. Davis, who was representing South Carolina in a companion case. During dinner conversation, the president stressed "what a great man Mr. Davis was." Then, after dinner, Eisenhower took Warren by the arm and, walking into another room, spoke about the Southern states in the segregation cases. "These are not bad people," the president told Warren. "All they are concerned about is that their sweet little girls are not required to sit in school alongside some big overgrown Negroes."[108]

Jackson's colorful line—"Blush or shudder, . . . mixture of blood has been making inroads on segregation faster than change in the law"—implicitly revealed why justices like Frankfurter and their clerks strove to avoid challenges to state antimiscegenation laws,[109] such as those in *Jackson v. Alabama* and *Naim v. Naim,* as well as other such cases beginning to arrive on the Court's docket.[110] By the early twentieth century, forty-two states had antimiscegenation laws. In fact, only Alaska, Connecticut, Hawaii, Minnesota, New Hampshire, New Jersey, Vermont, Wisconsin, and the District of Columbia never enacted such prohibitions. Those laws were increasingly under attack in the courts, and several state legislatures had abandoned them. By the 1940s, as noted earlier, thirty states still had such laws. Then, in the 1950s, ten of those laws were repealed by state legislatures or invalidated by their state courts.[111] This was largely due to publicity about the California supreme court's striking down that state's antimiscegenation law in 1948.[112]

More states followed suit. Consequently, by the time the Warren Court finally declared antimiscegenation laws unconstitutional, in *Loving v. Virginia* (1967),[113] only sixteen states still had such laws.

Shortly after the ruling in *Brown,* for instance, one of Justice Douglas's clerks, Harvey M. Grossman, wrote in a cert. memo on whether the Court should grant review of the petition challenging Alabama's antimiscegenation law in *Jackson v. State:* "It seems clear that the statute involved is unconstitutional." But, Grossman continued, granting "review at the present time would probably increase the tensions growing out of the school segregation cases . . . and, therefore, the Court may wish to defer action until a future time."[114] Frankfurter's former law clerk, Philip Elman, who then worked in the solicitor general's office but remained in close contact with the justice, later also recalled that "the last thing in the world the Justices wanted to deal with at that time was the question of interracial marriage."[115]

When the Court did finally invalidate bans on interracial marriages in *Loving,* it did so in a very brief opinion, as in *Brown,* delivered by the chief justice. Warren claimed, quoting from the opinion in *Brown,* that while "historical sources 'cast some light' they are not sufficient to resolve the problem; [a]t best, they are inconclusive. The most avid proponents of the post-War Amendments undoubtedly intended them to remove all legal distinctions among 'all persons born or naturalized in the United States.' Their opponents, just as certainly, were antagonistic to both the letter and spirit of the Amendments and wished them to have the most limited effect."[116]

The historical record actually points completely contrariwise. Bickel's article, "The Original Understanding and the Segregation Cases,"[117] and Jackson's own reading of the history of the Thirty-Ninth Congress both reached the opposite conclusion. Others subsequently disagreed as well.[118] Just as Congress had continued to fund segregated schools in the District of Columbia after the adoption of the Fourteenth Amendment, a majority of the states that ratified the amendment maintained antimiscegenation laws well into the mid-twentieth century.[119]

In addition, Jackson put his finger on precisely the fundamental taboo, identified in Myrdal's *American Dilemma,* that was the bedrock of the country's race problem. Fear of interracial sex and marriage is what lay at the very bottom of segregation in education, public accommodations, and virtually all else. As Myrdal explained, sex was "the principle around which the whole structure of segregation of the Negroes—down to disfranchisement and denial of equal opportunities in the labor market—is organized." He put it even more bluntly: "In cruder language, but with the same logic, the Southern man on the street responds to any plea for social equality: 'Would you like to have your daughter marry a Negro?'"[120]

Crucial for understanding race relations in America, Myrdal argued, was "the white man's theory of color caste," the essential elements of which were as follows:[121]

1. The concern for "race purity" is basic to the whole issue: the primary and essential command is to prevent amalgamation; whites are determined to utilize every means to this end.
2. Rejection of "social equality" is to be understood as a precaution to hinder miscegenation, and particularly intermarriage.
3. The danger of miscegenation is so tremendous that the segregation and discrimination inherent in the refusal of "social equality" must be extended to nearly all spheres of life. There must be segregation and discrimination in recreation, in religious services, in education, before the law, in politics, in housing, in stores, and in breadwinning.

Myrdal's findings were well understood even if they were considered inflammatory by many. President Truman's 1947 Committee on Civil Rights reached basically the same conclusion. That committee found that systematic racial discrimination "brands the Negro with the mark of inferiority and asserts that he is not fit to associate with white people."[122] A year later, Truman's Department of Justice, led by Attorney General, and future justice, Tom Clark, filed a brief in *Shelly v. Kramer* (1948), the case challenging racially restrictive covenants. Clark's brief cited Myrdal's *American Dilemma*.[123]

Notably, Myrdal's 1944 book also placed America's history of white supremacy in an international context. In particular, he analogized it to the racism of Nazi Germany, which was especially fresh in minds during the last battles of World War II. Nor could that point have been lost on the Court when it considered *Brown*. This was especially true for Jackson, who shortly after the war served as the chief prosecutor at the Nazi war crimes trials in Nuremberg, Germany.[124] Nuremberg, Frankfurter recalled after Jackson's death, "had a profound influence on his endeavor to understand the human situation. . . . [He] was there made to realize how ultimately fragile the forces of reason are and how precious the safeguards of law so painstakingly built up in the course of centuries."[125] Furthermore, in 1948 the United Nations had adopted the Universal Declaration of Human Rights, which specifically prohibited limitations on the right to marry "due to race."[126]

Nor was Jackson alone among the justices in thinking about America's racial segregation in relation to the country's international standing.[127] Justice Reed, for one, assigned law clerks to research international and comparative law bearing on segregation. He also asked other justices to send him any authoritative international documents dealing with the issue. Reed explained to them that "'segregation' as now presented does not mean 'discrimination' to me," but he also wondered whether "the attitude of the rest of the world toward segregation is worth consideration."[128]

The last draft continued with a brief discussion of why another fundamental change—the societal change in education—justified the ruling in *Brown*. As he firmly explained in the fourth draft, all laws "which classify persons for separate treatment in matters of education based solely on possession of colored blood" must be struck down. Since the late nineteenth century, public education had dramatically changed. Education was no longer a privilege but a right required by state laws, as well as a duty of all citizens in a democracy. Indeed, Jackson came close to suggesting that there was now a fundamental federal constitutional right to education.[129] In any event, given those changes, Jim Crow in elementary and high schools, no less than in graduate and law schools, no longer deserved or was entitled to support.[130] That was the second, though nonetheless crucial, social fact or factual premise, as Jackson saw it, which justified the ruling in *Brown*.

THE REMEDIAL DECREE

The last paragraph of the final version of Jackson's unpublished opinion concluded by observing: "I believe that the circumstances under which a large part of the country has grown into the existing system are such that only consideration of that in framing of the decree would be just. And, in the long run, I think only a reasonably considerate decree would be an expedient one for the persons it has sought to benefit hereby."

That paragraph encapsulated the much more lengthy discussions in previous drafts dealing with the Court's eventual remedial decree. In the first draft, for example, when thinking about the limits of judicial power compared with congressional legislation, Jackson stressed that it was obviously not enough to simply declare laws enforcing segregation "null and void." "That might be, and probably would be enough to end segregation in Delaware and Kansas, where it lingers by a tenuous lease of life, but," he added, "where the practice is really entrenched, it exists as a local usage, quite independently of any statute and striking down the statute will not be enough to end segregation." The reality Jackson explained was: "All we can say is that a school district must make some change, we don't know what, whenever the local judge tells them to." Clearly he envisioned at least some of the problems of court-ordered desegregation and the massive resistance that followed the ruling.

Indisputably, as the earlier and final drafts reveal, Jackson would un-doubtedly have signed on to the Court's remedial decree for proceeding "with all deliberate speed" in dismantling racially segregated schools.[131] The phrase "with all deliberate speed" was, as is well-known, inserted in *Brown II* at the suggestion of Frankfurter.[132] He borrowed it from Justice Holmes's opinion on how fast West Virginia had to repay its debt to Virginia after split-ting apart into a separate state.[133] Actually, attorneys for Virginia's Prince William County's companion case with *Brown* had suggested that the Court adopt precisely that course during oral arguments in April 1955.[134] They did so in countering the NAACP's arguments for the *immediate* desegregation of public schools.[135] Thurgood Marshall had argued for a "forthwith" remedial decree, contending that there was no "middle ground." Otherwise, accord-ing to the future justice, *Brown I* would "mean nothing until [a] time limit is set."[136]

After hearing oral arguments in *Brown II,* Chief Justice Warren indicated in conference discussions that more than a "bare bones" decree was needed. In response, however, Justice Black bluntly insisted, "The less we say the better off we are."[137] For once, Frankfurter and Black agreed. Subsequently, Warren circulated memos outlining various possible formulations for the decree.[138] Frankfurter responded in a letter restating that "with all deliber-ate speed" was preferable to "at the earliest practicable date."[139] In fact, years later, Frankfurter told Judge Hand that because of his "strong conviction that we shall be in for a long process & probably with some ugly episodes," he had "strongly urged the phrase 'with all deliberate speed.'" Frankfurter added that the reason "why the phrase wasn't quoted & the case [*Virginia v. West Virginia* (1911)] cited—the indication of a long drawn-out litigation—is another story."[140]

All of the justices agreed that the opinion in *Brown II,* as in *Brown I* a year earlier, should be unanimous and provide as much flexibility as possible. As Justice Holmes explained for the Court years earlier, when upholding Alabama's voter registration requirements and qualifications that were chal-lenged as discriminatory and effectively disenfranchising black voters, "In determining whether a court of equity can take jurisdiction, one of the first questions is what it can do to enforce any order that it may make."[141]

"The problem," one of Justice Reed's clerks astutely observed, was fram-ing the "mandate so as to allow such divergent results without making it so broad that evasion is encouraged."[142] Yet as Dennis Hutchinson later per-ceptively pointed out, "if *Brown I* was a clarion call, *Brown II*'s ambivalence implicitly diminished the moral imperative of the first decision."[143]

The phrase "with all deliberate speed" was understood by all to convey flexibility while countenancing accommodation of local school districts and delays in the implementation of desegregation. All the justices agreed— even if not fully understanding the extent—that the Court was embarking onto uncharted territory. With that, Jackson most assuredly would have agreed, with caution, in signing on to *Brown II*. If only he had lived.

CHAPTER FIVE

This Is the End

E. Barrett Prettyman Jr. was almost certainly correct in criticizing the organization and tone of the last draft of Jackson's unpublished opinion before the justice's meeting in the hospital with Chief Justice Warren. Prettyman's suggested reorganization made a good deal of sense. Yet Prettyman had not read earlier revisions and therefore could not appreciate how much Jackson's thinking evolved and why the final draft took the shape it did.

In earlier drafts, Jackson was preoccupied with Congress's responsibility to address the problem of segregation, along with the comparative advantages and difficulties of congressional legislation versus the Court's formulating an appropriate remedial decree. In the penultimate and last drafts, by contrast, Jackson paid much more attention to constitutional interpretation and to the justification for the Court's decision. Any hope for congressional action had long been abandoned.[1] Concerns about formulating a judicial remedy were relegated to the last two short paragraphs of later drafts,[2] suggesting rearguments on that question, just as the Court would order.

There is no denying that the unpublished opinion contained some highly inflammatory language. Indeed, it is hard to understand how he could have thought that publication of the opinion might have "blunted" criticism of the Court's reasoning and holding in *Brown*.[3] On the contrary, the unpublished opinion probably would have further outraged the South. Both Chief Justice Warren and Jackson strove to write nonaccusatorial opinions. Neither placed blame on prior justices and judges or Southerners. Still, Jackson's occasional prose would unquestionably have been incendiary to some. Southerners surely would have recoiled at the statement: "Blush or shudder, as many will, mixture of blood has been making inroads on segregation faster than change in the law." Clearly this was more provocative than footnote 11's mere—however controversial—citation of Myrdal's *American Dilemma*. Jackson's line highlighted one of Myrdal's central and most provocative findings—namely, that whites feared interracial intercourse and marriage as the ultimate threat to their supremacy.

Undoubtedly Jackson's opinion would have generated even greater opposition than did the Court's opinion by contending that all racial classifications were "irrational" per se, and therefore that all segregated public accommodations, along with antimiscegenation laws, logically must fall. However, Warren's opinion for the Court did not expressly overrule *Plessy*, simply holding

115

instead the "separate but equal" doctrine no longer applied in the field of public education.[4] But Jackson's unpublished opinion, by comparison, was considerably more extensive, with application beyond segregated schools to all segregated public accommodations. It was likewise more intrusive in affecting basic principles of federalism and local governance, and effectively preempting and rendering unnecessary the Civil Rights Act of 1964.

Prettyman was keenly aware of the limited scope of the Court's opinion when he appealed to Jackson's pragmatism in offering criticisms and suggestions.[5] Prettyman played to Jackson, just as years later Frankfurter did to Judge Hand when disabusing him of the scope of *Brown*'s holding. Political realities, judicial politics, and pragmatism sometimes outweigh blind-faith commitment to legal principles.[6] Jackson, always a principled pragmatist, gave way to that view, which Warren was urging as well, when deciding to set his unpublished opinion aside and agreeing to join the Court's opinion. By contrast, Hand did not abandon his faith in unbending legal principles. Only after Frankfurter's repeated attempts to persuade him of the limits of the ruling in *Brown* did Hand yield. But even then, he denounced *Brown* and the Court in his Holmes lectures.

Closely related, but no less controversial and important, are the different bases for the *Brown* decision given in the Court's opinion, and by contrast in Jackson's unpublished opinion. Chief Justice Warren's opinion focused on the psychological and sociological harms of segregation, drawing "attention to the moral deficiency of segregationists."[7] But Jackson emphasized the utter "irrationality" of any belief in the racial inferiority of blacks. For him, it was simply common sense, without any need for supporting sociological evidence. Arguably, Jackson's analysis rendered segregationists more blameworthy than did Warren's focus on the harmful effects of segregation. In short, Jackson's position was a more profound and potent rebuke, which undoubtedly would have further antagonized those already opposed to the ruling in *Brown*.

Ironically, over a decade later, Chief Justice Warren appeared to almost embrace Jackson's position. During the conference discussion of *Loving v. Virginia* (1967),[8] according to Justice Douglas's notes, the chief justice opened the deliberations by stating, "The Fourteenth Amendment was intended to wipe out discrimination on the basis of race. Miscegenation statutes maintain white supremacy. They should all go down the drain."[9] With little discussion, all the other justices agreed. Warren's opinion for the Court in *Loving,* as in *Brown,* noted that the history of the Fourteenth Amendment was "inconclusive," though now as to the matter of antimiscegenation laws. Warren then proceeded to reject Virginia's arguments that its law had "equal application" to the different races and hence had a rational basis. In other words, as Jackson had viewed it years earlier, before Prettyman and Warren persuaded him to agree to a more limited ruling in *Brown,* racial classifications were at least deserving of "strict scrutiny," if not completely "irrational." As it happened, however, Justice Byron White (1962–1993), during the Court's consideration of *Loving,* responded with a letter to Warren, explaining that the test should be "much more onerous than mere rationality where racial classifications are involved and that this heavier burden has not been met here."[10] White did so partially because he had used the higher "strict scrutiny" test when delivering the Court's unanimous decision in *McLaughlin v. Florida* (1964),[11] striking down a state law making it a crime for an interracial couple to "habitually live in and occupy in the nighttime the same room." Not surprisingly, Florida also had an antimiscegenation law and did not recognize interracial common-law marriages.[12] Ironically, though, White explained favoring the higher standard because "there are some racial classifications, although perhaps rare, which I would approve."

Ultimately, Warren agreed with White, and the draft opinion in *Loving* was revised to emphasize that racial classifications carry "the very heavy burden of justification" and that they must survive the "most rigid scrutiny" under the Fourteenth Amendment. That in turn prompted Justice Potter Stewart (1958–1981) to file a concurring opinion, just as he had done in *McLaughlin*. Stewart wanted to go further. He countered that it was "simply not possible for a state law to be valid under our Constitution which makes the criminality of an act depend upon the race of the actor."[13] The battle, so to speak, between nuanced and categorical rationales for asserting the Court's power to strike down laws based on race thus continued.

Another criticism leveled at Jackson's unpublished opinion was that his view of segregation was too simplistic. In particular, some critics targeted his emphasis on a universal instinct for some sort of separation, whether along racial, religious, ethnic, or some other line. Ostensibly Jackson's emphasis on the universality of an instinct for separation might have given too much credence to "the disingenuous arguments of segregationists."[14] It could have been interpreted to undercut "his efforts to demonstrate the unreasonableness of racial classifications."[15]

The "weakest point" in Jackson's opinion, according to other critics, flowed from his concern that the Court's ruling "would both harm efforts at desegregation and discredit the judiciary." For some critics, that posed the wrong consideration and resulted in an incomplete calculation. Jackson should have considered "what the cost of a decision upholding segregation would have been."[16] In short, Jackson was too explicit, too honest, and too judicious when weighing both sides. He may have also miscalculated the costs and benefits of the Court's ruling.[17]

Furthermore, Jackson's rejection of social science studies as the basis for the decision in *Brown* in favor of relying on common sense—as he put it, one would have to be "dumb" not to recognize the effects of segregation—was more than merely simplistic. Some critics charged that it was duplicitous and disingenuous. As one argued, "Jackson himself proposed a fact-based inquiry" and "manufactured" a "predicate to support its preferred result" without "providing any factual evidence of changes in the conditions of blacks." Consequently, he "left untouched the questions of how much change was necessary, and at what point laws become unconstitutional."[18]

Such criticisms nonetheless seem to be a bit of a reach, contrived, and off the mark. For one thing, as Paul Freund pointed out, Justice Holmes used to say that "we need education in the obvious more than investigation of the obscure."[19] That well characterized Jackson's thinking. For another, change was in the wind, and Jackson knew it. He did not need social science to tell him that. Again, quoting Freund on the obvious: "The old doctrine of separate-but-equal, announced in 1896, had been steadily eroded for at least a generation before the school cases, in a way that precedents are whittled down until they finally collapse."[20] In addition, psychosociological studies could not answer "questions of how much change" was necessary or "at what point laws become unconstitutional." Such criticisms of Jackson simply posed the wrong questions. To expect answers to these is a fool's errand. It is just as misguided as asking questions of history that cannot possibly be answered determinatively.

Finally, it is simply plain silly to fault Jackson's unpublished opinion for not demanding immediate compliance with *Brown*. Neither, of course, did Warren's opinion for the Court.[21] Like all of the other justices on the Court at that time, Jackson knew better. Immediate desegregation was an impossibility, and ordering it would have only exacerbated the inevitable pushback to the ruling.

Jackson was not in the least simplistic but rather complex and dialectical. He was principled. But he was also a realist and a pragmatist. All the while, he remained deeply concerned, as the various revisions of his unpublished opinion demonstrate, with the "reasoned elaboration" of the law.

Jackson's unpublished opinion underscores the basic fact that the decision in *Brown* was made neither lightly nor out of arrogant "liberal judicial activism," as that unanimous ruling has often been portrayed. Rather, the ruling in *Brown* was made with great reluctance and restraint. The Warren Court bet its institutional prestige on doing what was right, in full awareness of an anticipated pushback, even if the justices underestimated the extent of prolonged resistance that would follow. Jackson and the entire Warren Court did so with the hope that, in time, the country would forget its racially separated past in exchange for the promise of a more equal future, where people of all races would be treated with equal dignity and respect.

In the preface to *The Struggle for Judicial Supremacy,* Jackson observed that "Constitutional law had become, not the law of the Constitution, but the law *about* the Constitution."[22] In drafting and revising the unpublished opinion for *Brown,* Jackson thought and rethought first principles of constitutional interpretation and their factual premises. He struggled to convince himself, and potentially others, that the ruling in *Brown* was within the parameters of the Constitution. In doing so, he probed the depths of constitutional decision making, offering guidance for those who would follow. Jackson understood the future of race relations would resemble the past, only differently. The question was how different and how long it would take to become truly different—to move from one world to another.

PART TWO

Chapter Six

Justice Jackson's Unpublished Opinion

I.

Since the close of the Civil War, the United States has been "hesitating between two worlds—one dead, the other powerless to be born." Constitutions are easier amended than social customs, and even the North never fully conformed its racial practices to its professions.

One whose impressionable years were spent in public schools in a region where Negro pupils were very few and where economic, social and political motives united against segregating them is predisposed to the conclusion that segregation elsewhere has outlived whatever justification it may have had. The practice seems marked for early extinction. Whatever we might say today, within a generation it will be outlawed by decision of this Court because of the forces of mortality and replacement which operate upon it.

Decision of these cases would be simple if our personal opinion that school segregation is morally, economically or politically indefensible made it legally so. But it is not only established in the law of seventeen states and the national capital; it is deeply imbedded in social custom in a large part of this country. Its eradication involves nothing less than a substantial reconstruction of legal institution and of society. It persists because of fears, prides and prejudices which this Court cannot eradicate, which even in the North are latent, and occasionally ignite where the ratio of colored population to white passes a point of where the latter vaguely, and perhaps unreasonably, feel themselves insecure.

However sympathetic we may be with the resentments of those who are coerced into segregation, we cannot, in considering a recasting of society by judicial fiat, ignore the claims of those who are to be coerced out of it. We cannot deny the sincerity and passion with which many feel that their blood, lineage and culture are worthy of protection by enforced separatism of races and feel they have built their segregated institutions for many years on an almost universal understanding that segregation is not constitutionally forbidden.

It has seemed almost instinctive with every race, faith, state or culture to resort to some isolating device to protect and perpetuate those qualities, real or fancied, which it especially values in itself. Separatism, either by voluntary withdrawal or by imposed segregation, has been practiced in

123

some degree by many religions, nationalities and races, and by many—one almost can say all—governments, to alleviate tensions, prevent subversions and to quell or forestall violence. It is today being practiced on a voluntary basis by minorities, who discourage or forbid intermarriage, maintain separate denominational schools, and otherwise seek to prevent contacts which threaten dilution of blood or dissipation of faith. This instinct for self-preservation is enough to account for the prevalence of segregation in several of the Northern states.

But, in the South, the Negro appears to suffer from other antagonisms that are an aftermath of the great American white conflict. The white South harbors in historical memory, with deep resentment, the program of reconstruction and the deep humiliation of carpetbag government imposed by conquest. Whatever other motives were behind these offensive reconstruction measures and whatever their necessity or merit, the North made the Negro their emotional symbol and professed beneficiary, with the natural consequence of identifying him with all that was suffered from his Northern champions. Thus, I am convinced the race problem in the South involves more than mere racial prejudice. It is complicated emotionally with a white war and white politics.

Whether a use of the power of this Court to decree an end of segregation will diminish or increase racial tensions in the South I have no personal experience or knowledge to judge, nor is that my responsibility. But I am satisfied that it would retard acceptance of this decision if the Northern majority of this Court should make a Pharisaic and self-righteous approach to this issue or were inconsiderate of the conditions which have brought about and continued this custom or should permit a needlessly ruthless decree to be promulgated.

The plain fact is that the questions of constitutional interpretation and of the limitations on responsible use of judicial power in a federal system implicit in these cases are as far-reaching as any that have been before the Court since its establishment.

II. Does Existing Law Condemn Segregation?

Layman as well as lawyer must query how it is that the Constitution this morning forbids what for three-quarters of a century it has tolerated or approved. He must further speculate as to how this reversal of its meaning by the branch of the Government supposed not to make new law but only to declare existing law and which has exactly the same constitutional materials that so far as the states are concerned have existed since 1868 and in the case of the District of Columbia since 1791. Can we honestly say that the states which have maintained segregated schools have not, until today, been justified in understanding their practice to be constitutional?

Of course, for over three-quarters of a century majestic and sweeping generalities of the Due Process and Equal Protection Clauses of the Fourteenth Amendment were capable of being read to require a full and equal racial partnership in all matters with the reach of law. But neither of these clauses specifically mentions education or segregation. Yet, if these texts had such meaning to the age that wrote them, how could the identical Due Process Clause of the Fifth Amendment for half a century have tolerated slavery in the District of Columbia? And when those words were copied into the Fourteenth Amendment and the Equal Protection Clause added, why were they not deemed to assure the Negro the right to vote? The Fourteenth Amendment contemplated denial of the vote and provided a reduction of congressional representation for states which do not allow the Negro to exercise the franchise. It was nearly two years later (1870) when the Fifteenth Amendment was added to assure equal voting rights; but, even then, with the shortcomings of the Fourteenth Amendment obvious, nothing was included as to either segregation or education. Thus, there is no explicit prohibition of segregated schools and it can only be supplied by interpretation.

It is customary to turn to the original will and purpose of those responsible for adoption of a constitutional document as a basis for its subsequent interpretation. So much is implied by the questions we have asked of counsel. Their exhaustive research to uncover the original will and purpose expressed in the Fourteenth Amendment yields for me only one sure conclusion: it was a passionate, confused and deplorable era. Like most legislative history, that of the Amendment is misleading because its sponsors played down its consequences in order to quiet fears which might cause opposition, while its opponents exaggerated the consequence to frighten away support. Among its supporters may be found a few who hoped that it would bring about complete social equality and early assimilation of the liberated Negro into an amalgamated population. But I am unable to find any indication that their support was decision [*sic*], and certainly their view had no support from the great Emancipator himself. The majority was composed of more moderate men who appeared to be thinking in terms of ending all questions as to constitutionality of the contemporaneous statutes conferring upon the freed man certain limited civil rights. It is hard to find an indication that any influential body of the movement that carried the Civil War Amendments had reached the point of thinking about either segregation or education of the Negro as a current problem, and harder still to find that the Amendments were designed to be a solution.

If we turn from words to deeds as evidence of purpose, we find nothing to show that the Congress which submitted these Amendments understood or intended to prohibit the practice here in question. The very Congress that proposed the Fourteenth Amendment, and every Congress from that day to this, established or maintained segregated schools in the District of Columbia, where its power over purse and policy was complete. This system was notorious and must have been known to every Congressman who voted for District of Columbia appropriations down to this very day. Occasionally one protested, which only emphasized that the policy was firm and deliberate. Congress legislated concerning some Negro civil rights, such as the right to sit upon juries, but never has touched the segregation question. Congress readmitted representatives of the "reconstructed" Confederate States, which it required to accept the Fourteenth Amendment, but has never indicated a view that segregated schools constituted a breach of the condition of reinstatement in the Union.

Turning from Congress to look to the behavior of the States, we find that equally impossible to reconcile with any understanding that the Amendment would prohibit segregation in schools. Some inference might be drawn from the fact that five states which did have segregated schools when the Amendment was submitted to them abandoned them at about that time and that four which had segregated schools refused to ratify the Amendment. But nine Northern states and two border states either continued or established segregated schools after ratifying the Amendment. The eight reconstructed states all established segregated schools. Down to the present day, seventeen states of the Union by law permit or require separation of the races in the public school. Plainly, there was no consensus among state legislators or educators ratifying the Amendment any more than in Congress that it was to end segregation.

If we look to see how judicial precedent squares with the practice of legislators and administrators, we find that state courts of the North and this Court, where Northern men have predominated, have shared the understanding that these clauses of their own force do not prohibit the states from deciding that each race must obtain its education apart rather than by commingling. Almost a century of decisional law rendered by judges, many of whom risked their lives for the cause that produced these Amendments, is almost unanimous in the view that the Amendment tolerated segregation by state action, at least in the absence of congressional action to the contrary.

The custom of a people has always been recognized as a powerful lawmaker. Widespread usage has reinforced the view of legislators and educators and the opinions of the courts. This Court, in common with courts everywhere, has recognized the force of long custom and has been reluctant to use judicial power to try to recast social usages established among the people. Indeed, not long ago we decided that custom has nullified the constitutional plan for independent presidential electors. Today's decision is to uproot a custom deeply embedded not only in state statutes but in the habit and usage of people in their local communities.

Convenient as it would be to reach an opposite conclusion, I simply cannot find in the conventional material of constitutional interpretation any justification for saying that in maintaining segregated schools any state or the District of Columbia can be judicially decreed, up to the date of this decision, to have violated the Fourteenth Amendment.

III. DOES THE AMENDMENT CONTEMPLATE CHANGED CONDITIONS?

The Fourteenth Amendment does not attempt to say the last word on the concrete application of its pregnant generalities. It declares that "The Congress shall have power to enforce, by appropriate legislation, the provisions of this Article." It thus makes provision for giving effect from time to time to the changes of conditions and public opinion always to be anticipated in a developing society. A policy which it outlines only comprehensively it authorized Congress to complete in detail.

If the Amendment deals at all with state segregation and education, there can be no doubt that it gives Congress a wide discretion to enact legislation on that subject binding on all states and school districts. Admittedly, it explicitly enables Congress from time to time to exercise a wide discretion as to new laws to meet new conditions. The question is how far this Court should leave this subject to be dealt with by legislation, and any answer will have far-reaching implications.

The Court may decide the right of a particular plaintiff in a specific case and enforce its decision by contempt proceedings against the individuals who were defendants therein. But in embarking upon a widespread reform of social customs and habits of countless communities we must face the limitations on the nature and effectiveness of the judicial process.

The futility of effective reform of our society by judicial decree is demonstrated by the history of this very matter. For many years this Court has pronounced the doctrine that, while separate facilities for each race are permissible, they must be equal. Our pronouncement to that effect has remained a dead letter in a large part of the country. Why has the separate-but-equal doctrine declared by this Court so long been a mere promise to the colored ear to be broken to the hope?

It has remained an empty pronouncement because the courts have no power to enforce general declarations of law by applying sanction against any persons not before them in a particular litigation. Contempt proceedings as to those who disobey the court's order may be available, but only against those who were parties to the action.

I see no reason to expect a pronouncement that segregation is unconstitutional will be any more self-executing or any more efficiently executed than our pronouncement that unequal facilities are unconstitutional. A law suit must be maintained in every school district which shows persistent recalcitrance to lay the basis for a contempt charge. That is an effective sanction in a private controversy, but it is a weak reed to rely on in initiating a change in the social system of a large part of the United States. With no machinery except that of the courts to put the power of the Government behind it, it seems likely to result in a failure that will bring the court into contempt and the judicial process into discredit.

The Court can strike down legislation which supports educational segregation, but any constructive policy for abolishing it must come from Congress. Only Congress can enact a policy binding on all states and districts, and it can delegate its supervision to some administrative body provided with standards for determining the conditions under which sanctions should apply. It can make provisions for federal funds where changes required are beyond the means of the community, for mixing the races will require extensive changes in physical plants and will impose the largest burden on some of the nation's lowest income regions. Moreover, Congress can lift the heavy burden of private litigation from disadvantaged people and make the investigation and administrative proceedings against recalcitrant districts the function of some public agency that would secure enforcement of the policy.

A Court decision striking down state statutes or constitutional provisions which authorize or require segregation will not produce a social transition, nor is the judiciary the agency to which the people should look for that result. Our decision may end segregation in Delaware and Kansas, because there it lingers by a tenuous lease of life. But where the practice really is entrenched, it exists independently of any statute or decision as a local usage and deep-seated custom sustained by the prevailing sentiment of the community. School districts, from habit and conviction, will carry it along without aid of state statutes. To eradicate segregation by judicial action means two generations of litigation.

It is apparent that our decision does not end but begins the struggle over segregation. Representatives of the Negros contend with great force that if to enter white schools is a right at all it is a present and personal right and that deferred belief may be a denial of rights to those pupils who meanwhile pass school age. Counsel for the states contend that if segregation is abolished at all, the process must be adapted to varying local conditions which will require time and consideration and varying periods of adjustment. They point out in building their present administrative, education and physical structures they have relied on the teachings of this Court and the attitudes of Congress.

The Department of Justice concedes that uniform and immediate enforcement of a Court decree condemning segregation is impossible. It points out that school districts may have to be consolidated or divided, or their boundaries revised, and the teachers and pupils may have to be transferred. The Government points out that an essential part of the plan will involve placing white children under colored teachers, unless colored teachers are to be dismissed in some areas where they have been hired in substantial numbers. This is one of the most controversial problems of adjustment. Financial problems also obviously are involved. In some regions, the white schools are good, the Negro schools poor. If both classes are to be accommodated in both schools, it would require white pupils to shift to the Negro schools, a measure not likely to be accepted without strong local opposition. New facilities are necessarily to be provided, and that involves taxation, the sale of bonds, and the votes of taxpayers and affirmative actions by public bodies. It is impossible now to anticipate all of the difficulties or to determine the time necessary in any particular area to overcome them. While our decision may invalidate existing laws and regulations governing the school, the Court cannot substitute constructive laws and regulations for their governance. Local or state or federal action will have to build the integrated school systems if they are to exist. A gigantic administrative job has to be undertaken.

The Government advises that the courts assume this task and that we remand these cases to the District Courts under instructions to proceed with enforcement as rapidly as conditions make it appear practicable. The Government proposes that we affirmatively direct the District Courts to obtain from the local school authorities and approve "an effective program for accomplishing transition to a nonsegregated system." It adds, "in passing upon such a program, the lower court could receive the views not only of the parties but of interested persons and groups in the community."

I will not be a party to thus casting upon the lower courts a burden of continued litigation under circumstances which subject district judges to local pressures and provide them with no standards to justify their decisions to their neighbors, whose opinions they must resist. The Department offers us no standards, and none exist in the law, to determine when and how the school system should be revamped. For the courts to supervise the educational authorities with the aid of town meetings seems to me manifestly beyond judicial power or functions. Our sole authority is to decide an existing case or controversy between the parties. Nothing has raised more doubt in my mind as to the wisdom of our decision than the character of the decree which the Government conceives to be necessary to its success. We are urged, however, to supply means to supervise transition of the country from segregated to nonsegregated schools upon the basis that Congress may or probably will refuse to act. That assumes nothing less than that we must act because our representative system has failed. The premise is not a sound basis for judicial action.

IV. The Limits and Basis of Judicial Action

Until today Congress has been justified in believing that segregation does not offend the Constitution. In view of the deference habitually paid by other branches of the Government to this Court's interpretation of the Constitution, it is not unlikely that a considerable part of the inertia of Congress, if not of the country, has been due to the belief that the existing system is constitutional. The necessity for judicial action on this subject arises from the doctrine concerning it which is already on our books.

It is not, in my opinion, necessary or true to say that these earlier judges, many of whom were as sensitive to human values as any of us, were wrong in their own times. With their fundamental premise that the requirement of equal protection does not disable the state from making reasonable classifications of its inhabitants nor impose the obligation to accord identical treatment to all, there can be no quarrel. We still agree that it only requires that the classifications of different groups rest upon real and not upon feigned distinctions, that the distinction have some rational relation to the subject matter for which the classification is adopted, and that the differences in treatment between classes shall not go beyond what is reasonable in the light of the relevant differences. These legal premises are not being changed today.

But the second step in their reasoning, sometimes in reliance on precedents from slave days, sometimes from experience in their own time, was not a legal so much as a factual assumption. It was that there were differences between the Negro and the white races, viewed as a whole, such as to warrant separate classification and discrimination not only for their educational facilities but also for marriage, for access to public places of recreation, amusement or service and as passengers on common carriers and as the right to buy and own real estate.

Whether these early judges were right or wrong in their times I do not know. Certainly in the 1860's and probably throughout the Nineteenth Century the Negro population as a whole was a different people than today. Lately freed from bondage, they had little opportunity as yet to show their capacity for education or even self-support and management. There was strong belief in heredity, and the Negro's heritage was then close to primitive. Likewise, his environment from force of circumstances was not conducive to his mental development. I do not find it necessary to stigmatize as hateful or unintelligent the early assumption that Negro education presented problems that were elementary, special and peculiar and that the mass teaching of Negroes was an experiment not easily tied in with the education of pupils of more favored background. Nor, when I view the progress that was made under it, can I confidently say that the practice of each race pursuing its education apart has been, up to now, wholly to the Negro's disadvantage. My little experience in a nonsegregated school does not teach that to mingle closely with white pupils fully solves the Negro's psychological or educational problem. Indeed, Negro progress under segregation has been spectacular and, tested by the pace of history, his rise is one of the swiftest and most dramatic advances in the annals of man. It is that, indeed, which has enabled him to outgrow the system and to overcome the presumptions on which it was based.

The handicap of inheritance and environment has been too widely overcome today to warrant these earlier presumptions based on race alone. I do not say that every Negro everywhere is so advanced, nor would I know whether the proportion who have shown educational capacity is or is not in all sections similar. But it seems sufficiently general to require me to say that mere possession of colored blood, in whole or in part, no longer affords a reasonable basis for a classification for educational purposes and that each individual must be rated on his own merit. Retarded or subnormal ones, like the same kind in whites, may be accorded separate educational treatment. All that is required is that they be classified as individuals and not as a race for their learning, aptitude and discipline.

Moreover, we cannot ignore the fact that assimilation today has proceeded much beyond where it was at the earlier periods. Blush or shudder, as many will, mixture of blood has been making inroads on segregation faster than change in law. No clear line of separation between the races has been observed. More and more a large population with as much claim to white as to colored blood baffles any justice in classification for segregation.

Nor can we ignore the fact that the concept of the place of public education has markedly changed. Once a privilege conferred on those fortunate enough to take advantage of it, it is now regarded as a right of a citizen and a duty enforced by compulsory education laws. Any thought of public education as a privilege which may be given or withheld as a matter of grace has long since passed out of American thinking.

It is neither novel nor radical doctrine that statutes once held constitutional may become invalid by reason of changing conditions, and those held to be good in one state of facts may be held to be bad in another. A multitude of cases, going back far into judicial history, attest to this doctrine. In recent times, the practical result of several of our decisions has been to nullify the racial classification for many of the purposes as to which it was originally held valid.

I am convinced that present-day conditions require us to strike from our books the doctrine of separate-but-equal facilities and to hold invalid provisions of state constitutions or statutes which classify persons for separate treatment in matters of education based solely on possession of colored blood. In doing so, I have no doubt of the power of a court of equity to condition its remedies to do justice to both parties and I believe that the circumstances under which a large part of the country has grown into the existing system are such that only consideration of that in framing the decree would be just. And, in the long run, I think only a reasonably considerate decree would be an expedient one for the persons it has sought to benefit hereby.

Questions as to the contents of a decree have been shunned by both of the parties to the contest, although neither of them accept the Government's proposals. They obviously feared it would be inconsistent with their positions to discuss the contents of a decree lest they appear to be acquiescing in it.

I favor, at the moment, going no farther than to enter a decree that the state constitutions and statutes relied upon as requiring or authorizing segregation merely on account of race or color, are unconstitutional. I would order a reargument on the contents of our decree and request the Government and each of the parties to submit detailed proposed decrees applicable to each case.

Chapter Seven

Brown v. Board of Education of Topeka, Kansas[*]

347 U.S. 483 (1953)

MR. CHIEF JUSTICE WARREN delivered the opinion of the Court.

These cases come to us from the States of Kansas, South Carolina, Virginia, and Delaware. They are premised on different facts and different local conditions, but a common legal question justifies their consideration together in this consolidated opinion.[1]

In each of the cases, minors of the Negro race, through their legal representatives, seek the aid of the courts in obtaining admission to the public schools of their community on a nonsegregated basis. In each instance, they had been denied admission to schools attended by white children under laws requiring or permitting segregation according to race. This segregation was alleged to deprive the plaintiffs of the equal protection of the laws under the Fourteenth Amendment. In each of the cases other than the Delaware case, a three-judge federal district court denied relief to the plaintiffs on the so-called "separate but equal" doctrine announced by this Court in *Plessy v. Ferguson,* 163 U.S. 537. Under that doctrine, equality of treatment is accorded when the races are provided substantially equal facilities, even though these facilities be separate. In the Delaware case, the Supreme Court of Delaware adhered to that doctrine, but ordered that the plaintiffs be admitted to the white schools because of their superiority to the Negro schools.

The plaintiffs contend that segregated public schools are not "equal" and cannot be made "equal," and that hence they are deprived of the equal protection of the laws. Because of the obvious importance of the question presented, the Court took jurisdiction.[2] Argument was heard in the 1952 Term, and reargument was heard this Term on certain questions propounded by the Court.[3] Reargument was largely devoted to the circumstances surrounding the adoption of the Fourteenth Amendment in 1868. It covered exhaustively consideration of the Amendment in Congress, ratification by the states, then-existing practices in racial segregation, and the views of proponents and opponents of the Amendment.

This discussion and our own investigation convince us that, although these sources cast some light, it is not enough to resolve the problem with which we are faced. At best, they are inconclusive. The most avid proponents of the post-War Amendments undoubtedly intended them to remove all legal distinctions among "all persons born or naturalized in the United States." Their opponents, just as certainly, were antagonistic to both the letter and the spirit of the Amendments and wished them to have the most limited effect. What others in Congress and the state legislatures had in mind cannot be determined with any degree of certainty.

An additional reason for the inconclusive nature of the Amendment's history with respect to segregated schools is the status of public education at that time.[4] In the South, the movement toward free common schools, supported by general taxation, had not yet taken hold. Education of white children was largely in the hands of private groups. Education of Negroes was almost nonexistent, and practically all of the race were illiterate. In fact, any education of Negroes was forbidden by law in some states. Today, in contrast, many Negroes have achieved outstanding success in the arts and sciences, as well as in the business and professional world. It is true that public school education at the time of the Amendment had advanced further in the North, but the effect of the Amendment on Northern States was generally ignored in the congressional debates. Even in the North, the conditions of public education did not approximate those existing today. The curriculum was usually rudimentary; ungraded schools were common in rural areas; the school term was but three months a year in many states, and compulsory school attendance was virtually unknown. As a consequence, it is not surprising that there should be so little in the history of the Fourteenth Amendment relating to its intended effect on public education.

In the first cases in this Court construing the Fourteenth Amendment, decided shortly after its adoption, the Court interpreted it as proscribing all state-imposed discriminations against the Negro race.[5] The doctrine of "separate but equal" did not make its appearance in this Court until 1896 in the case of *Plessy v. Ferguson,* supra, involving not education but transportation.[6] American courts have since labored with the doctrine for over half a century. In this Court, there have been six cases involving the "separate but equal" doctrine in the field of public education.[7] In *Cumming v. County Board of Education,* 175 U.S. 528, and *Gong Lum v. Rice,* 275 U.S. 78, the validity of the doctrine itself was not challenged.[8] In more recent cases, all on the graduate school level, inequality was found in that specific benefits enjoyed by white students were denied to Negro students of the same educational qualifications. *Missouri ex rel. Gaines v. Canada,* 305 U.S. 337; *Sipuel v. Oklahoma,* 332 U.S. 631; *Sweatt v. Painter,* 339 U.S. 629; *McLaurin v. Oklahoma State Regents,* 339 U.S. 637. In none of these cases was it necessary to reexamine the doctrine to grant relief to the Negro plaintiff. And in *Sweatt v. Painter,* supra, the Court expressly reserved decision on the question whether *Plessy v. Ferguson* should be held inapplicable to public education.

In the instant cases, that question is directly presented. Here, unlike *Sweatt v. Painter,* there are findings below that the Negro and white schools involved have been equalized, or are being equalized, with respect to buildings, curricula, qualifications and salaries of teachers, and other "tangible" factors.[9] Our decision, therefore, cannot turn on merely a comparison of these tangible factors in the Negro and white schools involved in each of the cases. We must look instead to the effect of segregation itself on public education.

In approaching this problem, we cannot turn the clock back to 1868, when the Amendment was adopted, or even to 1896, when *Plessy v. Ferguson* was written. We must consider public education in the light of its full development and its present place in American life throughout the Nation. Only in this way can it be determined if segregation in public schools deprives these plaintiffs of the equal protection of the laws.

Today, education is perhaps the most important function of state and local governments. Compulsory school attendance laws and the great expenditures for education both demonstrate our recognition of the importance of education to our democratic society. It is required in the performance of our most basic public responsibilities, even service in the armed forces. It is the very foundation of good citizenship. Today it is a principal instrument in awakening the child to cultural values, in preparing him for later professional training, and in helping him to adjust normally to his environment. In these days, it is doubtful that any child may reasonably be expected to succeed in life if he is denied the opportunity of an education. Such an opportunity, where the state has undertaken to provide it, is a right which must be made available to all on equal terms.

We come then to the question presented: Does segregation of children in public schools solely on the basis of race, even though the physical facilities and other "tangible" factors may be equal, deprive the children of the minority group of equal educational opportunities? We believe that it does.

In *Sweatt v. Painter,* supra, in finding that a segregated law school for Negroes could not provide them equal educational opportunities, this Court relied in large part on "those qualities which are incapable of objective measurement but which make for greatness in a law school." In *McLaurin v. Oklahoma State Regents,* supra, the Court, in requiring that a Negro admitted to a white graduate school be treated like all other students, again resorted to intangible considerations: ". . . his ability to study, to engage in discussions and exchange views with other students, and, in general, to learn his profession."

Such considerations apply with added force to children in grade and high schools. To separate them from others of similar age and qualifications solely because of their race generates a feeling of inferiority as to their status in the community that may affect their hearts and minds in a way unlikely ever to be undone. The effect of this separation on their educational opportunities was well stated by a finding in the Kansas case by a court which nevertheless felt compelled to rule against the Negro plaintiffs: Segregation of white and colored children in public schools has a detrimental effect upon the colored children.

The impact is greater when it has the sanction of the law, for the policy of separating the races is usually interpreted as denoting the inferiority of the Negro group. A sense of inferiority affects the motivation of a child to learn. Segregation with the sanction of law, therefore, has a tendency to [retard] the educational and mental development of Negro children and to deprive them of some of the benefits they would receive in a racial[ly] integrated school system.[10]

Whatever may have been the extent of psychological knowledge at the time *of Plessy v. Ferguson,* this finding is amply supported by modern authority.[11] Any language in *Plessy v. Ferguson* contrary to this finding is rejected.

We conclude that, in the field of public education, the doctrine of "separate but equal" has no place. Separate educational facilities are inherently unequal.

Therefore, we hold that the plaintiffs and others similarly situated for whom the actions have been brought are, by reason of the segregation complained of, deprived of the equal protection of the laws guaranteed by the Fourteenth Amendment. This disposition makes unnecessary any discussion whether such segregation also violates the Due Process Clause of the Fourteenth Amendment.[12]

Because these are class actions, because of the wide applicability of this decision, and because of the great variety of local conditions, the formulation of decrees in these cases presents problems of considerable complexity. On reargument, the consideration of appropriate relief was necessarily subordinated to the primary question—the constitutionality of segregation in public education. We have now announced that such segregation is a denial of the equal protection of the laws. In order that we may have the full assistance of the parties in formulating decrees, the cases will be restored to the docket, and the parties are requested to present further argument on Questions 4 and 5 previously propounded by the Court for the reargument this Term.[13] The Attorney General of the United States is again invited to participate. The Attorneys General of the states requiring or permitting seg-regation in public education will also be permitted to appear as amici curiae upon request to do so by September 15, 1954, and submission of briefs by October 1, 1954.[14]

It is so ordered.

Chapter Eight

Bolling v. Sharpe

347 U.S. 497 (1954)

Mr. Chief Justice Warren delivered the opinion of the Court.

This case challenges the validity of segregation in the public schools of the District of Columbia. The petitioners, minors of the Negro race, allege that such segregation deprives them of due process of law under the Fifth Amendment. They were refused admission to a public school attended by white children solely because of their race. They sought the aid of the District Court for the District of Columbia in obtaining admission. That court dismissed their complaint. The Court granted a writ of certiorari before judgment in the Court of Appeals because of the importance of the constitutional question presented.

We have this day held that the Equal Protection Clause of the Fourteenth Amendment prohibits the states from maintaining racially segregated public schools.[1] The legal problem in the District of Columbia is somewhat different, however. The Fifth Amendment, which is applicable in the District of Columbia, does not contain an equal protection clause, as does the Fourteenth Amendment, which applies only to the states. But the concepts of equal protection and due process, both stemming from our American ideal of fairness, are not mutually exclusive. The "equal protection of the laws" is a more explicit safeguard of prohibited unfairness than "due process of law," and, therefore, we do not imply that the two are always interchangeable phrases. But, as this Court has recognized, discrimination may be so unjustifiable as to be violative of due process.[2]

Classifications based solely upon race must be scrutinized with particular care, since they are contrary to our traditions, and hence constitutionally suspect.[3] As long ago as 1896, this Court declared the principle that the Constitution of the United States, in its present form, forbids, so far as civil and political rights are concerned, discrimination by the General Government, or by the States, against any citizen because of his race.[4] And in *Buchanan v. Warley*, 245 U.S. 60, the Court held that a statute which limited the right of a property owner to convey his property to a person of another race was, as an unreasonable discrimination, a denial of due process of law.

Although the Court has not assumed to define "liberty" with any great precision, that term is not confined to mere freedom from bodily restraint.

Liberty under law extends to the full range of conduct which the individual is free to pursue, and it cannot be restricted except for a proper governmental objective. Segregation in public education is not reasonably related to any proper governmental objective, and thus it imposes on Negro children of the District of Columbia a burden that constitutes an arbitrary deprivation of their liberty in violation of the Due Process Clause.

In view of our decision that the Constitution prohibits the states from maintaining racially segregated public schools, it would be unthinkable that the same Constitution would impose a lesser duty on the Federal Government.[5] We hold that racial segregation in the public schools of the District of Columbia is a denial of the due process of law guaranteed by the Fifth Amendment to the Constitution.

For the reasons set out in *Brown v. Board of Education,* this case will be restored to the docket for reargument on Questions 4 and 5 previously propounded by the Court. 345 U.S. 972.

It is so ordered.

Timeline and Background for
Brown and Justice Jackson

1857	*Dred Scott v. Sanford,* 60 U.S. 393 (1857), holds that blacks, free or enslaved, are not citizens of the United States. Chief Justice Roger B. Taney bases the opinion on the original intentions of the framers and a strict construction of the Constitution, as well as the fact that blacks were subordinate and inferior "with no rights which the White man was bound to respect."
1865	The Bureau of Refugees, Freedmen, and Abandoned Lands is created to assist freedmen, and under its direction, black schools, such as Howard University in Washington, D.C., are established. At the same time, Southern states begin enacting black codes, which impose severe restrictions on freedmen, including prohibiting their right to vote and work in certain occupations.
1866	The Civil Rights Act of 1866 guarantees blacks basic economic rights to contract, sue, and own property.
July 9, 1868	The Fourteenth Amendment is ratified and *Dred Scott v. Sanford* overruled. Among its provisions, the amendment provides that "No State shall make or enforce any law which shall abridge the privileges or immunities of citizens of the United States; nor shall any State deprive any person of life, liberty, or property, without due process of law; nor deny to any person within its jurisdiction the equal protection of the laws." Section 5 further provides that "Congress shall have power to enforce, by appropriate legislation, the provisions of this article."
1873	*The Slaughterhouse Cases,* 83 U.S. 36 (1873), virtually eviscerates the Fourteenth Amendment in holding that citizens have dual citizenship—federal and

	state—and that most rights of citizenship remain under control of the states.
1875	The Civil Rights Act of 1875 prohibits interracial discrimination in public accommodations.
1883	The Supreme Court holds, in *The Civil Rights Cases,* 109 U.S. 3 (1883), that Congress exceeded its power under the Fourteenth Amendment in enacting the Civil Rights Act of 1875 and that the amendment does not prohibit discrimination by private individuals or businesses.
1883	Alabama's antimiscegenation law is upheld in *Pace v. Alabama,* 106 U.S. 583 (1883).
1887	Racial segregation associated with Jim Crow laws begins to emerge; Florida is the first state to require racial segregation in public accommodations, and eight other states follow.
February 13, 1892	Jackson is born in Spring Creek, Warren County, Pennsylvania. In 1897, his family moves to Frewsburg, New York, a village close to Jamestown, New York.
1896	*Plessy v. Ferguson,* 163 U.S. 537 (1896), upholds the doctrine of "separate but equal" in the area of public transportation. Justice Henry Brown interprets the Fourteenth Amendment to command "the absolute equality of the two races before the law," but he dismisses the claim that segregation is discriminatory with the observation that segregation does not "necessarily imply the inferiority of either race to the other." In dissent, Justice John Marshall Harlan declares that the Constitution is "colorblind."
1899	*Cumming v. Board of Education of Richmond County, Georgia,* 175 U.S. 528 (1899), upholds a school board's decision to close a free public black school because of fiscal constraints while continuing to maintain two all-white public schools.
1908	*Berea College v. Commonwealth of Kentucky,* 211 U.S. 45 (1908), upholds a state law forbidding interracial instruction in all schools and colleges.
1913–1934	After passing the bar exam, Jackson develops a legal

	practice in Jamestown, New York, and remains active in Democratic politics.
1927	*Gong Lum v. Rice,* 275 U.S. 78 (1927), holds that a Mississippi school board may require a Chinese American to attend a segregated black school rather than an all-white school on the basis of the "separate but equal" doctrine.
1931–1941	Jackson assumes various successive positions in the Roosevelt administration, rising from general counsel for the Internal Revenue Service, and moves to the District of Columbia (1931) to assistant attorney general for the tax division in the Department of Justice (1936) and for the antitrust division (1937), then to solicitor general (1938–1940) and attorney general (1940–1941), before his appointment to the Supreme Court.
1938	*State of Missouri ex rel. Gaines v. Canada,* 305 U.S. 337 (1938), rules that the state must provide a black student equal law school facilities rather than pay for tuition to attend an out-of-state law school. Chief Justice Hughes writes for the majority; justices James McReynolds and Pierce Butler dissent.
1941	Jackson is appointed and confirmed as associate justice, and Justice Harlan F. Stone is elevated to the chief justiceship.
1944	*Smith v. Allwright,* 321 U.S. 649 (1944), is handed down. Justice Reed delivers the Court's opinion holding that Texas's law permitting the exclusion of blacks from participating in the Democratic Party's primaries effectively disenfranchises blacks, in violation of the Fifteenth Amendment.
1945–1946	While still on the Court, Jackson assumes the position of U.S. chief Nuremberg war crimes prosecutor.
1948	In a landmark ruling in *Shelly v. Kraemer,* 334 U.S. 1 (1948), the Vinson Court unanimously (with Justices Jackson, Reed, and Rutledge recused) strikes down restrictive covenants in real estate contracts because they have to be judicially enforced and thus entail "state action," in violation of the Fourteenth Amendment.

1948	In a companion ruling with *Shelley v. Kraemer, Hurd v. Hodge Urciolo,* 334 U.S. 24 (1948), Chief Justice Vinson holds that the Fourteenth Amendment does not apply to restrictive covenants in the District of Columbia, but concludes that under the Civil Rights Act of 1866, D.C. residents should be treated the same as those in the states, and hence restrictive covenants in D.C. are unconstitutional. Justices Jackson, Reed, and Rutledge do not participate in the decision.
1948	*Sipuel v. Board of Regents of University of Oklahoma,* 322 U.S. 621 (1948), holds that Lois Ada Sipuel could not be denied admission to a state law school solely because of her race. The decision is handed down as a unanimous per curiam opinion.
June 5, 1950	*Sweatt v. Painter,* 339 U.S. 629 (1950), unanimously holds that the University of Texas Law School must admit a black student, Herman Sweatt, rather than create a separate all-black law school, because the latter does not provide equal facilities, resources, and career opportunities.
June 5, 1950	In *McLaurin v. Oklahoma State Regents,* 339 U.S. 637 (1950), Chief Justice Vinson delivers a unanimous ruling that a black student admitted to a graduate program who was required to sit apart from whites in classrooms, the library, and the cafeteria runs afoul of the Fourteenth Amendment.
1950	The NAACP Legal Defense Fund files a suit for a group of parents challenging segregated schools in the District of Columbia in *Bolling v. Sharpe,* which eventually becomes a companion case decided with *Brown v. Board of Education.*
February 1951	Oliver Brown and twelve other families file a class-action suit challenging the racial segregation of public schools in Topeka, Kansas, which under an 1879 law permitted school districts to operate separate elementary schools for blacks and whites; the Topeka high school was integrated since its inception in 1871, and the middle schools were integrated in 1941. Brown's daughter, Linda, was a third grader who had

to walk six blocks to a bus stop for a one-mile ride to her segregated elementary school, while an all-white elementary school was seven blocks from her house. In separate cases, segregated schools are challenged in Virginia and South Carolina in, respectively, *Davis et al. v. County School Board of Prince Edward County, Virginia,* and *Briggs et al. v. Elliott.* In another suit, school segregation is challenged in state courts in Delaware in a series of cases that were consolidated in *Belton (Bulah) v. Gebhart.*

August 1951	A federal district court holding, citing *Plessy v. Ferguson,* that upheld segregated schools is reversed in part by a three-judge panel of the court, which concludes that segregated schools have a detrimental effect on black children, but which denies relief on the grounds that Topeka's segregated schools are substantially equal with respect to curriculum, facilities, transportation, and teachers' qualifications. Brown and the NAACP Legal Defense Fund appeal that ruling.
November 19, 1951	Appeal in *Brown* is filed in the Court.
December 29, 1951	Statement as to jurisdiction is filed.
January 25, 1952	William H. Rehnquist arrives to clerk for Jackson.
March and April 1952	A federal district court rejects the request to order desegregation in Prince Edward County, Virginia, and orders the "equalization" of black schools instead. In Delaware, a state court orders the immediate admission of black students to white public schools. Both decisions are appealed.
June 7, 1952	At the justices' conference (according to Justice Reed's docket book), *Brown* is granted review by a unanimous vote, except Justice Jackson votes to hold and no vote is recorded for Chief Justice Vinson.
June 9, 1952	The Court announces that probable jurisdiction is noted and that it will hear oral arguments in *Brown v. Board of Education* and *Briggs v. Elliott* (South Carolina case) in the October 1952 term.
October 8, 1952	Before hearing oral arguments in *Brown* and *Briggs,* the Court issues a per curiam opinion that it will also grant appeals from the Delaware cases, *Davis v. Prince*

Edward County, Virginia, and the District of Columbia case in *Bolling v. Sharpe.* The cases are consolidated with *Brown* for oral arguments, with the petitioners invited to file petitions for certiorari before a judgment is issued in *Bolling v. Sharpe.* The solicitor general is requested to file an amicus curiae brief indicating the government's position and postpones oral arguments in all of the cases until December 9.

November 4, 1952 Dwight D. Eisenhower wins the presidential election. A per curiam opinion is issued requesting Kansas to present its views at oral argument, and if not, then the default will be construed as a concession that the segregation statute is invalid.

November 14, 1952 The solicitor general sends a letter requesting leave to file an amicus curiae brief in *Brown.*

December 9–11, 1952 First oral arguments are heard on *Brown v. Board of Education* and companion cases.

December 13, 1952 First conference discussion of *Brown.* Frankfurter suggests that the cases should be held over for reargument. Justices Jackson and Clark strongly support rearguments.

January 16, 1953 Oral arguments are heard in *Terry v. Adams.*

April 6, 1953 The Court grants review of *District of Columbia v. John R. Thompson Co., Inc.,* 345 U.S. 921 (1953), a challenge to segregated restaurants in the District of Columbia.

May 4, 1953 *Terry v. Adams,* 345 U.S. (1951), is announced by Justice Black, joined only by Burton, Douglas, and Frankfurter, holding that white-only preprimary Democratic Party elections, designed to disenfranchise Southern black voters, are unconstitutional under the Fifteenth Amendment. Justice Clark issues a concurring opinion, joined by Chief Justice Vinson and Justices Jackson and Reed, maintaining that the practice runs afoul of the holding in *Smith v. Allwright,* 321 U.S. 649 (1944).

May 27, 1953 Justice Frankfurter circulates a "Memorandum for the Conference" detailing questions that counsel for the parties should brief and address in rearguments.

May 29, 1953 At conference, a majority of the justices agree to put all of the questions proposed by Justice Frankfurter, with minor revisions, in an opinion requesting addition briefing and rearguments.

June 8, 1953   The Vinson Court requests additional briefing on five questions, restores *Brown* and companion cases to the docket, and schedules rearguments for Monday, October 12, 1953.

June 8, 1953   Justice Douglas hands down the unanimous decision in *District of Columbia v. John R. Thompson Co., Inc.,* 346 U.S. 100 (1953), holding that 1872 and 1873 Reconstruction laws prohibiting racial discrimination in restaurants in the District of Columbia are still enforceable, even though they had not been enforced for over eighty years and Congress's subsequent reorganizations of the District of Columbia's governance, which returned control to Congress, did not repeal those laws. Jackson does not participate in the decision.

June 30, 1953   William H. Rehnquist's clerkship ends.

September 8, 1953   Chief Justice Fred M. Vinson dies.

September 30, 1953   President Dwight D. Eisenhower names Earl Warren as chief justice in a recess appointment.

October 5, 1953   Chief Justice Warren takes his seat on the Court as a recess appointee, subject to Senate confirmation, which doesn't occur until March 1, 1954.

December 7, 1953   Justice Jackson prepares his first draft of the memo on *Brown.*

December 9–11, 1953   Second round of oral arguments on *Brown* and companion cases.

December 12, 1953   Second full conference discussion of *Brown,* with Chief Justice Warren now presiding.

January 6, 1954   Jackson revises the *Brown* draft for second time.

January 11, 1954   President Eisenhower formally nominates Earl Warren as chief justice, and Jackson revises the draft for a third time.

January 15, 1954   Justice Frankfurter circulates the memo to other justices on various alternatives for fashioning a decree.

January 16, 1954   Conference discussion and decision to schedule *Brown* for reargument on the issue of remedy.

February 15, 1954	Justice Jackson revises the draft for the fourth time.
March 1, 1954	Chief Justice Earl Warren is unanimously confirmed by Senate, and Justice Jackson makes a fifth revision of the *Brown* draft opinion.
March 15, 1954	Jackson works on the sixth and last draft of the opinion.
March 30, 1954	Jackson suffers a heart attack and enters Doctors Hospital, where he remains until May 17, 1954.
May 5, 1954	Chief Justice Warren prepares notes for conference discussion.
May 7, 1954	Chief Justice Warren circulates draft opinion to other justices.
May 8, 1954	Chief Justice Warren delivers the proposed draft opinions to Jackson in the hospital and discusses them with him. After Warren leaves, Jackson for the first time shares his draft opinion with his law clerk, E. Barrett Prettyman Jr., and asks for his reactions, which are later given in a memo.
May 13, 1954	Chief Justice Warren's final draft circulates.
May 15, 1954	Conference discussion.
May 17, 1954	Chief Justice Warren delivers the opinions for the Court in *Brown,* holding that *Plessy*'s doctrine of "separate but equal" is no longer applicable in the field of public education and that in *Bolling v. Sharpe* the ruling of *Brown* that segregated schools run afoul of the Fourteenth Amendment equal protection clause is no less applicable to the District of Columbia, based on the incorporation of the Fourteen Amendment's equal protection clause into the Fifth Amendment's due process clause. Warren also announces that the Court will set *Brown* over to the next term for rearguments on the issue of remedy and invites the attorney general to again participate as amicus curiae. Justice Jackson leaves the hospital in order to be present in the courtroom when the decisions are announced.
May 21, 1954	Chief Justice Warren makes minor changes in the opinion for the Court and circulates them to the other justices.

October 9, 1954	Justice Jackson dies. President Eisenhower subsequently nominates John Marshall Harlan, the grandson of the first John Marshall Harlan and dissenter in *Plessy v. Ferguson,* to fill Jackson's seat.
November 1954	The Senate Judiciary Committee decides to postpone action on the confirmation of Harlan, and the Court delays oral arguments on the remedial decree in *Brown* until spring 1955.
March 28, 1955	After a prolonged debate, the Senate confirms Justice Harlan, and he is sworn into office.
April 11–14, 1955	The Supreme Court hears the third round of arguments in *Brown,* focusing on the issue of remedies.
May 31, 1955	The Court announces its unanimous decision in *Brown v. Board of Education of Topeka, Kansas,* 349 U.S. 294 (1955) (*Brown II*), ordering desegregation in public schools with "all deliberate speed."
1967	*Loving v. Virginia,* 388 U.S. 1 (1967), strikes down antimiscegenation laws, quoting *Brown v. Board of Education.*

Notes

INTRODUCTION: A STORY RETOLD

1. See, e.g., Richard Kluger, *Simple Justice: The History of* Brown v. Board of Education *and Black America's Struggle for Equality* (New York: Knopf, 1975); Jack Greenberg, *Race Relations and American Law* (New York: Columbia University Press, 1959); and Michael Klarman, *From Jim Crow to Civil Rights: The Supreme Court and the Struggle for Racial Equality* (New York: Oxford University Press, 2004).

2. See, e.g., Mary Dudziak, *Cold War Civil Rights: Race and the Image of American Democracy* (Princeton, N.J.: Princeton University Press, 2002).

3. See, e.g., Paul Rosen, *The Supreme Court and Social Science* (Urbana: University of Illinois Press, 1972); I. A. Newby, *Challenge to the Court: Social Scientists and the Defense of Segregation, 1954–1966* (Baton Rouge: Louisiana State University Press, 1967); and David Faigman, *Laboratory of Justice: The Supreme Court's 200-Year Struggle to Integrate Science and the Law* (New York: Times Books, 2004).

4. See, e.g., Jack Bass, *Unlikely Heroes* (New York: Simon & Schuster, 1981); Jack Peltason, *Fifty-Eight Lonely Men: Southern Federal Judges and School Desegregation* (New York: Harcourt, Brace, & World, 1961); Mark Tushnet, *The NAACP's Legal Strategy against Segregated Education, 1925–1950* (Chapel Hill: University of North Carolina Press, 1988); Benjamin Muse, *Virginia's Massive Resistance* (Bloomington: Indiana University Press, 1961); Benjamin Muse, *Ten Years of Prelude: The Story of Integration Since the Supreme Court's 1954 Decision* (New York: Viking Press, 1964); Stephen Wasby, Anthony D'Amato, and Rosemary Metrailer, *Desegregation from* Brown *to* Alexander: *An Exploration of Supreme Court Strategies* (Carbondale: Southern Illinois University Press, 1977); and J. Harvey Wilkinson III, *From* Brown *to* Bakke: *The Supreme Court and School Integration, 1954–1978* (New York: Oxford University Press, 1979).

5. See Gerald Rosenberg, *The Hollow Hope: Can Courts Bring About Social Change?*, 2nd ed. (Chicago: University of Chicago Press, 2009).

6. See, e.g., Derrick Bell, "*Brown v. Board of Education* and the Interest–Convergence Dilemma," *Harvard Law Review* 93 (1980), 518; Derrick Bell, *Silent Covenants: Brown v. Board of Education and the Unfulfilled Hopes for Racial Reform* (New York: Oxford University Press, 2004); Austin Sarat, ed., *Race, Law, and Culture: Reflections on* Brown v. Board of Education (New York: Oxford University Press, 1997); and Risa Goluboff, *The Lost Promise of Civil Rights* (Cambridge, Mass.: Harvard University Press, 2007).

7. See Jack M. Balkin, ed., *What* Brown v. Board of Education *Should Have Said* (New York: New York University Press, 2001).

8. See, e.g., Paul Wilson, "The Genesis of *Brown v. Board of Education*," *Kansas*

Journal of Law and Public Policy 6 (1996), 7; Paul Wilson, "A Time to Lose," *Journal of Supreme Court History* 24 (1999), 170; Paul Wilson, *A Time to Lose: Representing Kansas* (Lawrence: University Press of Kansas, 1995); Jack Greenberg, Brown v. Board of Education: *Witness to a Landmark Decision* (New York: Twelve Tables, 2004); Herbert Brownell, "*Brown v. Board of Education* Revisited," *Journal of Supreme Court History* 18 (1993), 21; Philip Elman and Norman Silber, "The Solicitor General's Office, Justice Frankfurter, and Civil Rights Litigation, 1946–1960: An Oral History," *Harvard Law Review* 100 (1987), 817; and Norman I. Silber, *With All Deliberate Speed: The Life of Philip Elman, an Oral History Memoir* (Ann Arbor: University of Michigan Press, 2004). See also Mark Tushnet, *Making Civil Rights Law: Thurgood Marshall and the Supreme Court, 1936–1961* (New York: Oxford University Press, 1994).

9. See, e.g., Earl Warren, *The Memoirs of Chief Justice Earl Warren* (New York: Doubleday, 1977); and William O. Douglas, *The Court Years, 1939–1975: The Autobiography of William O. Douglas* (New York: Random House, 1980).

10. See, e.g., Gordon Davidson, Daniel Meador, Earl Pollock, and E. Barrett Prettyman Jr., "Supreme Court Law Clerks: Recollections of *Brown v. Board of Education II*," *St. John's Law Review* 79 (2005), 823; John Fassett, "Mr. Justice Reed and *Brown v. Board of Education*," *Yearbook of the Supreme Court Historical Society 1986* (1986), 48; John Fassett, Earl Pollock, E. Barrett Prettyman Jr., and Frank Sander, "Supreme Court Law Clerks' Recollections of *Brown v. Board of Education*," *St. John's Law Review* 78 (2004), 515; and John Fassett, *New Deal Justice: The Life of Stanley Reed of Kentucky* (New York: Vantage Press, 1994).

11. See Brad Synder, "How Conservatives Canonized *Brown v. Board of Education*," *Rutgers Law Review* 52 (2000), 383.

12. Alexander Bickel, "The Original Understanding and the Segregation Decision," *Harvard Law Review* 1 (1955), 69.

13. Robert H. Bork, *The Tempting of America: The Political Seduction of the Law* (New York: Free Press, 1990), 77.

14. See Michael McConnell, "Originalism and the Desegregation Decisions," *Virginia Law Review* 81 (1995), 947; "The Originalist Justification for *Brown:* A Reply to Professor Klarman," *Virginia Law Review* 81 (1995), 1937; and "The Originalist Case for *Brown v. Board of Education*," *Harvard Journal of Law and Public Policy* 19 (1996), 457. See also Reed Akil Amar, "Rethinking Originalism," *Slate,* September 21, 2005, http://www.slate.com/.

15. Michael J. Klarman, "*Brown,* Originalism, and Constitutional Theory: A Response to Professor McConnell," *Virginia Law Review* 81 (1995), 1881.

16. See especially Dennis Hutchinson, "Unanimity and Desegregation: Decisionmaking in the Supreme Court, 1949–1961," *Supreme Court Review* 1980 (1980), 143. See also Mark Tushnet and Katya Lezin, "What Really Happened in *Brown v. Board of Education*," *Columbia Law Review* 91 (1991), 1867.

17. See, e.g., Carlton Larson, "What If Chief Justice Fred Vinson Had Not Died of a Heart Attack in 1953? Implications for *Brown* and Beyond," *Indiana Law Review* 45 (2011), 131.

18. See, among others, Bernard Schwartz, "Chief Justice Earl Warren: Super Chief in Action," *Journal of Supreme Court History* 23 (1998), 112; Bernard Schwartz, *Super Chief: Earl Warren and His Supreme Court—A Judicial Biography* (New York: New

York University Press, 1983); Jim Newton, *Justice for All: Earl Warren and the Nation He Made* (New York: Riverhead Trade, 2007); Ed Cray, *Chief Justice: A Biography of Earl Warren* (New York: Simon & Schuster, 1997); and Sidney Ulmer, "Earl Warren and the *Brown* Decision," *Journal of Politics* 33 (1971), 689.

19. Warren, *Memoirs*, 4.

20. See, e.g., Jeffrey Hockett, *New Deal Justice: The Constitutional Jurisprudence of Hugo L. Black, Felix Frankfurter, and Robert H. Jackson* (Lanham, Md.: Rowman & Littlefield, 1996); William Domnarski, *The Great Justices, 1941–1954: Black, Douglas, Frankfurter, and Jackson in Chambers* (Ann Arbor: University of Michigan Press, 2006); and Noah Feldman, *Scorpions: The Battles and Triumphs of FDR's Great Supreme Court Justices* (New York: Twelve, 2010).

21. See Jeffrey Hockett, *A Storm over This Court: Law, Politics, and Supreme Court Decision Making in* Brown v. Board of Education (Charlottesville: University of Virginia Press, 2013).

22. Kluger, *Simple Justice*.

23. Eugene Gerhart, *America's Advocate: Robert H. Jackson* (New York: Bobbs-Merrill, 1958). See also Eugene Gerhart, *Lawyer's Judge* (Albany, N.Y.: Albany Q., 1961); both books were combined, with a foreword by Chief Justice William H. Rehnquist, in *Robert H. Jackson: Country Lawyer, Supreme Court Justice, and America's Advocate* (Buffalo, N.Y.: William S. Hein, 2003).

24. Charles Desmond, Paul Freund, Potter Stewart, and Lord Shawcross, eds., *Mr. Justice Jackson: Four Lectures in His Honor* (New York: Columbia University Press, 1965); and Glendon Schubert, ed., *Dispassionate Justice: A Synthesis of the Judicial Opinions of Robert H. Jackson* (New York: Bobbs-Merrill, 1969).

25. Excerpts of the opinion are in Mark Tushnet, ed., *I Dissent: Great Opposing Opinions in Landmark Supreme Court Cases* (Boston: Beacon Press, 2008); and in all ten editions of my casebook, *Constitutional Law and Politics*, vol. 2, *Civil Rights and Civil Liberties*, 11th ed. (New York: Norton, 2017).

26. See, e.g., Bernard Schwartz, "Chief Justice Rehnquist, Justice Jackson, and the *Brown* Case," *Supreme Court Review* 1988 (1988), 245; Laura K. Ray, "A Law Clerk and His Justice: What William Rehnquist Did Not Learn from Robert H. Jackson," *Indiana Law Review* 29 (1996), 535; Brad Snyder, "What Would Justice Holmes Do? Rehnquist's *Plessy* Memo, Majoritarianism, and *Parents Involved*," *Ohio State Law Journal* 69 (2008), 873; Brad Snyder, "The Judicial Genealogy (and Mythology) of John Roberts: Clerkships from Gray to Brandeis to Friendly to Roberts," *Ohio State Law Journal* 17 (2010), 1149; Brad Snyder and John Q. Barrett, "Rehnquist's Missing Letter: A Former Law Clerk's 1955 Thoughts on Justice Jackson and *Brown*," *Boston College Law Review* 53 (2010), 631; Hutchinson, "Unanimity and Desegregation"; and the discussion in Chapter 3.

27. For further discussion and examples, see O'Brien, *Storm Center*, chap. 5.

28. See David M. O'Brien, "John Marshall Harlan's Unpublished Opinions: Reflections on a Supreme Court at Work," *Journal of Supreme Court History* 1991 (1991), 42.

29. See Dennis Hutchinson, "'The Achilles Heel' of the Constitution: Justice Jackson and the Japanese Exclusion Cases," *Supreme Court Review* 2002 (2002), 455, 456–457 and footnote 10.

1. Paul A. Freund, "Mr. Justice Jackson and Individual Rights," in *Mr. Justice Jackson: Four Lectures in His Honor,* ed. Charles S. Desmond, Paul A. Freund, Justice Potter Stewart, and Lord Shawcross (New York: Columbia University Press, 1969), 36.

2. See, e.g., *West Virginia State Board of Education v. Barnette,* 319 U.S. 624 (1943), overruling *Minersville School District v. Gobitis,* 310 U.S. 568 (1940); initially upholding and then striking down compulsory flag-salute statutes, as further discussed below in this chapter.

3. Notably, Jackson saved two articles from the 1951 *Jamestown Sun Magazine* in the back of the binder for his draft autobiography. Robert Jackson Papers, Box 189, LC. One recalled that Jackson, at age twenty-five, read from the *Bhagavad Gita* at the funeral of a friend and theosophist, Eaton La Rue Moses.

4. Robert H. Jackson, Oral History Interview, Jackson Papers, Box 190, LC.

5. Robert H. Jackson, "Draft of Autobiography," Jackson Papers, Box 189, LC, 2–3, 5, 8, and 18.

6. Letter to Eugene C. Gerhart (January 19, 1950), quoted in Eugene C. Gerhart, *America's Advocate: Robert H. Jackson* (New York: Bobbs-Merrill, 1958), 62.

7. Michael Klarman, *From Jim Crow to Civil Rights: The Supreme Court and the Struggle for Racial Equality* (New York: Oxford University Press, 2004), 309. See also Laura K. Ray, "A Law Clerk and His Justice: What William Rehnquist Did Not Learn from Robert H. Jackson," *Indiana Law Review* 29 (1996), 535 and 537.

8. For further discussion, see John Barrett, "Albany in the Life Trajectory of Robert H. Jackson," *Albany Law Review* 68 (2005), 513, 516–525.

9. For further discussion, see David M. O'Brien, *Storm Center: The Supreme Court in American Politics,* 11th ed. (New York: Norton, 2017), chap. 2.

10. Quoted in Gerhart, *America's Advocate,* 36.

11. Oral history transcript, "The Reminiscences of Robert H. Jackson," based on interviews with Harlan B. Philips, CUOHP; and also in Jackson Papers, Boxes 190 and 191, as well as (same) Boxes 258–259, LC.

12. E. Barrett Prettyman Jr., "Robert H. Jackson: 'Solicitor General for Life,'" *Journal of Supreme Court History* 1992 (1992), 75, 76, and note 69, discussing discrepancies in the number of cases Jackson argued.

13. Quoted by Gerhart, *America's Advocate,* 191, and in Philip B. Kurland, "Robert H. Jackson," in *The Justices of the United States Supreme Court, 1789–1969,* ed. Leon Friedman and Fred Israel (New York: Chelsea House, 1969), 2557. See also Jackson's "Draft of Autobiography," Jackson Papers, Box 189, LC.

14. Jackson, Oral History Interview, Jackson Papers, Box 190, 1475–1476, LC.

15. Quoted and discussed in Prettyman, "Robert H. Jackson," 75–76.

16. Ibid., 77.

17. Ibid., 82.

18. In 2003, former deputy solicitor general Lawrence Wallace ended his career with 157 cases, and in the nineteenth century, when the Court's bar was much smaller and transportation more difficult, Senator Daniel Webster and Walter Jones are believed to have argued more cases. For further discussion, see William Har-

baugh, *Lawyer's Lawyer: The Life of John W. Davis* (New York: Oxford University Press, 1973).

19. See, e.g., Jeffrey Hockett, *New Deal Justice* (Lanham, Md.: Rowman & Littlefield, 1996), 220–226.

20. Robert H. Jackson, "Tribute to Country Lawyers: A Review," *American Bar Association Journal* 30 (1944), 136, 139.

21. Oral History Interview, Jackson Papers, Box 190, LC, 350; also available at CUOHP.

22. Robert H. Jackson, 1 *Unpublished Speeches* 12, Jackson Papers, Box 31, LC.

23. According to James Marsh as retold to the author by Dennis J. Hutchinson.

24. William H. Rehnquist, "Robert H. Jackson: A Perspective Twenty-Five Years Later," *Albany Law Review* 44 (1980), 533, 536.

25. Jackson, Oral History Interview, 1104–1105.

26. Based on Linda A. Blandford and Patricia Russell Evans, eds., *Supreme Court of the United States, 1789–1980: An Index to Opinions Arranged by the Justice,* vol. 2, *1902–1980,* (New York: Kras International, 1983), 861–871. Note, however, that omitted from that list is Justice Jackson's opinion for the Court in *West Virginia State Board of Education v. Barnette,* 319 U.S. 624 (1943), which is included here.

27. *Wickard v. Filburn,* 317 U.S. 111 (1942).

28. The ruling in *Wickard* was reaffirmed, for example, in *Gonzales v. Raich,* 545 U.S. 1 (2005). For further discussion see, e.g., David M. O'Brien, *Constitutional Law and Politics,* vol. 1, *Struggles for Power and Governmental Accountability,* 11th ed. (New York: Norton, 2017), 589–668.

29. *West Virginia State Board of Education v. Barnette,* 319 U.S. 624 (1943).

30. *Youngstown Sheet & Tube Co. v. Sawyer,* 343 U.S. 579 (1952).

31. *Korematsu v. United States,* 323 U.S. 214 (1944).

32. Paul A. Freund, "Address of Paul A. Freund at a Meeting of the Bar of the Supreme Court of the United States" (1955), Jackson Center, http://www.robert hjackson.org/.

33. Philip Kurland, "Justice Robert H. Jackson—Impact on Civil Rights and Civil Liberties," *Law Forum* 1977 (1977), 551, 555.

34. James Marsh, "The Genial Justice: Robert H. Jackson," *Albany Law Review* 68 (2004), 41, 47.

35. Felix Frankfurter, "Mr. Justice Jackson," *Harvard Law Review* 68 (1955), 937, reprinted in Philip Kurland, *Felix Frankfurter on the Supreme Court: Extrajudicial Essays on the Court and the Constitution* (Cambridge, Mass.: Harvard University Press, 1970), 510.

36. *Edwards v. California,* 314 U.S. 160 (1941).

37. A "Bibliography of Extrajudicial Writings by Robert H. Jackson" is available from the RHJC and at http://www.roberthjackson.org/.

38. Edward Douglas White, "The Supreme Court of the United States," *American Bar Association Journal* 7 (1921), 341.

39. Robert H. Jackson, *Full Faith and Credit: The Lawyer's Clause of the Constitution* (New York: Columbia University Press, 1945).

40. Robert H. Jackson, *The Case against the Nazi War Criminals* (New York: Knopf, 1946); and *The Nürenberg Case* (New York: Knopf, 1947).

41. Robert H. Jackson, with an introduction and edited by John Q. Barrett, *That Man: An Insider's Portrait of Franklin D. Roosevelt* (New York: Oxford University Press, 2003).

42. Robert H. Jackson, *The Supreme Court in the American System of Government* (Cambridge, Mass.: Harvard University Press, 1955).

43. Ibid., 53.

44. Ibid., 9.

45. Ibid., 79.

46. See, e.g., Hugo L. Black, *A Constitutional Faith* (New York: Knopf, 1968).

47. See, e.g., Wilfred Rumble, *American Legal Realism: Skepticism, Reform, and the Judicial Process* (Ithaca, N.Y.: Cornell University Press, 1968); and William W. Fisher III, Morton J. Horwitz, and Thomas A. Reed, eds., *American Legal Realism* (New York: Oxford University Press, 1993).

48. Oliver Wendell Holmes, "The Path of Law," *Harvard Law Review* 10 (1897), 457.

49. *Southern Pacific Co. v. Jensen,* 244 U.S. 205 (1917).

50. Letter to Edward Corwin (November 5, 1942), Harlan Fiske Stone Papers, Box 10, LC.

51. Letter to Justice Black (December 15, 1939), Frankfurter Papers, Box 13, LC.

52. *James B. Beam Distilling Co. v. Georgia,* 501 U.S. 529, 549 (1991) (Scalia, J., con. op.) (emphasis in the original). In *James Beam,* six justices held that *Bacchus Imports, Ltd. v. Dias,* 468 U.S. 263 (1984), was a constitutional ruling (holding that a state tax on local liquor sales discriminated against interstate commerce).

53. See and compare the opinions of Justices Reed, Black, Frankfurter, and Jackson in *Adamson v. California,* 332 U.S. 46 (1947), on the incorporation of the guarantees of the Bill of Rights into the Fourteenth Amendment and their application to the states.

54. *Youngstown Sheet & Tube Co. v. Sawyer,* 343 U.S. 579 (1952) (Jackson, J., con. op.), 646–647.

55. Jackson, *Supreme Court in American Government,* 61; see also 62–68.

56. Ibid., 18–19.

57. Ibid., 31.

58. Ibid., 54 (quoting Justice Cardozo).

59. Charles D. Breitel in Desmond et al., *Mr. Justice Jackson,* 31.

60. Felix Frankfurter, *Law and Politics,* ed. E. F. Prichard Jr., and Archibald MacLeish (New York: Harcourt, Brace, 1939), 6.

61. Jackson, *Supreme Court in American Government,* 56.

62. Felix Frankfurter in Kurland, *Felix Frankfurter on the Supreme Court,* 508–511.

63. See, e.g., Justice Frankfurter's opinions in *Colegrove v. Green,* 328 U.S. 549 (1946) (on the "political question" doctrine); and *Poe v. Ullman,* 367 U.S. 497 (1961) (on standing, mootness, and ripeness).

64. *Ashwander v. T.V.A.,* 297 U.S. 288 (1936).

65. Justice Jackson quoting Justice Frankfurter in *Struggle for Judicial Supremacy,* 305–306.

66. Ibid., 306.

67. *Minersville School District v. Gobitis,* 310 U.S. 568 (1940).

68. *Douglas v. City of Jeannette,* 319 U.S. 157 (1943) (Jackson, J., con. op.), 179.

69. Ibid., 174.

70. See, e.g., *Prince v. Massachusetts,* 321 U.S. 158 (1944) (Jackson, J., con. op.).

71. *Terminiello v. Chicago,* 337 U.S. 1 (1949) (Jackson, J., dis. op.), 37.

72. See, e.g., Justice Holmes's opinions in *Schenck v. United States,* 249 U.S. 47 (1919) and *Abrams v. United States,* 250 U.S. 616 (1919). See also Justice Jackson's concurring opinion in *Dennis v. United States,* 341 U.S. 494 (1951); and his separate opinion in *American Communications Association v. Douds,* 339 U.S. 382 (1950).

73. For further discussion, see Justice Frankfurter's former law clerk and Yale Law School professor Alexander Bickel's *The Least Dangerous Branch: The Supreme Court at the Bar of Politics* (New York: Bobbs-Merrill, 1962), 1–33 and 111–198; and his article "The Supreme Court, 1960 Term—Foreword: The Passive Virtues," *Harvard Law Review* 75 (1961), 40.

74. For further discussion, see Gerald Gunther, "The Subtle Vices of the 'Passive Virtues,'" *Columbia Law Review* 64 (1964), 1, and compare Bickel, *Least Dangerous Branch.*

75. *Everson v. Board of Education,* 330 U.S. 1 (1947) (Jackson, J., dis. op.), 19.

76. *Craig v. Harney,* 331 U.S. 367 (1947) (Jackson, J., dis. op.), 396.

77. *Brown v. Allen,* 344 U.S. 443 (1953) (Jackson, J., con. op.), 540.

78. *Plessy v. Ferguson,* 163 U.S. 537 (1896). See generally Charles Lofgren, *The Plessy Case: A Legal-Historical Interpretation* (New York: Oxford University Press, 1987).

CHAPTER 2. NINE SCORPIONS IN A BOTTLE

1. This discussion draws on David M. O'Brien, *Storm Center: The Supreme Court in American Politics,* 11th ed. (New York: Norton, 2017), chap. 3.

2. The title of chap. 1 in Drew Pearson and Robert S. Allen, *The Nine Old Men* (Garden City, N.Y.: Doubleday, Doran, 1936).

3. Quoted in ibid., 36.

4. For a further discussion, see David M. O'Brien, "Inside the Court: The 1937 'Constitutional Crisis' and the Court's 'Switch-in-Time-that-Saved-Nine,'" in *Constitutional Law and Politics,* vols. 1 and 2, 10th ed. (New York: Norton, 2017), chap. 1; letter from Justice Frankfurter to Paul Freund (October 18, 1953), Felix Frankfurter Papers, Box 184, LC; and, more generally, James Simon, *FDR and Chief Justice Hughes: The President, the Supreme Court, and the Epic Struggle over the New Deal* (New York: Simon & Schuster, 2012).

5. Robert H. Jackson, *The Struggle for Judicial Supremacy* (New York: Knopf, 1949), vii.

6. Robert H. Jackson, *The Supreme Court in the American System of Government* (1955; reprint, Harper Torchbooks, 1961).

7. Ibid., 16.

8. Robert H. Jackson Papers, "Oral History Interview," Jackson Papers, Box 190, 1104–1105, LC. In 1998, additional materials and oral history transcript, "The Reminiscences of Robert H. Jackson," based on the interviews of Harlan B. Phillips, were added and processed in 2001; they are available in Boxes 258 and 259.

9. John M. Harlan, "A Glimpse of the Supreme Court at Work," *University of Chicago Law School Record* 11 (1963), 1.

10. Justice Lewis Powell, "What the Justices Are Saying . . .," *A.B.A. Journal* 62 (1976), 1454.

11. Felix Frankfurter, "Chief Justices I Have Known," *University of Virginia Law Review* 39 (1953), 883, reprinted in Philip Kurland, ed., *Felix Frankfurter on the Supreme Court* (Chicago: University of Chicago Press, 1970), 491.

12. Letter (February 2, 1955), Frankfurter Papers, Box 1, HLS.

13. The source of this expression remains unclear. Some scholars attribute it to Justice Holmes as told to longtime Court watcher Max Lerner. In his book *Nine Scorpions in a Bottle* (New York: Arcade, 1994), however, Max Lerner does not indicate the source. Ronald Collins, an editor of Holmes's works, finds no such reference (e-mail to author). Dennis J. Hutchinson attributed it to Alexander Bickel, a law clerk to Justice Frankfurter, in "The Black–Jackson Feud," *Supreme Court Review* 1988 (1988), 203, 238, but without further specification. In *Scorpions: The Battles and Triumphs of FDR's Great Supreme Court Justices* (New York: Twelve Books, 2010), Noah Feldman appears to base that view on a reference to "two scorpions in a bottle, each capable of killing the other, but only at the risk of his own life," in J. Robert Oppenheimer's article on the U.S.–U.S.S.R. arms race in "Atomic Weapons and American Policy," *Foreign Affairs* 31 (1953), 52, 59. The phrase received coverage, and Bickel, a law clerk in 1952–1953, might have picked it up. But there remains no direct support for that, and it is not likely given the tone and style of Bickel's other writings.

14. Based on O'Brien, *Storm Center.*

15. The point is that although there were of course disagreements throughout the nineteenth century, they were publicly suppressed, and a higher premium was placed on institutional opinions for the Court than in the twentieth century.

16. C. Herman Pritchett, *The Roosevelt Court: A Study in Judicial Politics and Values, 1937–1947* (New York: Macmillan, 1948), 40.

17. For further discussion, see O'Brien, *Storm Center,* chap. 5, and David M. O'Brien, "Institutional Norms and Supreme Court Opinions: On Reconsidering the Rise of Individual Opinions," in *Supreme Court Decision-Making: New Institutional Approaches,* ed. Cornell Clayton and Howard Gilman (Chicago: University of Chicago Press, 1999), 91. See also Pamela Corley, Amy Steigerwalt, and Artemus Ward, "Revisiting the Roosevelt Court: The Critical Juncture from Consensus to Dissensus," *Journal of Supreme Court History* 38 (2013), 20.

18. Pritchett, *Roosevelt Court,* 40. See also David J. Danelski, "The Influence of the Chief Justice in the Decisional Process of the Supreme Court," in *American Court Systems: Readings in Judicial Process and Behavior,* ed. Sheldon Goldman and Austin Sarat, 2nd ed. (White Plains, N.Y.: Longman, 1989), 486; and Thomas Walker, Lee Epstein, and William Dixon, "On the Mysterious Demise of Consensual Norms in the United States Supreme Court," *Journal of Politics* 50 (1988), 362.

19. Edwin McElwain, "The Business of the Supreme Court as Conducted by Chief Justice Hughes," *Harvard Law Review* 63 (1949), 18.

20. Quoted in David Danelski and Joseph Tulchin, eds., *The Autobiographical Notes of Charles Evans Hughes* (Cambridge, Mass.: Harvard University Press, 1973), xxvi.

21. Quoted in O'Brien, *Storm Center,* 228; and see, generally, Alpheus T. Mason, *Harlan Fiske Stone: Pillar of the Law* (New York: Viking Press, 1956).

22. William O. Douglas, *The Court Years, 1939–1975: The Autobiography of William O. Douglas* (New York: Random House, 1980), 223. Emphasis in original.

23. Memo to Brethren (October 22, 1942), Jackson Papers, Box 125, LC.

24. Memorandum to the Conference by Justice Frankfurter, 1951, 1953–1961, SC; also in John M. Harlan Papers, Boxes 499 and 587, MLPU; in the Tom C. Clark Papers, UT. For a good discussion of Frankfurter's efforts, see Dennis Hutchinson, "Felix Frankfurter and the Business of the Supreme Court, O.T. 1946–O.T. 1961," in *Supreme Court Review* 1980 (1980), 143.

25. See Memorandum for the Conference by Chief Justice Warren (October 7, 1957), Frankfurter Papers, Box 220, LC.

26. Letter from Justice Douglas to Justice Frankfurter (October 13, 1960), Frankfurter Papers, Box 152, HLS.

27. Letter from Justice Black to Justice Frankfurter (October 13, 1960), Frankfurter Papers, Box 152, HLS.

28. See Stacia L. Haynie, "Leadership and Consensus on the U.S. Supreme Court," *Journal of Politics* 54 (1992), 1167.

29. See Lee Epstein, Jeffrey Segal, Harold Spaeth, and Thomas Walker, eds., *The Supreme Court Compendium* (Washington, D.C.: CQ Press, 1994), table 3-1, 147–148; and William Domnarski, *The Great Justices, 1941–1954: Black, Douglas, Frankfurter, and Jackson in Chambers* (Ann Arbor: University of Michigan Press, 2006), tables on 169–175.

30. See Wilfred Rumble, *American Legal Realism: Skepticism, Reform, and the Judicial Process* (Ithaca, N.Y.: Cornell University Press, 1968); and William Fisher, Morton J. Horwitz, and Thomas Reed, eds., *American Legal Realism* (New York: Oxford University Press, 1993).

31. See, generally, Melvin I. Urofsky, *Division and Discord: The Supreme Court under Stone and Vinson, 1941–1953* (Columbia: University of South Carolina Press, 1997); and Phillip J. Cooper, *Battles on the Bench: Conflict Inside the Supreme Court* (Lawrence: University Press of Kansas, 1995).

32. Correspondence between Frankfurter and Vinson (November 29 and December 1, 2, and 3, 1948), Fred Vinson Papers, Box 215, UK.

33. See Antonin Scalia, "The Dissenting Opinion," *Journal of Supreme Court History* 19 (1994), 33; Ruth Bader Ginsburg, "The Role of Dissenting Opinions," Leo and Berry Memorial Lecture, October 21, 2007, discussed in O'Brien, *Storm Center,* chap. 5.

34. See, e.g., Sidney Ulmer, "Earl Warren and the *Brown* Decision," *Journal of Politics* 33 (1971), 702 ("The unanimous opinion in the case [*Brown*] must, of course, be attributed to Warren"); Bernard Schwartz, *The Unpublished Opinions of the Warren Court* (New York: Oxford University Press, 1985), 446 (both the decision and the unanimity were attributable directly to Warren); Jim Newton, *Justice for All: Earl Warren and the Nation He Made* (New York: Riverhead Trade, 2007); Bernard Schwartz, "Chief Justice Earl Warren: Super Chief in Action," *Journal of Supreme Court History* 1 (1998), 477; and, generally, Bernard Schwartz, *Super Chief: Earl Warren and His Supreme Court—A Judicial Biography* (New York: New York University Press, 1983).

35. See, e.g., "Memorandum, Segregation Cases" (May 17, 1954), William O. Douglas Papers, Box 1149, LC; Harold Burton Papers, Box 337, LC; and S. Sidney Ulmer, "Bricolage and Assorted Thoughts on Working in the Papers of Supreme Court Justices," *Journal of Politics* 35 (1973), 286; Mary Frances Berry, *Stability, Security, and Continuity: Mr. Justice Burton and Decision-Making in the Supreme Court, 1945–1958* (Westport, Conn.: Greenwood Press, 1978), 125; and Richard Kluger, *Simple Justice: The History of* Brown v. Board of Education *and the Struggle for Racial Equality* (New York: Knopf, 1975), chap. 23.

36. See, e.g., Letter from Felix Frankfurter to Justice Reed (May 20, 1954), Reed Papers, UK; and discussed by, among others, his former law clerk, John Fassett, "Mr. Justice Reed and *Brown v. Board of Education*," *Yearbook of the Supreme Court Historical Society* 1986 (1986), 48, 63.

37. See, e.g., Feldman, *Scorpions,* 376–377.

38. See, e.g., Michael J. Klarman, *From Jim Crow to Civil Rights: The Supreme Court and the Struggle for Racial Equality* (New York: Oxford University Press, 2004), 298. See also Mark Tushnet and Katya Lezin, "What Really Happened in *Brown v. Board of Education,*" *Columbia Law Review* 91 (1991), 1867.

39. Reed quoted in Roger K. Newman, *Hugo Black: A Biography* (New York: Pantheon, 1994), 438; and Interview with Justice Tom C. Clark, *"Brown v. Board of Education,"* Richard Kluger Papers, Box 1, YU.

40. Letter from Justice Frankfurter to Justice Harlan (November 6, 1956), Frankfurter Papers, HLS; discussed in Schwartz, *Super Chief,* 95.

41. For more on Byrnes's attack on *Brown,* see the discussion in Chapter 3.

42. Letter from Justice Frankfurter to Judge Hand (February 13, 1958), Frankfurter Papers, Box 199, HLS.

43. *West Coast Hotel v. Parrish,* 300 U.S. 379 (1937).

44. *National Labor Relations Board v. Jones & Laughlin Steel Corporation,* 301 U.S. 1 (1937).

45. For further discussion, see Letter to Paul Freund (October 18, 1953), Frankfurter Papers, Box 184, LC; O'Brien, *Constitutional Law and Politics,* vol. 1, 66–69. See also Merlo J. Pusey, "Justice Roberts' 1937 Turnaround," *Yearbook of the Supreme Court Historical Society* 1983 (1983), 102.

46. Radio address of Senator Hugo L. Black on the Mutual Broadcasting System, Station WOL, Washington, D.C. (February 23, 1937), discussed in Elizabeth Black, "Hugo Black: A Memorial Portrait," *Yearbook of the Supreme Court Historical Society* 1982 (1982), 72.

47. "The Black Controversy," Jackson Papers, Box 26, LC; "1945–1946—Black–Jackson Feud," Hugo L. Black Papers, Box 531, LC. See also Hutchinson, "Black–Jackson Feud," 240–247; *Supreme Court Review* 1988 (1988), 203; and Eugene Gerhart, *America's Advocate: Robert H. Jackson* (New York: Bobbs-Merrill, 1958), 240–247.

48. Statement appended to Letter to Virginia Hamilton (a biographer) (April 7, 1968), Black Papers, Box 31; see also materials in Box 224, Black Papers, LC; and Homer Cummings Diaries, UVA.

49. See Howard Ball and Phillip J. Cooper, *Of Power and Right: Hugo Black, William O. Douglas, and America's Constitutional Revolution* (New York: Oxford University Press, 1999).

50. William O. Douglas Interviews with Walter Murphy, 1961–1963, MLPU.

51. Undated note, Felix Frankfurter Papers, Box 170, File 9, HLS.

52. Quoted in Newman, *Hugo Black,* 546.

53. Arthur Krock notes (January 8, 1947), reprinted in Gerhart, *America's Advocate,* 274.

54. Newton, *Justice for All,* 270.

55. Newman, *Hugo Black,* 419–420.

56. Domnarski, *Great Justices,* 119.

57. See Tom C. Clark Oral History Interview, 50, UK; and William J. Brennan Jr., "A Remembrance of William O. Douglas," *Journal of Supreme Court History* 1991 (1991), 104.

58. See Domnarski, *Great Justices,* 119.

59. Douglas note to Justice Clark (asking for confirmation of his recollection) (May 3, 1968), Clark Papers, UT; discussed in O'Brien, *Storm Center;* and Douglas, *Court Years,* 226.

60. *Bridges v. California,* 314 U.S. 252 (1941), further discussed in James Simon, *Antagonists: Hugo Black, Felix Frankfurter, and Civil Liberties in Modern America* (New York: Simon & Schuster, 1990), 121–129.

61. See, generally, Hugo L. Black, *A Constitutional Faith* (New York: Knopf, 1968); and Paul Freund, "Mr. Justice Black and the Judicial Function," *U.C.L.A. Law Review* 14 (1967), 467, 468.

62. See, e.g., defenses of Frankfurter's "balancing" stance by (former law clerk) Wallace Mendelson, "On the Meaning of the First Amendment: Absolutes in the Balance," *California Law Review* 50 (1962), 821; and Dean Alfange Jr., "The Balancing of Interests in Free Speech Cases: In Defense of an Abused Doctrine," *Law in Transition Quarterly* 2 (1965), 35.

63. Although recounted in numerous places, see Newton, *Justice for All,* 271.

64. See and compare Charles Fairman, "Does the Fourteenth Amendment Incorporate the Bill of Rights? The Original Understanding," *Stanford Law Review* 2 (1949), 5; Charles Fairman, "The Supreme Court, 1955 Term—Foreword: The Attack on the Segregation Cases," *Harvard Law Review* 70 (1956), 83; Alexander Bickel, "The Original Understanding and the Segregation Decision," *Harvard Law Review* 69 (1955), 1; and Felix Frankfurter, "Memorandum on 'Incorporation' of the Bill of Rights into the Due Process of the Fourteenth Amendment," *Harvard Law Review* 78 (1965), 746; with Stanley Morrison, "Does the Fourteenth Amendment Incorporate the Bill of Rights? The Judicial Interpretation," *Stanford Law Review* 2 (1949), 140; William W. Crosskey, "Charles Fairman, 'Legislative History,' and the Constitutional Limits on State Authority," *University of Chicago Law Review* 22 (1954), 1; John P. Frank and Robert F. Munro, "The Original Understanding of the 'Equal Protection of the Laws,'" *Washington University Law Quarterly* 1972 (1972), 421; Hugo L. Black, "Justice Black and the Bill of Rights," Interview by Eric Sevareid and Martin Agronsky, *CBS News* special (December 3, 1968), printed in *Southwestern University Law Review* 9 (1977), 937. See also, more generally, Pamela Brandwein, *Reconstructing the Reconstruction: The Supreme Court and the Production of Historical Truth* (Durham, N.C.: Duke University Press, 1999); Richard L. Aynes, "On Misreading John Bingham and the Fourteenth Amendment," *Yale Law Journal*

103 (1993), 57; and Richard L. Aynes, "Charles Fairman, Felix Frankfurter, and the Fourteenth Amendment," *Chicago-Kent Law Review* 70 (1995), 1197.

65. *Adamson v. California,* 332 U.S. 46 (1947).

66. *Griswold v. Connecticut,* 381 U.S. 479 (1965).

67. *Brown v. Board of Education,* 349 U.S. 294 (1955). See "Notes of December 12, 1952, Segregation," Jackson Papers, Box 184, LC; "Memorandum for the Conference: *Re: The Segregation Cases*" from Justice Frankfurter, Black Papers, Box 314, Jackson Papers, Box 184, and other justices' papers, LC. See also Klarman, *From Jim Crow to Civil Rights,* 293–294; Newman, *Hugo Black,* 428–429; and Kluger, *Simple Justice,* 592–595.

68. Interview with Eric Sevareid and Martin Agronsky, reported in Homer Bigart, "Black Believes Warren Phrase Slowed Integration," *New York Times,* December 4, 1968.

69. *Alexander v. Holmes County Board of Education,* 396 U.S. 19 (1969).

70. See, e.g., Ulmer, "Earl Warren and the *Brown* Decision"; Berry, *Stability, Security, and Continuity;* and Kluger, *Simple Justice,* 594–595.

71. Correspondence with Sidney Ulmer, Black Papers, Box 53, LC; further discussed in Kluger, *Simple Justice,* 594–595; Newman, *Hugo Black,* 610; and Tinsley Yarbrough, *Mr. Justice Black and His Critics* (Durham, N.C.: Duke University Press, 1988), 237–239.

72. Hugo Black Jr., *My Father: A Remembrance* (New York: Random House, 1978), 261.

73. Homer Cummings Diaries, UVA; Stanley Reed Interview, 3–25, CUOHP; and Stanley Reed Papers, Boxes 282 and 370, UK.

74. Jackson's draft autobiography (June 8, 1944), 145, Jackson Papers, Box 189, LC.

75. John D. Fassett, *New Deal Justice: The Life of Stanley F. Reed of Kentucky* (New York: Vantage Press, 1994), chap. 30; and Fassett, "Mr. Justice Reed."

76. They are now available in the Reed Papers, UK.

77. See Fassett, "Mr. Justice Reed," 51–54.

78. Letters to clerks (July 14, 1953, and August 14, 1953), quoted in ibid., 51, 54.

79. Quoted by Fassett, *New Deal Justice,* 487.

80. *Missouri ex rel Gaines v. Canada,* 305 U.S. 337 (1938).

81. Justice Burton's conference notes on *Sipuel v. Oklahoma State Regents,* 332 U.S. 631 (1941) (per curiam), quoted in Fassett, *New Deal Justice,* 557.

82. *Smith v. Allwright,* 321 U.S. 649 (1944).

83. *Sweatt v. Painter,* 339 U.S. 629 (1950).

84. *McLaurin v. Oklahoma State Regents,* 339 U.S. 637 (1950).

85. *Henderson v. United States,* 339 U.S. 816 (1950).

86. *District of Columbia v. John R. Thompson Co., Inc.,* 436 U.S. 100 (1953) (further discussed in Chapter 3).

87. Quoted in Kluger, *Simple Justice,* 595.

88. Recounted in *From the Diaries of Felix Frankfurter,* ed. Joseph P. Lash (New York: Norton, 1975), 333–335.

89. See Schwartz, *Super Chief,* 129.

90. Conference notes of Justices Burton, Douglas, Jackson, and Clark, com-

piled and reprinted in Del Dickson, ed., *Supreme Court in Conference, 1940–1985* (New York: Oxford University Press, 2001), 646–662.

91. Ibid., 665–666 (emphasis in original).

92. See Kluger, *Simple Justice*, 692–694; Fassett, "Mr. Justice Reed," 55–57.

93. Quoted in Fassett, *New Deal Justice*, 567 (emphasis in original).

94. See Schwartz, *Super Chief*, 87; and Kluger, *Simple Justice*, 692–699.

95. Kluger's notes on interview with Mickum; and Kluger, *Simple Justice*, 698; but see Fassett, *New Deal Justice*, 745n54.

96. Douglas, *Court Years*, 115.

97. Douglas Interview with Murphy, 279.

98. Justice Thurgood Marshall Interview with Dennis J. Hutchinson (1979), as told to the author (e-mail, August 16, 2016).

99. Kluger's notes of interview with George Mickum (October 20, 1974), Kluger Papers, Box 5, YU.

100. Cummings Diaries, UVA.

101. Henry Morgenthal Diaries, Box 69:308, Roosevelt Papers, RPL.

102. Interview with Justice Frankfurter by Gerald Gunther, Frankfurter Papers, Box 291, HLS.

103. See, e.g., *West Virginia State Board of Education v. Barnette*, 319 U.S. 624 (1943), in which Jackson overturned an earlier ruling, written by Frankfurter, holding that the First Amendment bars compulsory saluting of the American flag at the start of the day in public schools (as further discussed in Chapter 1).

104. See, e.g., Bruce Allen Murphy, *The Brandeis / Frankfurter Connection: The Secret Political Activities of Two Supreme Court Justices* (New York: Oxford University Press, 1982).

105. For further discussion, see O'Brien, *Storm Center*, chap. 2.

106. Quoted in Frankfurter, *Diaries*, 155 (commenting to Justice Murphy on Justice Douglas's presidential aspirations and that the Court was becoming "a jumping-off place for politics").

107. Quoted in ibid., 77.

108. Quoted in ibid., 76.

109. F. Alley Allen Interview, Reed Papers, UK.

110. Quoted in Fassett, *New Deal Justice*, 584.

111. Douglas, *Court Years*, 173. See also John Sapieza Oral History Interview, Reed Papers, UK; and William Oliver Oral History Interview, BLUC.

112. The memorandum was subsequently published; see Alexander Bickel, "The Original Understanding and the Segregation Decision," *Harvard Law Review* 69 (1955), 1.

113. Reported in John Frank (a former Black law clerk), *The Marble Temple* (New York: Knopf, 1958), 105.

114. Memo, Douglas Papers, Box 228, LC.

115. Francis A. Allen, "Remembering *Shelly v. Kraemer:* Of Public and Private Worlds," *Washington University Law Quarterly* 67 (1989), 709, 719–720.

116. Philip Elman and Norman Silber, "The Solicitor General's Office, Justice Frankfurter, and Civil Rights Litigation," *Harvard Law Review* 100 (1987), 817, 840.

117. Mickum Interview, Kluger Papers, YU.

118. Oliver Interview, 6, BLUC; and author interview with E. Barrett Pretty-man Jr., Hogan & Hartson, Washington, D.C. (March 1987).

119. G. Edward White, *Earl Warren: A Public Life* (New York: Oxford University Press, 1982), 183; *Cooper v. Aaron,* 358 U.S. 1 (1958).

120. Letter to Justice Harlan (September 8, 1958), Frankfurter Papers, Box 169, HLS.

121. See letters and memos, Earl Warren Papers, Boxes 353 and 574, LC; and letters to Justice Hugo Black (May 7, 1963, and December 15, 1964), Black Papers, Box 60, LC.

122. Schwartz, *Super Chief,* 151; and Schwartz, *Unpublished Opinions,* 11. See also Fassett, *New Deal Justice,* 583–584.

123. *Naim v. Naim,* 350 U.S. 985 (1956), further discussed in Chapter 4.

124. *Loving v. Virginia,* 388 U.S. 1 (1967).

125. See Del Dickson, "State Court Defiance and the Limits of Supreme Court Authority: *Williams v. Georgia* Revisited," *Yale Law Journal* 103 (1994), 1423, 1427; Memorandum from Justice Felix N. Frankfurter to Conference on *Naim v. Naim* (November 4, 1955), Frankfurter Papers, Box 249, LC, reprinted in Dennis Hutchinson, "Unanimity and Segregation: Decisionmaking in the Supreme Court, *1948–1958*," *Georgetown Law Journal* 68 (1979), 1, 55; and cert. memo in Justice Burton Papers, quoted in Hutchinson, 63; as well as Bernard Schwartz, "Felix Frankfurter and Earl Warren: A Study of a Deteriorating Relationship," *Supreme Court Review* 1980 (1980), 115, 118–122.

126. See, e.g., Schwartz, *Super Chief,* 205–206; and O'Brien, *Storm Center.*

127. Quoted in Michael Parrish, "Felix Frankfurter, the Progressive Tradition, and the Warren Court," in *The Warren Court in Historical and Political Perspective,* ed. Mark Tushnet (Charlottesville: University of Virginia Press, 1996), 52.

128. Quoted in Leonard Baker, *Brandeis and Frankfurter: A Dual Biography* (New York: Harper & Row, 1989), 415.

129. Conference notes reprinted in Dickson, *Supreme Court in Conference,* 64.

130. *American Federation of Labor v. American Sash & Door Company,* 335 U.S. 538 (1946), 555–556.

131. Frankfurter Memo on *Brown* (September 26, 1952), Warren Papers, Box 571, LC.

132. Subsequently, in response to Judge Learned Hand's 1958 Holmes Lecture, *The Bill of Rights* (Cambridge, Mass.: Harvard University Press, 1958), criticizing the overreaching and limitation of judicial power, Columbia Law School professor and supporter of the NAACP's assault on segregation Herbert Wechsler sought to make sense of the scope of the ruling in *Brown* in "Toward Neutral Principles of Constitutional Law," *Harvard Law Review* 73 (1959), 1.

133. Letter from Judge Hand, Correspondence with Judge Hand (March 7 to December 6, 1955), Frankfurter Papers, Box 184, HLS. (The Frankfurter and Hand correspondence is further discussed in Chapter 4.)

134. Felix Frankfurter Memorandum on Segregation Decree, Warren Papers, Box 574, LC.

135. Memorandum to Brethren (January 15, 1954), Burton Papers, LC.

136. Elman and Silber, "Solicitor General's Office," 827–828.

137. See Frankfurter Notes (April 16, 1955), LC; discussed by Kluger, *Simple Justice*, 738–741; Hutchinson, "Unanimity and Segregation"; and Dickson, "State Court Defiance," 1467.

138. Norman I Silber, *With All Deliberate Speed: The Life of Philip Elman, an Oral History Memoir* (Ann Arbor: University of Michigan Press, 2004), 207–208. See also Bernard Schwartz, *Unpublished Opinions*, 450.

139. See, e.g., Fassett, *New Deal Justice*, 580.

140. Earl Warren, *The Memoirs of Chief Justice Earl Warren* (New York: Doubleday, 1977), 4.

141. Memo from Frank Murphy, Papers as President, PSF Box 77, RPL.

142. Douglas Interview with Murphy, 2–15, MLPU.

143. See, e.g., William O. Douglas, *Points of Rebellion* (New York: Random House, 1969); William O. Douglas, *Being an American* (New York: John Day, 1940).

144. Douglas Interview with Murphy, 78–79.

145. *West Virginia State Board of Education v. Barnette* (discussed further in Chapter 1); and Douglas Interview with Murphy, 51.

146. Steven B. Duke, "Justice Douglas and Criminal Law," in *"He Shall Not Pass This Way Again": The Legacy of Justice William O. Douglas*, ed. Stephen L. Wasby (Pittsburgh: University of Pittsburgh Press, 1990), 133.

147. See the further discussion in Chapter 3.

148. Kluger, *Simple Justice*, 602.

149. See Marshall L. Small, "William O. Douglas Remembered: A Collective Memory by WOD Law Clerks," *Journal of Supreme Court History* 32 (2007), 297; and Melvin Urofsky, "William O. Douglas and His Law Clerks," *Western Legal History* 3 (1990), 3.

150. See and compare, e.g., Bruce Allen Murphy, *Wild Bill: The Legend and Life of William O. Douglas* (New York: Random House, 2003), with James Simon, *Independent Journey: The Life of William O. Douglas* (New York: Harper & Row, 1980).

151. Conference notes in Dickson, *Supreme Court in Conference*, 640.

152. Ibid., 652.

153. Ibid., 288.

154. Ibid., 275.

155. Ibid., 278 and 286.

156. Jackson Interview, 779, CUOHP; and Jackson Papers, LC.

157. Notes on "H.F.S. & C.J. ship," Frankfurter Papers, Box 172, HLS.

158. Jackson Interview, 1084–1087, CUOPH; and Jackson Papers, Box 259, LC.

159. Robert H. Jackson and John Q. Barrett, *That Man: An Insider's Portrait of Franklin D. Roosevelt* (New York: Oxford University Press, 2003).

160. *Morgan v. Virginia*, 328 U.S. 373 (1946).

161. See Berry, *Stability, Security, and Continuity*, 95.

162. Quoted in Kluger, *Simple Justice*, 611 (emphasis in original).

163. Conference notes reprinted in Dickson, *Supreme Court in Conference*, 640, 643, and 652.

164. Ibid., 658–659.

165. See, generally, Simon, *Antagonists*; and Domnarski, *Great Justices*, 102.

166. Jackson Oral History Interview, Columbia University Oral History Project, 8, 527, CUOHP. See also Dennis Hutchinson, "The Black–Jackson Feud," 226.

167. Fred Vinson Papers, Box 218, UK; Stanley Reed Papers, Box 325, UK; White House Central Files, WHCF-PSF, Boxes 221 and 231, and OF Box 212, TPL.

168. Letter (June 11, 1946), reprinted in *Off the Record: The Private Papers of Harry S. Truman,* ed. R. Ferrell (New York: Harper & Row, 1980), 90.

169. Tom Clark Oral History Interview, UK.

170. William Rogers Oral History Interview, UK.

171. Douglas, *Court Years,* 248–249.

172. Frankfurter, *Diaries,* 274.

173. Urofsky, *Division and Discord,* 151.

174. See, e.g., Kluger, *Simple Justice,* 590; Klarman, *From Jim Crow to Civil Rights,* 294 and 298; and Feldman, *Scorpions,* 374.

175. Francis A. Allen, "Chief Justice Vinson and the Theory of Constitutional Government: A Tentative Appraisal," *Northwestern University Law Review* 49 (1954), 3. See also, generally, James E. St. Clair and Linda Gugin, *Chief Justice Fred M. Vinson of Kentucky: A Political Biography* (Lexington: University Press of Kentucky, 2002).

176. *Shelley v. Fraemer,* 334 U.S. 1 (1948).

177. *Hurd v. Hodge,* 334 U.S. 24 (1948).

178. *Sipuel v. Board of Regents, University of Oklahoma,* 332 U.S. 631 (1948).

179. Conference notes reprinted in Dickson, *Supreme Court in Conference,* 641–642 (emphasis in original).

180. Ibid., 638.

181. Ibid., 647 (emphasis in original).

182. Newton Minow Oral History Interview, 27–28, UK. See also Conference Lists, Black Papers, Box 310, LC.

183. See Mimi Clark Gronlund, *Supreme Court Justice Tom C. Clark: A Life of Service* (Austin: University of Texas Press, 2010); and Alexander Wohl, *Father, Son, and Constitution: How Justice Tom Clark and Attorney General Ramsey Clark Shaped American Democracy* (Lawrence: University Press of Kansas, 2013).

184. See Linda C. Gugin and James E. St. Clair, *Sherman Minton: New Deal Senator, Cold War Justice* (Indianapolis: Indiana Historical Society, 1997); and William Franklin Radcliff, *Sherman Minton: Indiana's Supreme Court Justice* (Indianapolis: Guild Press of Indiana, 1996).

185. Quoted in Merle Miller, *Plain Speaking—An Oral Biography of Harry S. Truman* (New York: Berkley, 1973), 225–226.

186. See Kluger, *Simple Justice,* 270–271 and 611–612.

187. President's Committee on Civil Rights, *To Secure These Rights* (Ann Arbor: University of Michigan Press, 1947).

188. Tom C. Clark and Philip B. Perlman, *Prejudice and Property: A Historical Brief against Racial Covenants* (Washington, D.C.: Public Affairs Press, 1948).

189. Quoted in Schwartz, *Super Chief,* 89.

190. Memorandum on *Sweatt* and *McLaurin* from Mr. Justice Tom C. Clark to the Conference (April 7, 1950), Frankfurter Papers, Box 218, LC; reprinted as an appendix in Hutchinson, "Unanimity and Segregation," 89. See also Gary M. Lavergne, *Before* Brown: *Herman Marion Sweatt, Thurgood Marshall, and the Long Road to Justice* (Austin: University of Texas Press, 2010), 249–250.

191. Conference notes reprinted in Dickson, *Supreme Court in Conference*, 642–643.

192. Transcript of Tom C. Clark Oral History Interview I (October, 7, 1969), by Joes B. Frantz, Internet copy, 21, LBJ.

193. Tom C. Clark Oral History Interview, 9–10, UK (emphasis in original).

194. Quoted in Kluger, *Simple Justice*, 612.

195. Quoted in Radcliff, *Sherman Minton*, 160.

196. Letter from Sherman Minton to the Senate Judiciary Committee, explaining his refusal to testify (October 1, 1949), *Congressional Record* 95 (1949), 13803.

197. Conference notes reprinted in Dickson, *Supreme Court in Conference*, 653 (emphasis in original).

198. Ibid., 659–660. See also David N. Atkinson, "Opinion Writing on the Supreme Court, 1949–1956: The Views of Justice Sherman Minton," *Temple Law Quarterly* 49 (1975), 105, 111.

199. Associated Press Release (October 20, 1960), in Burton Papers, LC, quoted in David N. Atkinson, "Justice Sherman Minton and the Protection of Minority Rights," *Washington and Lee Law Review* 34 (1977), 97, 107.

200. Herbert Brownell Oral History Interview, 6–11, EPL; Herbert Brownell Interview, 60–65, BLUC; and Dwight D. Eisenhower Diary (DDE Diary), Box 4, EPL.

201. DDE Diary (October 8, 1954), Box 4; and letter to Edgar Eisenhower, WHCF-NS, Box 11, EPL. For further discussion of Warren's role in the 1952 Republican Party convention, see the discussion and sources in O'Brien, *Storm Center*, chap. 2.

202. Quoted in "Warren: Out of the Storm Center," *Time*, June 28, 1968, http://www.time.com/.

203. See, e.g., Wallace Mendelson, *Justices Black and Frankfurter: Conflict in the Court* (Chicago: University of Chicago Press, 1961).

204. Notes on Interview with Earl E. Pollock, former clerk to Chief Justice Warren, Kluger Papers, Box 5, YU.

205. Quoted in "Earl Warren's Way: 'Is It Fair?'" *Time*, July 22, 1974, 66.

206. Conference notes reprinted in Dickson, *Supreme Court in Conference*, 654.

207. Notes on Interview with Earl Warren, Kluger Papers, Box 5, 1, YU.

208. Ibid., 2. See also Warren, *Memoirs*, 3–4; and, for further discussion, see Hutchinson, "Unanimity and Segregation," 34–44.

209. Author interview with Justice Stevens (April 5, 1985), Supreme Court.

210. Notes on Interview with Earl Warren, Kluger Papers, 3, YU.

CHAPTER 3. JUSTICE AND COMPANY

1. See the discussion in Chapter 1.

2. See Chapter 2 and, generally, David M. O'Brien, "Institutional Norms and Supreme Court Opinions: On Reconsidering the Rise of Individual Opinions," in *Supreme Court Decision-Making: New Institutionalist Approaches*, ed. Cornell Clayton and Howard Gillman (Chicago: University of Chicago Press, 1999), 91.

3. See, generally, David M. O'Brien, *Storm Center: The Supreme Court in American Life*, 11th ed. (New York: Norton, 2017), chap. 3. For further discussion of the

evolution of justices' working relationships with their law clerks, see Todd Peppers, *Courtiers of the Marble Palace: The Rise and Influence of the Supreme Court Law Clerk* (Stanford: Stanford University Press, 2006); Artemus Ward and David Weiden, *Sorcerers' Apprentices: 100 Years of Law Clerks at the United States Supreme Court* (New York: New York University Press, 2006); and John Knox, *The Forgotten Memoir of John Knox: A Year in the Life of a Supreme Court Clerk in FDR's Washington,* ed. Dennis Hutchinson and David Garrow (Chicago: University of Chicago Press, 2002).

4. Robert H. Jackson, *The Supreme Court in the American System of Government* (1955; reprint, New York: Harper Torchbooks, 1961).

5. Quoted in Letter from Justice Frankfurter to Justice Reed (December 3, 1941), Reed Papers, Box 171, UK.

6. Arthur Rosett Oral History Interview, Reed Papers, UK.

7. Quoted in Sidney Fine, *Frank Murphy: The Washington Years* (Ann Arbor: University of Michigan Press, 1984). Justice Frank Murphy's Papers, in the Bentley Historical Library at the University of Michigan, contain a large number of case files in which the clerks' handwritten draft opinions are attached to typewritten copies with the justice's comments and changes.

8. William H. Rehnquist, "Are the Old Times Dead?," Mac Swinford Lecture, University of Kentucky, September 23, 1983, quoted in O'Brien, *Storm Center,* 133.

9. William J. Brennan Jr., Dean's Day Address, New York University Law School (1979), as quoted in Ward and Weiden, *Sorcerers' Apprentices,* 202. See also Paul Freund, *The Supreme Court of the United States: Its Business, Purposes, and Performance* (Cleveland: The World Publishing Co., 1961), 145–170.

10. Quoted in Peppers, *Courtiers,* 149 (quoting the Diary of Dallin Oaks, who clerked for the chief justice in the 1958 term).

11. Jesse H. Choper, "Clerking for Chief Justice Earl Warren," in *In Chambers: Stories of Supreme Court Law Clerks and Their Justices,* ed. Todd Peppers and Artemus Ward (Charlottesville: University of Virginia Press, 2012), 265.

12. William H. Rehnquist, "Who Writes Decisions of the Supreme Court?" *U.S. News & World Report,* December 13, 1957, 74.

13. William H. Rehnquist, "Remarks," Ninth Circuit Conference, Corodano, California (July 17, 1982) (printed draft copy at 24, on file with the author), quoted in O'Brien, *Storm Center,* 142. See also William H. Rehnquist, *The Supreme Court: How It Was, How It Is* (New York: Morrow, 1987), 297–301.

14. William H. Rehnquist, Remarks at the Jefferson Literary Society and Debating Society Meeting, Charlottesville, Virginia, September 20, 1985, and interviews on *This Honorable Court* (PBS, 1988) and *Book Notes* (C-SPAN, October 25, 1998).

15. Chief Justice Roberts, Fourth Judicial Conference Talk (aired on C-SPAN, June 25, 2011), discussed in O'Brien, *Storm Center,* 138. See also Brad Snyder, "The Judicial Genealogy (and Mythology) of John Roberts: Clerkships from Gray to Brandeis to Friendly to Roberts," *Ohio State Law Journal* 71 (2010), 1149.

16. See, generally, Edward Lazarus, *Closed Chambers: The First Eyewitness Account of the Epic Struggles Inside the Supreme Court* (New York: Times Books, 1998). Other empirical studies based on interviews with a large number of former law clerks confirm the growing role and influence of recent clerks. See, e.g., Todd Peppers

and Christopher Zorn, "Law Clerk Influence on Supreme Court Decision Making: An Empirical Assessment," *De Paul Law Review* 58 (2008), 5; and, generally, Peppers, *Courtiers;* and Ward and Weiden, *Sorcerers' Apprentices.*

17. Alexander M. Bickel, "The Court: An Indictment Analyzed," *New York Times Magazine* 16 (April 27, 1958), 54.

18. E. Barrett Prettyman Jr., Lecture at the Chautauqua Institution (August 10, 2010), discussed in Brad Synder and John Q. Barrett, "Rehnquist's Missing Letter: A Former Law Clerk's 1955 Thoughts on Justice Jackson and *Brown,*" *Boston College Law Review* 53 (2012), 631.

19. See April 7, 1953, letter from Jackson to Phil C. Neal, a former clerk and Stanford University Law School professor, who was a feeder of clerks for the justice, Jackson Papers, Box 17, LC. See also letter from Elsie L. Douglas, explaining to an applicant for a clerkship that no additional clerks would be hired for the next term because the current clerk, Prettyman, "proved so very satisfactory the Justice has asked him to stay another year." Letter to Richard E. Sherwood (February 26, 1954), Jackson Papers, Box 188, LC.

20. Peppers, *Courtiers,* 126.

21. Quoted in ibid., 126–127, based on James M. Marsh, "Supreme Court Justice without a College Degree," *Philadelphia Lawyer* 63 (1999), 1. See also John Q. Barrett, "No College, No Prior Clerkship: How Jim Marsh Became Justice Jackson's Law Clerk," in *Of Courtiers and Kings: More Stories of Supreme Court Law Clerks and the Justices,* ed. Todd C. Peppers and Clare Cushman (Charlottesville: University of Virginia Press, 2015), 170.

22. Letter to Paul S. Andrews, Dean of Syracuse University College of Law (December 28, 1949), Jackson Papers, Box 165, LC.

23. Rehnquist, *Supreme Court,* 20.

24. Letter from William H. Rehnquist to Justice Jackson (undated), Jackson Papers, Box 19, LC.

25. Correspondence with William H. Rehnquist, Jackson Papers, Box 19, LC.

26. Correspondence with Phil C. Neal, Jackson Papers, Box 17, LC.

27. Correspondence with Donald B. Cronson, Jackson Papers, Box 177, LC.

28. "Office Memo" and "Responsibility for Security and Work in the Office of Mr. Justice Jackson," 1950 October Term, Jackson Papers, Box 165, LC. See also "Summary of Discussion at Mr. Justice Frankfurter's home, Monday evening, June 6, 1955," with his clerks and those of Justice Jackson, Chief Justice Warren, and other chambers, Felix Frankfurter Papers, File 17, Box 182, HLS; "Memorandum for Law Clerks," Earl Warren Papers, Box 398, LC; "Law Clerk's Instructions," William O. Douglas Papers, Box 1120, LC; and "Memorandum," John M. Harlan Papers, Box 561, MLPU.

29. Rehnquist, *Supreme Court,* 10–11.

30. Memorandum, "Responsibility for Security" (emphasis added), Jackson Papers, Box 165, LC.

31. James M. Marsh, "Affirm, If Possible: How a United States Supreme Court Justice's Confidence in This Clerk Turned a Tentative 5–4 Vote into an 8–1 Decision," *Philadelphia Lawyer* 62 (1997), 1.

32. Rehnquist, "Who Writes Decisions?," 74. See also William H. Rehnquist,

"Robert H. Jackson: A Perspective Twenty-Five Years Later," *Albany Law Review* 44 (1980), 533 (stating that "like most of his other clerks, I worked closely with him on several opinions which he wrote").

33. Letter to Philip Kurland (September 24, 1964), in Philip Kurland File, Frankfurter Papers, Reel 44, Box 73, LC.

34. Kurland never completed the planned biography of Jackson. Mark De Wolfe Howe completed only two volumes of his biography of Justice Holmes—*Justice Oliver Wendell Holmes: The Shaping Years, 1841–1870* (Cambridge, Mass.: Harvard University Press, 1957), and *Justice Oliver Wendell Holmes: The Proving Years, 1870–1882* (Cambridge, Mass.: Harvard University Press, 1963)—and completed a couple of edited volumes of the justice's speeches and letters—*The Occasional Speeches of Justice Oliver Wendell Holmes* (Cambridge, Mass.: Harvard University Press, 1962), and *Holmes–Laski Letters,* 2 vols. (Cambridge, Mass.: Harvard University Press, 1953). Another clerk, Alexander Bickel, never completed a biography of Justice Brandeis but edited *The Unpublished Opinions of Mr. Justice Brandeis* (Cambridge, Mass.: Harvard University Press, 1957). See also Gerald Gunther, *Learned Hand: The Man and the Judge* (New York: Oxford University Press, 2010).

35. Letter from James Marsh to Eugene Gerhart (December 9, 1954), quoted in Eugene Gerhart, *Lawyer's Judge* (Albany: Albany Q., 1961). Gerhart also published *America's Advocate: Robert H. Jackson* (New York: Bobbs-Merrill, 1958). The two books were combined and republished with a foreword by Chief Justice Rehnquist as *Robert H. Jackson: Country Lawyer, Supreme Court Justice, America's Advocate* (Buffalo: William S. Hein, 2003).

36. Letter to Philip Kurland (September 21, 1964), in Philip Kurland File, Frankfurter Papers, Reel 44, Box 73, LC.

37. Undated letter to Justice Jackson, Jackson Papers, Box 19, LC.

38. Ibid.

39. See Rehnquist, *Supreme Court,* chaps. 1 and 2.

40. Ibid., 77.

41. See Jill Lepore, "The Great Paper Caper: Someone Swiped Justice Frankfurter's Papers. What Else Has Gone Missing?" *New Yorker,* December 1, 2014; and Synder and Barrett, "Rehnquist's Missing Letter."

42. Prettyman, Lecture at the Chautauqua Institution.

43. Letter from E. Barrett Prettyman Jr., to Justice Felix Frankfurter (October 13, 1955), reprinted as an appendix in Snyder and Barrett, "Rehnquist's Missing Letter," 658; in Frankfurter Papers, File 6, Box 170, Reel 2, 327–331, HLS; and Frankfurter Papers, Box 194, Reel 94, 315–318, LC.

44. Interview quoted in Noah Feldman, *Scorpions: The Battles and Triumphs of FDR's Great Supreme Court Justices* (New York: Twelve Books, 2010), 393.

45. Warner Gardner was an assistant to Jackson in the solicitor general's office, and after the justice's death, he similarly recalled that "beneath his poise and his affability, was a reserved man; our acquaintanceship of many years included no degree of personal intimacy." Warner W. Gardner, "Government Attorney," *Columbia Law Review* 55 (1955), 438.

46. Paul Freund, *On Law and Justice* (Cambridge, Mass.: Harvard University Press, 1968), 181.

47. Memo (December 7, 1955), Frankfurter Papers, Box 177, File 1, HLS.

48. See O'Brien, *Storm Center,* 120–121; and Melvin I. Urofsky, *Louis D. Brandeis: A Life* (New York: Pantheon, 2009), 587.

49. See, e.g., Drew Pearson and Robert S. Allen, *The Nine Old Men* (New York: Doubleday, Doran, 1936).

50. William H. Rehnquist, "A Random Thought on the Segregation Cases," Jackson Papers, Box 184, LC.

51. See Rehnquist, *Supreme Court,* 36–37, 48–49, and 62.

52. James F. Byrnes, "The Supreme Court Must Be Curbed," *U.S. News &World Report,* May 18, 1956, 50, 52.

53. See O'Brien, *Storm Center,* 92; and James F. Byrnes, *All in One Lifetime* (New York: Harper & Brothers, 1958).

54. See letters and memos in Warren Papers, Boxes 353 and 574, LC.

55. "The Bright Young Men Behind the Bench," *U.S. News &World Report,* July 17, 1957, 45.

56. Ibid., 46.

57. "New Clerks Begin High Court Tasks: Recent Law Graduates Aid Justices with Their Facts but Not Their Decisions," *New York Times,* October 14, 1957.

58. Rehnquist, "Who Writes Decisions?," 74.

59. "Sway of Clerks on Court Cited," *New York Times,* December 10, 1957, 23.

60. William D. Rogers, "Clerks' Work Is 'Not Decisive of Ultimate Result'" *U.S. News &World Report,* February 21, 1958, 114.

61. William H. Rehnquist, "Another View: Clerks Might 'Influence' Some Actions," *U.S. News &World Report,* February 21, 1958, 116.

62. John C. Stennis, Speech in the Senate (May 6, 1958), reprinted as "Investigate Supreme Court 'Law Clerk' System?" *U.S. News &World Report,* May 16, 1958, 117. See also "Stennis Is Wary of Court's Clerks," *New York Times,* May 7, 1958.

63. See, e.g., Alexander M. Bickel, *Politics and the Warren Court* (New York: Harper & Row, 1955); Alexander M. Bickel, *The Least Dangerous Branch: The Supreme Court at the Bar of Politics* (New York: Bobbs-Merrill, 1962); and Philip B. Kurland, *Politics, the Constitution, and the Warren Court* (Chicago: University of Chicago Press, 1970).

64. Bickel, "The Court: An Indictment Analyzed."

65. Alexander Bickel, "Supreme Court Law Clerks," Frankfurter Papers, Part II, Reel 31, 970, HLS.

66. Letter from Frankfurter to Bickel (August 28, 1955), Frankfurter Papers, Part II, Reel 31, 970, HLS.

67. Ibid.

68. William H. Rehnquist, "The Making of a Supreme Court Justice," *Harvard Law Record* 7 (October 8, 1959), 10.

69. See Herman J. Obermayer, *Rehnquist: A Personal Portrait of the Distinguished Chief Justice of the United States* (New York: Threshold Editions, 2009), 33–48; and, generally, John A. Jenkins, *The Partisan: The Life of William Rehnquist* (New York: Public Affairs, 2012).

70. *New York Times Company v. United States,* 403 U.S. 670 (1971). See Daniel Ellsberg, *Secrets: A Memoir of Vietnam and the Pentagon Papers* (New York: Viking Press,

2003); and David Rudenstine, *The Day the Presses Stopped: A History of the Pentagon Papers* (Berkeley: University of California Press, 1996).

71. John Dean, *The Rehnquist Choice: The Untold Story of the Nixon Appointment That Redefined the Supreme Court* (New York: Touchstone, 2001), 86.

72. Ibid., 27.

73. See, generally, John P. Frank, *Clement Haynsworth, the Senate, and the Supreme Court* (Charlottesville: University of Virginia Press, 1991).

74. See, generally, Robert Harris, *Decision: The Intense Minute by Minute Account of the Senate's Defeat of the Nomination of G. Harrold Carswell* (New York: Ballantine Books, 1972).

75. See Dean, *Rehnquist Choice,* 31–240; and, generally, Henry J. Abraham, *Justices, Presidents, and Senators: A History of the U.S. Supreme Court Appointments from Washington to Bush II,* 5th ed. (Lanham, Md.: Rowman & Littlefield, 2008), 233–274.

76. Abraham, *Justices, Presidents, and Senators,* 199–264; and Jenkins, *Partisan,* 103–136.

77. Quoted in Dean, *Rehnquist Choice,* 191.

78. Quoted in Abraham, *Justices, Presidents, and Senators,* 252.

79. See "Justice Letter on Haynsworth and the Bowling Lane Case," *Washington Post,* September 21, 1969, A8 (reprinting a letter to Senator James Eastland), and William H. Rehnquist, "Letter to the Editor: A Reply to Two Editorials on the Carswell Nomination," *Washington Post,* February 14, 1971, A14.

80. "Supreme Court: Memo from Rehnquist," *Newsweek,* December 6, 1971, 32. The memo is in Justice Jackson's Papers, Box 184, LC, and was introduced into the *Congressional Record—Senate,* 45,200 (December 7, 1971).

81. Quoted in John P. Mackenzie, "Controversy Deepens over Rehnquist Memo," *Washington Post,* December 10, 1971, A6.

82. Ibid.

83. Letter from Elsie Douglas to Senator Edward M. Kennedy, August 8, 1986, Joseph Rauh Papers, Box 287, Folder 5, LC, quoted in Snyder and Barrett, "Rehnquist's Missing Letter," 633.

84. See "The Brooke Memorandum," in *Congressional Record,* 45816-16 (December 9, 1971), reprinted in Mark Whitman, ed., *The Record of* Brown v. Board of Education (Princeton, N.J.: Markus Wiener, 1993), 200–204.

85. Excerpted in Dean, *Rehnquist Choice,* 276.

86. Quoted in ibid., 275.

87. *Congressional Record—Senate,* 45,440 (December 8, 1971).

88. Dean, *Rehnquist Choice,* 276–277.

89. *Congressional Record—Senate,* 92nd Cong., 1st Sess., 46,115–46,116 (December 10, 1971).

90. Quoted and further discussed in Laura K. Ray, "A Law Clerk and His Justice: What William Rehnquist Did Not Learn from Robert Jackson," *Indiana Law Review* 29 (1996), 535, 555.

91. Anthony Lewis, "Ex-Colleague Says Rehnquist Opposed Segregation," *New York Times,* December 10, 1971, A28, reprinted in *Congressional Record—Senate,* 46,112.

92. Cronson's memo is in Jackson Papers, Box 184, LC.

93. *District of Columbia v. John R. Thompson, Co.,* 346 U.S. 100 (1953).

94. See, for example, Senator Bayh's comments and inserts in the *Congressional Record—Senate,* 117th Cong., 45,815–45,816 and 45,803–45,805; as well as, more generally, U.S. Congress, 92nd Cong., 1st Sess., Senate Committee on the Judiciary, *Hearings on the Nominations of William H. Rehnquist of Arizona, and Lewis F. Powell, Jr., of Virginia, to be Associate Justices of the Supreme Court of the United States, November 3, 4, 8, 9 and 10, 1971* (Washington, D.C.: Government Printing Office, 1971); as well as Senate Judiciary Committee, *Nomination of William H. Rehnquist, S. Exec. Doc. No.* 16, reprinted in Roy M. Mersky and J. Myron Jacobstein, eds., *The Supreme Court of the United States: Hearings and Reports on Successful and Unsuccessful Nominations of Supreme Court Justices by the Senate Judiciary Committee, 1916–1975,* vol. 8 (Buffalo, N.Y.: W. S. Hein, 1975).

95. See, e.g., Richard Kluger, *Simple Justice: The History of* Brown v. Board of Education *and the Struggle for Racial Equality* (New York: Knopf, 1975), 606–608; Ray, "A Law Clerk and His Justice," 554–555; Brad Snyder, "How Conservatives Canonized *Brown v. Board of Education,*" *Rutgers Law Review* 52 (2000), 383, 442–443; Vincent Bugliosi, *The Betrayal of America: How the Supreme Court Undermined the Constitution and Chose Our President* (New York: Nation Books, 2009), 82–85; generally, S. Sidney Ulmer, "Earl Warren and the *Brown* Decision," *Journal of Politics* 33 (1971), 689.

96. Kluger, *Simple Justice,* 604–609.

97. Cronson letter to Rehnquist (December 9, 1975), and other correspondence, in William H. Rehnquist Papers, Box 107, HIA. Cronson's proposed memorandum is also reproduced in Peppers and Ward, *In Chambers,* 413–415.

98. A clerk for Justice Reed in the 1953 term confirms their lively lunchtime meetings; see John Fassett, "Mr. Justice Reed and *Brown v. Board of Education,*" *Yearbook of the Supreme Court Historical Society* 1986 (1986), 48, 53.

99. See Kluger, *Simple Justice,* 606–607.

100. John A. Jenkins, "The Partisan," *New York Times Magazine* 3 (March 3, 1985). See also Jenkins, *Partisan.*

101. For a list of solo dissenters from 1953 to 1991, see L. Epstein, J. Segal, H. Spaeth, and T. Walker, eds., *The Supreme Court Compendium: Data, Decisions and Developments,* 2nd ed. (Washington, D.C.: C.Q. Press, 2001), 502.

102. *Terry v. Adams,* 345 U.S. 461 (1953).

103. In *Nixon v. Herndon,* 273 U.S. 536 (1927), the Court struck down all-white Democratic primary elections authorized by the state; *Nixon v. Condon,* 286 U.S. 73 (1932), invalidated white primaries authorized by a state Democratic party's executive committee; and *Smith v. Allwright,* 321 U.S. 649 (1949), struck down all-white primaries authorized by a state party-membership resolution. These rulings dealt with governmental or public exclusion of African Americans voting. *Terry v. Adams* involved a preprimary Democratic candidate nominating process by a private political "club" in Texas, the Jaybird Democratic Association.

104. Cert. memo on *Terry v. Adams,* Jackson Papers, Box 179, LC.

105. Jackson's draft opinion is in ibid. For further discussion, see Brad Snyder, "What Would Justice Holmes Do? Rehnquist's *Plessy* Memo, Majoritarianism, and *Parents Involved,*" *Ohio State Law Journal* 69 (2008), 873, 883–884.

106. *Nomination of Justice William Hubbs Rehnquist: Hearings before the Senate Com-*

mittee on the Judiciary, 99th Cong., 2nd Sess. (Washington, D.C.: U.S. Government Publications Office, 1986), 322–323.

107. *Rehnquist Nomination Hearings* 1986, 276–277.

108. Ibid., 296.

109. Besides Dean, *Rehnquist Choice,* see Bugliosi, *Betrayal of America.*

110. See Bernard Schwartz, "Chief Justice Rehnquist, Justice Jackson, and the *Brown* Case," *Supreme Court Review* 1988 (1988), 245.

111. See, e.g., Kluger, *Simple Justice,* 607–609; Michael Klarman, *From Jim Crow to Civil Rights: The Supreme Court and the Struggle for Racial Equality* (New York: Oxford University Press, 2004), 304–309; Ray, "A Law Clerk and His Justice," 553–559; Gregory Chernack, "The Clash of Two Worlds: Justice Robert H. Jackson, Institutional Pragmatism, and *Brown,*" *Temple Law Review* 72 (1999), 51, 54n21. But see also Dennis Hutchinson, "Unanimity and Desegregation: Decisionmaking in the Supreme Court, 1948–1958," *Georgetown Law Journal* 68 (1979), 1.

112. Kluger, *Simple Justice,* 609.

113. Mark Tushnet and Katya Lezin, "What Really Happened in *Brown v. Board of Education,*" *Columbia Law Review* 91 (1991), 1867, 1911. See also Mark Tushnet, *A Court Divided: The Rehnquist Court and the Future of Constitutional Law* (New York: Norton, 2005), 20–21.

114. See Saul Brenner, "The Memos of Supreme Court Law Clerk William Rehnquist: Conservative Tracts or Mirrors of His Justice's Mind?" *Judicature* 76 (1993), 77. But for an analysis contrariwise, see Ray, "A Law Clerk and His Justice," 557–558.

115. See, generally, William Harbaugh, *Lawyer's Lawyer: The Life of John W. Davis* (New York: Oxford University Press, 1973).

116. See Synder, "What Would Justice Holmes Do?"

117. First draft of opinion, in Jackson Papers, Box 184, LC.

118. Note of Elsie Douglas, Jackson Papers, Box 184, and author interview with E. Barrett Prettyman Jr., Hogan & Hartson (Washington, D.C., March 1987).

119. See Felix Frankfurter letter to Phillip Kurland (September 21, 1964), Kurland File, Frankfurter Papers, Box 73, Reel 44, LC; and E. Barrett Prettyman File, Jackson Papers, Box 18, LC.

120. Correspondence (November 10, 1952), Jackson Papers, Box 18, LC.

121. E. Barrett Prettyman Jr., "On Becoming a Law Clerk," speech (March 14, 2012), Robert H. Jackson Center, available on YouTube.

122. See Kluger, *Simple Justice,* 691–696; and "Notes re Segregation Decision" (December 15, 1954), E. Barrett Prettyman Jr., Papers, MS 86-5, Special Collections, University of Virginia Law School Library (UVA).

123. Earl Warren, "To The Members of the Court," May 7, 1954, Jackson Papers, Box 184, LC.

124. *Brown v. Board of Education,* 347 U.S. 483 (1954), 490. See also Interview with Cullen Couch, "Behind the Scenes of *Brown,* E. Barrett Prettyman, Jr., '53 Sensed History in the Making," *University of Virginia Lawyer* 1 (Fall 2004); and Prettyman, "Notes re Segregation Decision" (December, 15, 1954), Prettyman Papers, UVA.

125. Prettyman, "Notes re Segregation Decision," Prettyman Papers, UVA.

126. Prettyman Memo, "Re Nos. 1–4" (undated), Jackson Papers, Box 184, LC.

127. Ibid. See also Prettyman's more detained recommendations on the formu-

lation of a judicial decree in "Notes re Segregation Cases" (undated), Jackson Paper, Box 184, LC.

128. Prettyman, "Re Nos. 1–4," Jackson Papers, LC.

129. See E. Barrett Prettyman Jr., "Thoughts on Justice Jackson's 'Unpublished Opinion,'" Athenaeum Hotel, Chautauqua, New York (November 8, 2003), available at the Robert H. Jackson Center, http://www.roberthjackson.org/.

130. Kluger, *Simple Justice,* 880–881.

131. *Brown v. Board of Education (Brown II),* 349 U.S. 294 (1955).

CHAPTER 4. CROSSING THE RUBICON

1. For the contrary view, see, Mark Tushnet and Katya Lezin, "What Really Happened in *Brown v. Board of Education,*" *Columbia Law Review* 91 (1991), 1867; and compare Dennis J. Hutchinson, "'The Achilles Heel' of the Constitution: Justice Jackson and the Japanese Exclusion Cases," *Supreme Court Review* 2002 (2002), 455.

2. See Dennis J. Hutchinson, "Unanimity and Desegregation: Decisionmaking in the Supreme Court, 1948–1958," *Georgetown Law Journal* 69 (1979), 1, 39–41 and note 331.

3. *Korematsu v. United States,* 323 U.S. 214 (1944). See also Hutchinson, "Achilles Heel," 456–457 and note 10.

4. Unpublished opinion for *Brown v. Board of Education,* fifth draft, Robert H. Jackson Papers, Box 184, LC. All subsequent quotations, unless otherwise noted, are to these drafts.

5. See the discussion of Jackson's literary style and background in Chapter 1.

6. *West Virginia State Board of Education v. Barnette,* 319 U.S. 624 (1943), further discussed in Chapter 1.

7. Robert H. Jackson, *The Supreme Court in the American System of Government* (Cambridge, Mass.: Harvard University Press, 1955), 57–58.

8. See Raoul Berger, *Government by the Judiciary: The Transformation of the Fourteenth Amendment* (Cambridge, Mass.: Harvard University Press, 1977); Robert H. Bork, *The Tempting of America: The Political Seduction of The Law* (New York: Free Press, 1990); and Steven Calabresi, ed., *Originalism: A Quarter-Century of Debate* (Washington, D.C.: Regnery Publishing, 2007); and compare Leonard Levy, *Original Intent and the Framers' Constitution* (New York: Macmillan, 1988); and Jack Rakove, *Original Meanings: Politics and Ideas in the Making of the Constitution* (New York: Knopf, 1997). See also David M. O'Brien, ed., *Judges on Judging: Views from the Bench,* 5th ed. (Washington, D.C.: C.Q. Press, 2016), especially Judge Robert H. Bork, "Tradition and Morality in Constitutional Law," 197–203; Justice Antonin Scalia, "Originalism: The Lesser Evil," 209–217; Justice Clarence Thomas, "Judging," 218–224; and compare Justice Thurgood Marshall, "The Constitution: A Living Document," 225–229; Justice William J. Brennan, "The Constitution of the United States: Contemporary Ratification," 230–241; Justice John Paul Stevens, "Originalism and History," 242–246; and Justice David H. Souter, "On Constitutional Interpretation," 247–254.

9. See Benjamin N. Cardozo, *The Nature of the Judicial Process* (New Haven, Conn.: Yale University Press, 1921); Beryl Harold Levy, ed., *Cardozo and the Frontiers of Le-*

gal Thinking (New York: Oxford University Press, 1938); and, generally, Andrew L. Kaufman, *Cardozo* (Cambridge, Mass.: Harvard University Press, 1998).

10. Robert H. Jackson, *The Struggle for Judicial Supremacy* (New York: Knopf, 1941), x–xi.

11. Tushnet and Lezin, "What Really Happened in *Brown v. Board of Education*," 1880.

12. *Katz v. United States,* 389 U.S. 347 (1967) (Black, J., dis. op.); and *Griswold v. Connecticut,* 381 U.S. 479 (1965) (Black, J., dis. op.).

13. See correspondence with Charles Fairman, Felix Frankfurter Papers, Box 184, HLS. See also Richard L. Aynes, "Charles Fairman, Felix Frankfurter, and the Fourteenth Amendment," *Chicago-Kent Law Review* 70 (1995), 1197.

14. See the discussion in Chapter 2 and sources cited about the debate of the incorporation of the Bill of Rights into the Fourteenth Amendment's due process clause and application to the states; Charles Fairman File, Jackson Papers, Box 12, LC; and, generally, Pamela Brandwein, *Reconstructing Reconstruction: The Supreme Court and the Production of Historical Truth* (Durham, N.C.: Duke University Press, 1999).

15. *Missouri v. Holland,* 252 U.S. 416 (1920). See also Oliver Wendell Holmes, "The Path of Law," published originally in *Harvard Law Review* 10 (1897), 457, and reprinted in *Harvard Law Review* 110 (1997), 991; and O'Brien, *Judges on Judging,* 151. For an interesting exchange of views on the Holmesian position, see and compare Justice William H. Rehnquist, "The Notion of a Living Constitution," *Texas Law Review* 54 (1976), 693, with Judge William Wayne Justice, "A Relativistic Constitution," *University of Colorado Law Review* 52 (1980), 19, both excerpted and reprinted in *Judges on Judging,* 163–172 and 173–184.

16. See, generally, Raoul Berger, *Government by the Judiciary: The Transformation of the Fourteenth Amendment* (Cambridge, Mass.: Harvard University Press, 1977).

17. See, e.g., Justice Scalia's opinion for the Court in *Michael H. v. Gerald D.,* 491 U.S. 110 (1989); and his dissenting opinion in *McIntyre v. Ohio Elections Commission,* 514 U.S. 334 (1995).

18. See, generally, James F. Simon, *In His Own Image: The Supreme Court in Nixon's America* (Philadelphia: David McKay, 1974).

19. See, e.g., Ronald Dworkin, *Taking Rights Seriously* (Cambridge, Mass.: Harvard University Press, 1977), 131–149; Judge Richard A. Posner, "What Am I, a Potted Plant? The Case against Strict Constructionism" *New Republic* 197 (1987), 23, reprinted in O'Brien, *Judges on Judging,* 204–208; and Leonard Levy, *Against the Law: The Nixon Court and Criminal Justice* (New York: Harper & Row, 1974).

20. Brennan, "Constitution of the United States," 231 and 234–235; Marshall, "Constitution"; and, among other works, see, generally, David A. Strauss, *The Living Constitution* (New York: Oxford University Press, 2010).

21. Quoted and discussed in Roger K. Newman, *Hugo Black: A Biography* (New York: Pantheon, 1994), 431–432.

22. Learned Hand, *The Bill of Rights* (Cambridge, Mass.: Harvard University Press, 1962), 54–55, and further discussed in this chapter.

23. *Heart of Atlanta Motel, Inc. v. United States,* 379 U.S. 241 (1964), and *Katzenbach v. McClung,* 379 U.S. 294 (1964), and, more generally, Richard C. Cortner,

Civil Rights and Public Accommodations: The Heart of Atlanta Motel *and* McClung *Cases* (Lawrence: University Press of Kansas, 2001).

24. "Conference Notes of Justice Clark on the *Segregation Cases*" (December 13, 1952), Tom Clark Papers, UT (when the author went through the papers in 1984, they had not yet been processed and cataloged into boxes). The memo, however, is reprinted in Hutchinson, "Unanimity and Desegregation," 91–92.

25. See, e.g., Roscoe Pound, *An Introduction to the Philosophy of Law* (New Haven, Conn.: Yale University Press, 1922); and Bernard Schwartz, *Main Currents in American Legal Thought* (Durham, N.C.: Carolina Academic Press, 1993), 465–473.

26. James Reston, "A Sociological Decision," *New York Times,* May 18, 1954, A14.

27. J. Harvie Wilkinson, *From* Brown *to* Bakke: *The Supreme Court and School Integration, 1954–1978* (New York: Oxford University Press, 1979), 31.

28. See, e.g., Edmond Cahn, "Jurisprudence," *New York University Law Review* 30 (1957), 157; Kenneth B. Clark, "The Desegregation Cases: Criticism of the Social Scientist's Role," *Villanova Law Review* 5 (1959–1960), 224; Ernst Van Den Haag, "Social Science Testimony in the Desegregation Cases—A Reply to Professor Kenneth Clark," *Villanova Law Review* 6 (1960–1961), 69; and excerpts of articles and chapters on both sides of the debate over the use of social science, collected in Mark Whitman, ed., *Removing the Badge of Slavery: The Record of* Brown v. Board of Education (Princeton, N.J.: Markus Wiener, 1993). Also useful is Leon Friedman, ed., Brown v. Board of Education: *The Landmark Oral Argument before the Supreme Court* (New York: New Press, 1969); Philip Kurland and Gerard Casper, eds., *Landmark Briefs and Arguments of the Supreme Court of the United States,* vol. 49–49A (Arlington, Va.: University Publications of America, 1975); I. A. Newby, *Challenge to the Court: Social Scientists and the Defense of Segregation, 1954–1966* (Baton Rouge: Louisiana State University Press, 1967); and David L. Faigman, *Laboratory of Justice: The Supreme Court's 200 Year Struggle to Integrate Science and the Law* (New York: Times Books, 2004), 161–204.

29. Notes of Interview with Earl E. Pollock, "*Brown v. Board of Education,*" Richard Kluger Papers, Box 5, YU. Kluger tells it slightly differently in *Simple Justice: The History of* Brown v. Board of Education (New York: Knopf, 1975), 706.

30. *Dred Scott v. Sanford,* 19 How. (60 U.S.) 393 (1857).

31. Quoted in Kluger, *Simple Justice,* 706.

32. In addition to the discussion in the text and sources cited, see the similar discussion of Justice Burton's law clerks in Mary Frances Berry, *Stability, Security, and Continuity: Mr. Justice Burton and Decision-Making in the Supreme Court, 1945–1958* (Westport, Conn.: Greenwood Press, 1973).

33. Quoted in Kluger, *Simple Justice,* 321.

34. Quoted in ibid., 707 and 713.

35. Quoted in ibid., 706.

36. *Beauharnais v. Illinois,* 343 U.S. 250 (1952).

37. James F. Byrnes, "The Supreme Court Must Be Curbed," *U.S. News & World Report,* May 18, 1956, 50, 53–54, and 56.

38. *Ray v. Blair,* 343 U.S. 214 (1952).

39. See *Nixon v. Herndon,* 273 U.S. 536 (1927); *Nixon v. Condon,* 286 U.S. 73 (1932); *Smith v. Allwright,* 321 U.S. 649 (1949); and *Terry v. Adams,* 345 U.S. 461 (1953), discussed in Chapter 3.

40. Jackson, *Supreme Court*, 55.

41. Ibid., 11–13.

42. Letter from Frankfurter to Hand (February 13, 1958), Learned Hand Papers, Box 105D-23, HLS.

43. Earl Warren, *The Memoirs of Chief Justice Earl Warren* (New York: Doubleday, 1977), 286–287 (emphasis in the original).

44. Jackson, *Supreme Court*, 79–80 and 82.

45. Learned Hand, "The Spirit of Liberty" (1944), in *The Spirit of Liberty: Papers and Addresses of Learned Hand*, collected and ed. Irving Dillard (New York: Knopf, 1952), 189–190.

46. See, e.g., among many other articles and books, Lino Gralia, *Disaster by Decree* (Ithaca, N.Y.: Cornell University Press, 1976); and Numan Bentley, *The Rise of Massive Resistance: Race and Politics in the South during the 1950s* (Baton Rouge: Louisiana State University Press, 1969).

47. All of the decisions are discussed in Chapter 2.

48. See James Patterson, Brown v. Board of Education: *A Civil Rights Milestone and Is Troubled Legacy* (New York: Oxford University Press, 2001), xiii; and Jack Slater, "1954 Revisited," *Ebony* 29 (May 1974), 126.

49. George Frederick Zook, The President's Commission on Higher Education, *Higher Education for American Democracy: Report of the President's Commission on Higher Education* (Washington, D.C.: Government Printing Office, 1947), 2:31 and 2:35. See also John R. Thelin, *A History of American Higher Education* (Baltimore, Md.: Johns Hopkins University Press, 2004).

50. See *Jackson v. Alabama*, 72 So.2d 114 (Ala. Ct. App.), cert. denied, 72 So.2d 116 (Ala.), and cert. denied, 348 U.S. 888 (1954) (challenge to Alabama's antimiscegenation law); and *Naim v. Naim*, 87 S.E.2d 749 (Va.), vacated and remanded, 350 U.S. 891 (1955) (per curiam); the Virginia supreme court adhered to its prior ruling upholding the state's antimiscegenation law, 90 S.E. 849 (Va.), and motion for reconsideration was denied, 350 U.S. 985 (1956); further discussed below. See also Ed Cray, *Chief Justice: A Biography of Earl Warren* (New York: Simon & Schuster, 1997), 309–310.

51. See Del Dickson, "State Court Defiance and the Limits of Supreme Court Authority: *Williams v. Georgia* Revisited," *Yale Law Journal* 103 (1994), 1423; and E. Barrett Prettyman Jr., *Death and the Supreme Court* (New York: Harcourt, Brace & World, 1961). See also Bernard Schwartz, *Super Chief: Earl Warren and His Supreme Court—A Judicial Biography* (New York: New York University Press, 1983), 159.

52. *Pace v. Alabama*, 106 U.S. 583 (1883).

53. *Jackson v. Alabama*, 72 So.2d 114 (Ala. Ct. App.), cert. denied, 72 So.2d 116 (Ala.), and cert. denied, 348 U.S. 888 (1954).

54. "Memorandum from Justice Felix N. Frankfurter to the Conference on *Naim v. Naim*" (November 4, 1955), Frankfurter Papers, Box 249, LC; reprinted in Hutchinson, "Unanimity and Desegregation," 95–96, and discussed at 62–66.

55. Quoted and further discussed in Gregory Michael Dorr, "Principled Expediency: *Naim v. Naim* and the Supreme Court," *American Journal of Legal History* 42 (1988), 119, 156; and file on *Naim v. Naim,* Warren Papers, Box 369, LC.

56. Further discussed in Dorr, "Principled Expediency," 146; and Schwartz, *Super Chief,* 159–160.

57. *Naim v. Naim,* 350 U.S. 891 (1955).

58. *Naim v. Naim,* 197 Va. 734 (1956), 735.

59. "Virginia Rejects Order of U.S. Supreme Court," *Richmond News Leader,* January 18, 1956, A1.

60. The Southern Manifesto was published on March 11, 1956, and reprinted as "Text of 96 Congressmen's Declaration on Integration," *New York Times,* March 12, 1956, A10.

61. Conference of Chief Justices, *Report of the Committee on Federal–State Relationships as Affected by Judicial Decisions* (Chicago: Conference of Chief Justices, 1958).

62. See *Colegrove v. Green,* 328 U.S. 549 (1946). In Frankfurter's last year on the Court while ill, the Warren Court abandoned that doctrine in *Baker v. Carr,* 369 U.S. 186 (1962), and laid the foundation for "one person, one vote" and the "reapportionment revolution." See, generally, Gordon E. Baker, *The Reapportionment Revolution: Representation, Political Power, and the Supreme Court* (New York: Random House, 1967).

63. Letter of Justice Frankfurter to Judge Hand (February 13, 1958), Frankfurter Papers, Box 199, HLS.

64. Letter from Frankfurter to Learned Hand (September 17, 1957), Hand Papers, Box 105D-23, HLS.

65. Quoted in Walter Murphy, *The Elements of Judicial Strategy* (Chicago: University of Chicago Press, 1964), 193. The justice who told Murphy that, though it was certainly not his view, was undoubtedly Justice Douglas who was interviewed by Murphy numerous times. See William O. Douglas Interviews with Walter Murphy, MLPU. On Justice Black's position, see the draft of the per curiam opinion, *Naim v. Naim,* Frankfurter Papers, Box 86, HLS.

66. Letter to Frankfurter (September 9, 1957), Hand Papers, Box 105D-23, HLS.

67. Alexander Bickel, "The Original Understanding and the Segregation Decision," *Harvard Law Review* 69 (1955), 1, 56.

68. Ibid., and for a brief analysis of the article's conclusion on what was and what was not "inconclusive" about the history of the Fourteenth Amendment compared with the Court's opinion in *Brown,* see the article reprinted as an appendix in Alexander Bickel, *Politics and the Warren Court* (New York: Harper & Row, 1965), 260–261.

69. Letter to Frankfurter (September 25, 1957), Hand Papers, HLS.

70. See, e.g., Herbert Wechsler, "Toward Neutral Principles of Constitutional Law," *Harvard Law Review* 73 (1959), 1, especially 34. Wechsler disagrees with Judge Hand's criticism of *Brown* in the 1958 Oliver Wendell Holmes Lecture at Harvard Law School, but he shares his devotion to the "rule of law" and attempts to make sense of the scope and neutral application of the ruling in *Brown.*

71. See Justice Scalia's dissenting opinion in *Lawrence v. Texas,* 539 U.S. 558 (2003) (striking down Texas's law criminalizing homosexual sodomy); and *Obergefell v. Hodges,* 135 S.Ct. 2584 (2015) (striking down state bans on same-sex marriages).

72. Letter from Frankfurter to Hand (September 27, 1957), Hand Papers, HLS.

73. Gerald Gunther, *Learned Hand: The Man and the Judge* (Cambridge, Mass.: Harvard University Press, 1994), 665–672.

74. Hand, *Bill of Rights.*

75. Letter to Frankfurter (October 10, 1957), Hand Papers, Box 105D-23, HLS.

76. Hand, *Bill of Rights,* 54–55.

77. See, e.g., Dorothy Thompson, "Judge Hand on Judicial Power: Famed Jurist Seen Supporting Argument Integration Decision Was a Usurpation," *Evening Star* (Washington, D.C.), February 12, 1958, A21; and Maurice Goldbloom, "The Bill of Rights, by Learned Hand," *Commentary,* June 1, 1958, https://www.comment arymagazine.com/.

78. Letter from Frankfurter to Learned Hand (October 12, 1957), quoting *Brown v. Board of Education,* 495, Hand Papers, Box 105D-23, HLS.

79. Letter from Justice Frankfurter to Judge Hand (February 13, 1958), Frankfurter Papers, Box 199, HLS.

80. Alexander Bickel, *The Least Dangerous Branch: The Supreme Court at the Bar of Politics* (Indianapolis, Ind.: Bobbs-Merrill, 1962), 174.

81. Wechsler, "Toward Neutral Principles."

82. Herbert Wechsler, "Neutral Principles of Constitutional Law," in *Principles, Politics, and Fundamental Law: Selected Essays* (Cambridge, Mass.: Harvard University Press, 1961), 47.

83. Hand, *Bill of Rights,* 70.

84. For a discussion of the difference between hedgehogs and foxes, see Isaiah Berlin, *The Hedgehog and the Fox,* 2nd ed. (Princeton, N.J.: Princeton University Press, 2013); and Ronald Dworkin, *Justice for Hedgehogs* (Cambridge: Oxford University Press, 2011). Dworkin was one of Judge Hand's most highly regarded former law clerks, and later a professor at, simultaneously, Oxford University and New York University Law School. Whereas Hand was cautious and often deeply torn, Dworkin confidently defended taking rights seriously. See, e.g., his *Taking Rights Seriously* (Cambridge: Oxford University Press, 1977); *A Matter of Principle* (Cambridge, Mass.: Harvard University Press, 1985); and *Law's Empire* (Cambridge: Oxford University Press, 1986).

85. See, e.g., Jack Bass, *Unlikely Heroes* (New York: Simon & Schuster, 1981); Jack Peltason, *Fifty-Eight Lonely Men: Southern Federal Judges and School Desegregation* (New York: Harcourt, Brace & World, 1961); Benjamin Muse, *Ten Years of Prelude: The Story of Integration since the Supreme Court's 1954 Decision* (New York: Viking Press, 1964); James T. Patterson, *Brown v. Board of Education;* and Stephen Wasby, Anthony D'Amato, and Rosemary Metrailer, *Desegregation from Brown to Alexander: An Exploration of Supreme Court Strategies* (Carbondale: Southern Illinois University Press, 1977).

86. See Gerlad Rosenberg, *The Hollow Hope: Can Courts Bring About Social Change?,* 2nd ed. (Chicago: University of Chicago Press, 2009); Donald Horowitz, *Courts and Social Change* (Washington, D.C.: Brookings Institution, 1977); and Mark Kozlowski, *The Myth of the Imperial Judiciary: Why the Right Is Wrong about the Courts* (New York: New York University Press, 2003).

87. See, e.g., Gary Orfield and Carole Ashkinaze, *The Closing Door: Conservative Policy and Black Opportunity* (Chicago: University of Chicago Press, 1991); and Gary

Orfield and Susan Eaton, *Dismantling Desegregation: The Quiet Reversal of* Brown v. Board of Education (New York: New Press, 1996).

88. See, generally, Bass, *Unlikely Heroes;* and Peltason, *Fifty-Eight Lonely Men.*

89. Warren, *Memoirs,* 300.

90. For a further discussion see the author's articles, "The Seduction of the Judiciary: Social Science and the Courts," *Judicature* 64 (1980), 8; and "Of Myths, Motivations, and Justifications: A Postscript on Social Science and the Law," *Judicature* 64 (1980), 285.

91. See, e.g., David Faigman, "Normative Constitutional Fact-Finding: Exploring the Empirical Component of Constitutional Interpretation," *University of Pennsylvania Law Review* 139 (1991), 541; and Morgan Marietta and Tyler Farley, "The Prevalence and Justification of Social Facts in Landmark Decisions of the Supreme Court," *Journal of Law and Courts* 6 (Fall 2016), 243.

92. *Planned Parenthood of Southeastern Pennsylvania v. Casey,* 505 U.S. 835 (1992).

93. *Roe v. Wade,* 410 U.S. 113 (1973).

94. *Lochner v. New York,* 198 U.S. 45 (1905).

95. *West Coast Hotel Co. v. Parrish,* 300 U.S. 379 (1937).

96. *Planned Parenthood of Southeastern Pennsylvania v. Casey,* 861–862, quoting Jackson, *Struggle for Judicial Supremacy,* 85. For criticism of *Casey's* analogies and reliance on Jackson's arguments, see Gregory Chernack, "The Clash of Two Worlds: Justice Robert H. Jackson, Institutional Pragmatism, and *Brown," Temple Law Review* 72 (1999), 51, 104. However, Chernack concedes, "Although it did not focus on the factual changes that Jackson did, the *Casey* Court nevertheless tried to provide an explanation similar to Jackson's" (105).

97. *Casey,* 855. See also Justice Souter's 2010 Harvard Law School Commencement Address, "On Constitutional Interpretation," in O'Brien, *Judges on Judging,* 247–254.

98. *Lawrence v. Texas,* 539 U.S. 558 (2003).

99. *Bowers v. Hardwick,* 478 U.S. 186 (1986).

100. *Obergefell v. Hodges,* 135 S.Ct. 2584 (2015).

101. Jackson's prescient observation has proven correct. According to the U.S. Bureau of the Census, interracial marriages constituted only 0.4 percent of all marriages in 1960, but after the Court's ruling in *Loving v. Virginia,* 388 U.S. 1 (1967), striking down antimiscegenation laws, interracial marriages rose to 0.7 in 1970 and 2.0 percent in 1980, and remained about the same in 1990. See http://www.census/gov/population/socdemo/race/interractabl.txt. By 2013, interracial marriages rose to 12 percent, according to the Pew Research Center; see Wendy Wang, "Interracial Marriage: Who Is 'Marrying Out'?" *Pew Research,* June 12, 2015, http://www.pewresearch.org/.

102. See Harvey Applebaum, "Miscegenation Statutes: A Constitutional and Social Problem," *Georgetown Law Journal* 53 (1964), 49, 51.

103. For a list of the statutes, see, e.g., ibid., 51–53; and Notes, "The Constitutionality of Anti-Miscegenation Statutes," *Yale Law Journal* 58 (1949), 472, 480–481.

104. "Memorandum on *Sweatt* and *McLaurin* from Mr. Justice Clark to the Conference" (April 7, 1950), Frankfurter Papers, Box 218, LC; and reprinted in Hutchinson, "Unanimity and Desegregation," 89–90.

105. Justice Reed in conference discussion, in Conference notes of Justices Burton, Douglas, Jackson, and Clark, compiled and reprinted in Del Dickson, ed., *The Supreme Court in Conference, 1940–1985* (New York: Oxford University Press, 2001), 665–666. Reed's position is further discussed in Chapter 2.

106. Conference Notes, "No. 8 *Brown v. Board of Education*" (December 13, 1952), William O. Douglas Papers, Box 1150, LC.

107. Ibid.

108. Quoted and discussed in David M. O'Brien, *Storm Center: The Supreme Court in American Politics,* 11th ed. (New York: Norton, 2017), in chap. 2.

109. For different perspectives—cultural, social, historical, and legal—on state antimiscegenation laws, see the following: Notes, "Constitutionality of Anti-Miscegenation Statutes"; Applebaum, "Miscegenation Statutes"; Walter Waddington, "The *Loving* Case: Virginia's Anti-Miscegenation Statute in Historical Perspective," *Virginia Law Review* 52 (1966), 1189; Peter Wallenstein, "Race, Marriage, and the Supreme Court from *Pace v. Alabama* (1883) to *Virginia v. Loving* (1967)," *Journal of Supreme Court History* 1998 (1998), 65; Gregory Michael Dorr, *Segregation's Science: Eugenics and Society in Virginia* (Charlottesville: University of Virginia Press, 2008); Randall Kennedy, *Interracial Intimacies: Sex, Marriage, Identity, and Adoption* (New York: Pantheon Books, 2003); Kevin Maillard and Rose Culson Villazoe, eds., *Loving v. Virginia in a Post-Racial World: Rethinking Race, Sex, and Marriage* (New York: Cambridge University Press, 2012); Phyl Newbeck, *Virginia Hasn't Always Been for Lovers: Interracial Marriage Bans and the Case of Richard and Mildred Loving* (Carbondale: Southern Illinois University Press, 2008); Peggy Pascoe, *What Comes Naturally: Miscegenation Law in the Making of Race in America* (New York: Oxford University Press, 2009); Werner Sollars, *Interracialism: Black–White Intermarriage in American History, Literature, and Law* (New York: Oxford University Press, 200); Peter Wallenstein, *Tell the Court I Love My Wife: Marriage and Law—An American History* (New York: Palgrave-Macmillan, 2002); and Peter Wallenstein, *Race, Sex, and the Freedom to Marry:* Loving v. Virginia (Lawrence: University Press of Kansas, 2014).

110. See also, e.g., *Jackson v. State,* 37 Ala. App. 519 (1954), *Jackson v. State,* 260 Ala. 698 (1954); and *Jackson v. Alabama,* 348 U.S. 888 (1954). For further discussion, see Peter Wallenstein, "Race, Marriage, and the Law of Freedom: Alabama and Virginia, 1860s–1960s," *Chicago-Kent Law Review* 70 (1994), 371, 414–416.

111. Applebaum, "Miscegenation Statutes," 50.

112. *Perez v. Sharp,* 32 Cal. 2d 711, 198 P. 2d 17 (1948).

113. *Loving v. Virginia,* 388 U.S. 1 (1967). See, generally, Wallenstein, *Tell the Court I Love My Wife.*

114. Memo on *Jackson v. State,* Douglas Papers, Box 1156, LC.

115. Philip Elman and Norman Silber, "The Solicitor General's Office, Justice Frankfurter, and Civil Rights Litigation, 1946–1960: An Oral History," *Harvard Law Review* 100 (1997), 817, 845–847.

116. *Loving v. Virginia,* 388 U.S. 1 (1967), 9 (quoting *Brown v. Board of Education*).

117. See the discussion in the text at supra note.

118. See, e.g., R. Carter Pittman, "The Fourteenth Amendment: Its Intended Effect on Anti-Miscegenation Laws," *North Carolina Law Review* 43 (1964), 92, 100–107; and Applebaum, "Miscegenation Statutes."

119. See Pittman, "Fourteenth Amendment," 104–107.

120. Myrdal, *American Dilemma*, vol. 2, 575–576; also reprinted in Mark Whitman, ed., *Removing the Badge of Slavery: The Record of* Brown v. Board of Education (Princeton, N.J.: Markus Wiener, 1993), 25.

121. Myrdal, *American Dilemma*, vol. 1, 27.

122. President's Committee on Civil Rights, *To Secure These Rights* (New York: Simon & Schuster, 1947), 79.

123. *Shelley v. Kraemer,* 334 U.S. 1 (1948); and Tom C. Clark, *Prejudice and Property: An Historic Brief against Racial Covenants* (Washington, D.C.: Public Affairs Press, 1948).

124. See, generally, Robert H. Jackson, *The Case against the Nazi War Criminals* (New York: Knopf, 1946); and Robert H. Jackson, *The Nurnberg Case* (New York: Knopf, 1945). See also Paul Freund, "Individual and Commonwealth in the Thought of Mr. Justice Jackson," in *On Law and Justice* (Cambridge, Mass.: Harvard University Press, 1968), 172.

125. Felix Frankfurter, "Foreword," *Columbia Law Review* 55 (1955), 435, 435.

126. Article 16 of the United Nations Universal Declaration of Human Rights provides that "men and women of full age, without limitation due to race, nationality or religion, have the right to marry and found a family."

127. See, e.g., Constance Baker Motley, "The Historical Setting of *Brown* and Its Impact on the Supreme Court Decision," *Fordham Law Review* 61 (1992), 9, 12; and, generally, Mary Dudziak, *Cold War Civil Rights: Race and the Image of American Democracy* (Princeton, N.J.: Princeton University Press, 2002).

128. The letter and memos from John Fassett are reproduced and discussed in "Mr. Justice Reed and *Brown v. Board of Education*," *Yearbook of the Supreme Court Historical Society* 1986 (1986), 48, 53–55.

129. The Burger Court, however, rejected such a claim in *San Antonio Independent School District v. Rodriguez,* 411 U.S. 2 (1973).

130. See Hope Franklin, "Jim Crow Goes to School: The Genesis of Legal Segregation in Southern Schools," *Southern Atlantic Quarterly* 58 (1959), 225; and, more generally, John Hope Franklin, *From Slavery to Freedom: A History of African Americans,* 9th ed. (New York: McGraw-Hill, 2010).

131. *Brown v. Board of Education of Topeka, Kansas (Brown II),* 349 U.S. 294 (1955).

132. See "Memorandum on the Segregation Decree: 1955 & Updated," Frankfurter Papers, Box 219, Reel 139, 245, LC; and Warren Papers, Box 574, LC.

133. In *Virginia v. West Virginia,* 222 U.S. 17 (1911), 19–20, Justice Holmes observes, "It is enough if it proceeds, in the language of the English Chancery, with all deliberate speed." In correspondence with Frederick Pollock, referring to *United States v. Shipp,* 203 U.S. 563 (1906), and 214 U.S. 386 (1909), Holmes also observes, "In your chancery's delightful phrase, with all deliberate speed." Letter (March 7, 109), reprinted in Mark deWolfe Howe, ed., *Holmes–Pollock Letters: The Correspondence of Mr. Justice Holmes and Sir Frederick Pollock, 1874–1932,* vol. 1 (Cambridge, Mass.: Harvard University Press, 1946), 152. The phrase, however, apparently was not an English chancery phrase but from an 1893 poem by Francis Thompson; see Kluger, *Simple Justice,* 743–744; and Jim Chen, "Poetic Justice," *Cardozo Law Review* 28 (2006), 581, 586.

134. See transcript of argument of Archibald G. Robinson, reprinted in Kurland and Casper, *Landmark Briefs and Arguments,* vol. 49A, 39.

135. For further discussion, see Kluger, *Simple Justice,* 741–757; and Klarman, *From Jim Crow to Civil Rights: The Supreme Court and the Struggle for Racial Equality* (New York: Oxford University Press, 2004), 312–325.

136. Quoted and discussed in Mark Tushnet, *Making Civil Rights Law: Thurgood Marshall and the Supreme Court, 1936–1961* (New York: Oxford University Press, 1994), 244 and 228.

137. Chief Justice Warren's Conference Notes, Warren Papers, Box 574, LC. See also Newman, *Hugo Black,* 439–440.

138. "Memorandum" (April 28, 1955) and "Outline of Possible Provisions for Decree" (undated), Warren Papers, Box 574, LC.

139. Letter to Chief Justice Warren (May 24, 1955), Warren Papers, Box 574, LC.

140. Letter from Justice Frankfurter to Judge Learned Hand (September 8, 1957), Hand Papers, Box 105D-23, HLS.

141. *Giles v. Harris,* 289 U.S. 475 (1903).

142. John Fassett, "Memo to Justice Reed re Integration Materials," in Stanley Reed Papers, Box 331, UK; also reproduced in John D. Fassett, *New Deal Justice: The Life of Stanley Reed of Kentucky* (New York: Vantage Press, 1994), 577.

143. Dennis J. Hutchinson, "*Brown v. Board of Education,*" in *The Oxford Companion to the Supreme Court of the United States,* 2nd ed., ed. Kermit Hall (New York: Oxford University Press, 2005), 112.

CHAPTER 5. THIS IS THE END

1. In the second draft of the unpublished opinion, for example, there was a five-page section, "Judicial and Legislative Powers Compared," which remained in the third draft, but which was then shortened and subsequently dropped as a section in the opinion.

2. By comparison, the third, fourth, and fifth drafts each include five-page sections on "The Decree."

3. For that suggestion, see Jeffrey Hockett, "Justice Robert H. Jackson and Segregation: A Study of the Limitations and Proper Basis of Judicial Action," in *Black, White, and Brown: The Landmark School Desegregation Case in Retrospective,* ed. Clare Cushman and Melvin Urofsky (Washington, D.C.: C.Q. Press, 2004), 89.

4. Hockett discusses this important distinction in ibid., 96 and 104–105.

5. See the discussion of Prettyman's reactions to Jackson's last draft in Chapter 3.

6. For further discussion, see Chapter 4 on the exchanges between Justice Frankfurter and Judge Hand on what *Brown* meant.

7. Hockett, "Justice Robert H. Jackson and Segregation," 104–105.

8. *Loving v. Virginia,* 388 U.S. 1 (1967).

9. Justice Douglas's Conference Notes on *Loving v. Virginia* are published in Del Dickson, *The Supreme Court in Conference, 1940–1985* (New York: Oxford University Press, 2001), 695–696.

10. "Dear Chief" Letter (May 31, 1967), Byron White Papers, Box 105, LC.

11. *McLaughlin v. Florida,* 379 U.S. 184 (1964).

12. See *McLaughlin v. Florida* File, White Papers, Box 54, LC.

13. Justice Stewart concurring in *Loving,* quoting his concurrence in *McLaughlin v. Florida,* 379 U.S. 184, 198. See also Potter Stewart Papers, Folder No. 287, Box 33, YU.

14. Hockett, "Justice Robert H. Jackson and Segregation," 103–104.

15. Ibid., 104.

16. Gregory Chernack, "The Clash of Two Worlds: Justice Robert H. Jackson, Institutional Pragmatism, and *Brown*," *Temple Law Review* 72 (1999), 51, 101.

17. As Hockett argues, "Jackson did not [sufficiently] differentiate between the concerns of those opposed to and those in support of segregation," and consequently "asserted that this struggle had two sides, both of which made legitimate claims." Hockett, "Justice Robert H. Jackson and Segregation," 93.

18. Chernack, "Clash of Two Worlds," 106. See also Mark Tushnet and Katya Lezin, "What Really Happened in *Brown v. Board of Education*," *Columbia Law Review* 91 (1991), 1867, 1918.

19. Paul Freund, *The Supreme Court of the United States: Its Business, Purposes, and Performance* (Cleveland: World Publishing, 1961), 172.

20. Ibid., 173.

21. Hockett, "Justice Robert H. Jackson and Segregation," 100, makes the same point.

22. Robert H. Jackson, *The Struggle for Judicial Supremacy* (New York: Knopf, 1941), xv (emphasis in original).

CHAPTER 7. *BROWN V. BOARD OF EDUCATION* *OF TOPEKA, KANSAS*

*Together with No. 2, *Briggs et al. v. Elliott et al.,* on appeal from the United States District Court for the Eastern District of South Carolina, argued December 9–10, 1952, reargued December 7–8, 1953; No. 4, *Davis et al. v. County School Board of Prince Edward County, Virginia, et al.,* on appeal from the United States District Court for the Eastern District of Virginia, argued December 10, 1952, reargued December 7–8, 1953, and No. 10, *Gebhart et al. v. Belton et al.,* on *certiorari* to the Supreme Court of Delaware, argued December 11, 1952, reargued December 9, 1953.

1. In the Kansas case, *Brown v. Board of Education,* the plaintiffs are Negro children of elementary school age residing in Topeka. They brought this action in the United States District Court for the District of Kansas to enjoin enforcement of a Kansas statute which permits, but does not require, cities of more than 15,000 population to maintain separate school facilities for Negro and white students. Pursuant to that authority, the Topeka Board of Education elected to establish segregated elementary schools.

Other public schools in the community, however, are operated on a nonsegregated basis. The three-judge District Court . . . found that segregation in public education has a detrimental effect upon Negro children, but denied relief on the ground that the Negro and white schools were substantially equal with respect to buildings, transportation, curricula, and educational qualifications of teachers. The case is here on direct appeal.

In the South Carolina case, *Briggs v. Elliott,* the plaintiffs are Negro children of both elementary and high school age residing in Clarendon County. They brought this action in the United States District Court for the Eastern District of South Carolina to enjoin enforcement of provisions in the state constitution and statutory code which require the segregation of Negroes and whites in public schools. The three-judge District Court . . . denied the requested relief. The court found that the Negro schools were inferior to the white schools, and ordered the defendants to begin immediately to equalize the facilities. But the court sustained the validity of the contested provisions and denied the plaintiffs admission to the white schools during the equalization program. This Court vacated the District Court's judgment and remanded the case for the purpose of obtaining the court's views on a report filed by the defendants concerning the progress made in the equalization program. On remand, the District Court found that substantial equality had been achieved except for buildings and that the defendants were proceeding to rectify this inequality as well. The case is again here on direct appeal. . . .

In the Virginia case, *Davis v. County School Board,* the plaintiffs are Negro children of high school age residing in Prince Edward County. They brought this action in the United States District Court for the Eastern District of Virginia to enjoin enforcement of provisions in the state constitution and statutory code which require the segregation of Negroes and whites in public schools. The three-judge District Court . . . denied the requested relief. The court found the Negro school inferior in physical plant, curricula, and transportation, and ordered the defendants forthwith to provide substantially equal curricula and transportation and to "proceed with all reasonable diligence and dispatch to remove" the inequality in physical plant. But, as in the South Carolina case, the court sustained the validity of the contested provisions and denied the plaintiffs admission to the white schools during the equalization program. The case is here on direct appeal.

In the Delaware case, *Gebhart v. Belton,* the plaintiffs are Negro children of both elementary and high school age residing in New Castle County. They brought this action in the Delaware Court of Chancery to enjoin enforcement of provisions in the state constitution and statutory code which require the segregation of Negroes and whites in public schools. The Chancellor gave judgment for the plaintiffs and ordered their immediate admission to schools previously attended only by white children, on the ground that the Negro schools were inferior with respect to teacher training, pupil-teacher ratio, extracurricular activities, physical plant, and time and distance involved in travel. The Chancellor also found that segregation itself results in an inferior education for Negro children, but did not rest his decision on that ground. The Chancellor's decree was affirmed by the Supreme Court of Delaware, which intimated, however, that the defendants might be able to obtain a modification of the decree after equalization of the Negro and white schools had been accomplished. The defendants, contending only that the

Delaware courts had erred in ordering the immediate admission of the Negro plaintiffs to the white schools, applied to this Court for *certiorari.* The writ was granted. The plaintiffs, who were successful below, did not submit a cross-petition.

2. 344 U.S. 1, 141, 891.

3. 345 U.S. 972. The Attorney General of the United States participated both Terms as *amicus curiae.*

4. For a general study of the development of public education prior to the Amendment, see Butts and Cremin, *A History of Education in American Culture* (1953), Pts. I, II; Cubberley, *Public Education in the United States* (1934 ed.), cc. II–XII. School practices current at the time of the adoption of the Fourteenth Amendment are described in Butts and Cremin, *supra,* at 269–275; Cubberley, *supra,* at 288–339, 408–431; Knight, *Public Education in the South* (1922), cc. VIII, IX. See also H. Ex.Doc. No. 315, 41st Cong., 2d Sess. (1871). Although the demand for free public schools followed substantially the same pattern in both the North and the South, the development in the South did not begin to gain momentum until about 1850, some twenty years after that in the North. The reasons for the somewhat slower development in the South (e.g., the rural character of the South and the different regional attitudes toward state assistance) are well explained in Cubberley, *supra,* at 408–423. In the country as a whole, but particularly in the South, the War virtually stopped all progress in public education. Id. at 427–428. The low status of Negro education in all sections of the country, both before and immediately after the War, is described in Beale, *A History of Freedom of Teaching in American Schools* (1941), 112–132, 175–195. Compulsory school attendance laws were not generally adopted until after the ratification of the Fourteenth Amendment, and it was not until 1918 that such laws were in force in all the states. Cubberley, *supra,* at 563–565.

5. *Slaughter-House Cases,* 16 Wall. 36, 67–72 (1873); *Strauder v. West Virginia,* 100 U.S. 303, 307–308 (1880): It ordains that no State shall deprive any person of life, liberty, or property, without due process of law, or deny to any person within its jurisdiction the equal protection of the laws. What is this but declaring that the law in the States shall be the same for the black as for the white; that all persons, whether colored or white, shall stand equal before the laws of the States, and, in regard to the colored race, for whose protection the amendment was primarily designed, that no discrimination shall be made against them by law because of their color? The words of the amendment, it is true, are prohibitory, but they contain a necessary implication of a positive immunity, or right, most valuable to the colored race—the right to exemption from unfriendly legislation against them distinctively as colored—exemption from legal discriminations, implying inferiority in civil society, lessening the security of their enjoyment of the rights which others enjoy, and discriminations which are steps towards reducing them to the condition of a subject race. See also *Virginia v. Rives,* 100 U.S. 313, 318 (1880); *Ex parte Virginia,* 100 U.S. 339, 344–345 (1880).

6. The doctrine apparently originated in *Roberts v. City of Boston,* 59 Mass. 198, 206 (1850), upholding school segregation against attack as being violative of a state constitutional guarantee of equality. Segregation in Boston public schools was eliminated in 1855. But elsewhere in the North, segregation in public education has persisted in some communities until recent years. It is apparent that such segregation has long been a nationwide problem, not merely one of sectional concern.

7. See also *Berea College v. Kentucky,* 211 U.S. 45 (1908).

8. In the *Cumming* case, Negro taxpayers sought an injunction requiring the defendant school board to discontinue the operation of a high school for white children until the board resumed operation of a high school for Negro children.

Similarly, in the *Gong Lum* case, the plaintiff, a child of Chinese descent, contended only that state authorities had misapplied the doctrine by classifying him with Negro children and requiring him to attend a Negro school.

9. In the Kansas case, the court below found substantial equality as to all such factors. In the South Carolina case, the court below found that the defendants were proceeding "promptly and in good faith to comply with the court's decree." In the Virginia case, the court below noted that the equalization program was already "afoot and progressing"; since then, we have been advised, in the Virginia Attorney General's brief on reargument, that the program has now been completed. In the Delaware case, the court below similarly noted that the state's equalization program was well under way.

10. A similar finding was made in the Delaware case: I conclude from the testimony that, in our Delaware society, State-imposed segregation in education itself results in the Negro children, as a class, receiving educational opportunities which are substantially inferior to those available to white children otherwise similarly situated.

11. K. B. Clark, *Effect of Prejudice and Discrimination on Personality Development* (Mid-century White House Conference on Children and Youth, 1950); Witmer and Kotinsky, *Personality in the Making* (1952), c. VI; Deutscher and Chein, "The Psychological Effects of Enforced Segregation: A Survey of Social Science Opinion," 26 *J. Psychol.* 259 (1948); Chein, "What Are the Psychological Effects of Segregation under Conditions of Equal Facilities?" *International Journal of Opinion and Attitude Research* 3 (1949), 229; Brameld, "Educational Costs," in *Discrimination and National Welfare* (MacIver, ed., 1949), 44–48; Frazier, *The Negro in the United States* (1949), 674–681. And see generally Myrdal, *An American Dilemma* (1944).

12. See *Bolling v. Sharpe, post,* p. 497, concerning the Due Process Clause of the Fifth Amendment.

13. . . . . 4. Assuming it is decided that segregation in public schools violates the Fourteenth Amendment (a) would a decree necessarily follow providing that, within the limits set by normal geographic school districting, Negro children should forthwith be admitted to schools of their choice, or (b) may this Court, in the exercise of its equity powers, permit an effective gradual adjustment to be brought about from existing segregated systems to a system not based on color distinctions?

5. On the assumption on which questions 4(a) and (b) are based, and assuming further that this Court will exercise its equity powers to the end described in question 4(b),(a) should this Court formulate detailed decrees in these cases;(b) if so, what specific issues should the decrees reach;(c) should this Court appoint a special master to hear evidence with a view to recommending specific terms for such decrees;(d) should this Court remand to the courts of first instance with directions to frame decrees in these cases and, if so, what general directions should the decrees of this Court include and what procedures should the courts of first instance follow in arriving at the specific terms of more detailed decrees?

14. See Rule 42, *Revised Rules of this Court* (effective July 1, 1954).

CHAPTER 8. *BOLLING V. SHARPE*

1. *Brown v. Board of Education, ante,* 483.

2. *Detroit Bank v. United States,* 317 U.S. 329; *Currin v.Wallace,* 306 U.S. 1, 13–14; *Steward Machine Co. v. Davis,* 301 U.S. 548, 585.

3. *Korematsu v. United States,* 323 U.S. 214, 216; *Hirabayashi v. United States,* 320 U.S. 81, 100.

4. *Gibson v. Mississippi,* 162 U.S. 565, 591. *Cf. Steele v. Louisville & Nashville R. Co.,* 323 U.S. 192, 198–199.

5. *Cf. Hurd v. Hodge,* 334 U.S. 24

Bibliography

PRIMARY SOURCES

BLUC   Bancroft Library, Oral History Project, University of California, Berkeley, California.
        Brownell, Herbert, Interview.
        Oliver, William, Interview.

CLE   Clemson University, Cooper Library, Clemson, South Carolina.
        Byrnes, James F., Papers.

CUOHP   Columbia University, Butler Library, Oral History Project, New York, New York.
        Jackson, Robert H., Interview.
        Reed, Stanley, Interview.

EPL   Dwight D. Eisenhower Presidential Library, Abilene, Kansas.
        Brownell, Herbert, Interview.
        Dwight D. Eisenhower Diary.
        Shaney, Bernard, Papers.
        White House Central Files (WHCF).

HIA   Hoover Institution Archives, Stanford, California.
        Rehnquist, William H., Papers.

HLS   Harvard Law School, Manuscripts Room, Cambridge, Massachusetts.
        Frankfurter, Felix, Papers.
        Hand, Learned, Papers.

LBJ   Lyndon Baines Johnson Presidential Library, Austin, Texas.
        Clark, Tom C., Oral History Interview.

LC   Library of Congress, Manuscript Division, Washington, D.C.
        Black, Hugo L., Papers.
        Brennan, William J., Jr., Papers.
        Burton, Harold H., Papers.
        Douglas, William O., Papers.
        Frankfurter, Felix, Papers.
        Jackson, Robert H., Papers.
        Marshall, Thurgood, Papers.
        Rutledge, Wiley, Papers.
        Stone, Harlan Fiske, Papers.
        Warren, Earl, Papers.
        White, Byron, Papers.

MLPU   Seeley G. Mudd Library, Princeton University, Princeton, New Jersey.
        Douglas, William O., Interviews with Walter Murphy.
        Harlan, John Marshall, Papers.

RHJC   Robert H. Jackson Center, Jamestown, New York.
RPL   Franklin D. Roosevelt Presidential Library, Hyde Park, New York.
        Morgenthau, Henry, Papers.
        Papers as President.
TPL   Harry S. Truman Presidential Library, Independence, Missouri.
        Minton, Sherman, Papers.
        White House Central Files.
UK   University of Kentucky, Special Collections Library, Lexington, Kentucky.
        Allan, F. Alley, Oral History Interview.
        Clark, Tom C., Oral History Interview.
        Minow, Newton, Oral History Interview.
        Reed, Stanley F., Papers.
        Rogers, William, Oral History Interview.
        Sapieza, John, Oral History Interview.
        Vinson, Fred M., Papers.
UM   University of Michigan, Bentley Historical Library, Ann Arbor, Michigan.
        Murphy, Frank, Papers.
UT   University of Texas, Law School Library, Special Collections, Austin, Texas.
        Clark, Tom C., Papers.
UV   University of Virginia, Law School Library, Special Collections, Charlottesville, Virginia.
        Prettyman, E. Barrett, Jr., Papers.
UVA   University of Virginia, Alderman Library, Special Collections, Charlottesville, Virginia.
        Cummings, Homer, Papers.
YU   Yale University Library, Manuscripts and Archives, New Haven, Connecticut.
        Kluger, Richard, Papers.
        Stewart, Potter, Papers.

WORKS CITED

Abraham, Henry J. *Justices, Presidents, and Senators: A History of U.S. Supreme Court Appointments from Washington to Bush II.* Lanham, Md.: Rowman & Littlefield, 2008.

Alfange, Dean, Jr. "The Balancing Interests of an Abused Doctrine." *Law in Transition Quarterly* 2 (1965), 35.

Allen, Francis A. "Chief Justice Vinson and the Theory of Constitutional Government: A Tentative Appraisal." *Northwestern University Law Review* 49 (1954), 3.

————. "Remembering *Shelly v. Kraemer:* Of Public and Private Worlds." *Washington University Law Quarterly* 67 (1989), 709.

Alton, Stephen R. "Loyal Lieutenant, Able Advocate: The Role of Robert H. Jackson in Franklin D. Roosevelt's Battle with the Supreme Court." *William & Mary Bill of Rights Journal* 5 (1997), 527.

Applebaum, Harvey. "Miscegenation Statutes: A Constitutional and Social Problem." *Georgetown Law Journal* 53 (1964), 49.

Armstrong, Scott. "Supreme Court Clerks as Judicial Actors and as Sources." *Marquette Law Review* 98 (2014), 387.

Atkinson, David N. "Justice Sherman Minton and the Protection of Minority Rights." *Washington & Lee Law Review* 34 (1977), 97.

————. "Opinion Writing on the Supreme Court, 1949–1956: The Views of Justice Sherman Minton." *Temple Law Quarterly* 49 (1975), 105.

Aynes, Richard L. "Charles Fairman, Felix Frankfurter, and the Fourteenth Amendment." *Chicago-Kent Law Review* 70 (1995), 1197.

————. "On Misreading Bingham and the Fourteenth Amendment." *Yale Law Journal* 103 (1993), 68.

Baker, Gordon E. *The Reapportionment Revolution: Representation, Political Power, and the Supreme Court.* New York: Random House, 1967.

Baker, Leonard. *Brandeis and Frankfurter: A Dual Biography.* New York: Harper & Row, 1989.

Baker, Liva. "John Marshall I and a Color Blind Constitution: The Frankfurter–Harlan II Conversations." *Journal of Supreme Court History* 1992 (1992), 27.

Balkin, Jack M., ed. *What* Brown v. Board of Education *Should Have Said.* New York: New York University Press, 2001.

Ball, Howard, and Phillip J. Cooper. *Of Power and Right: Hugo Black, William O. Douglas, and America's Constitutional Revolution.* New York: Oxford University Press, 1992.

Barrett, John. "Albany in the Life Trajectory of Robert H. Jackson." *Albany Law Review* 68 (2005), 513.

————. "A Jackson Portrait for Jamestown, 'A Magnet in the Room.'" *Buffalo Law Review* 50 (2002), 809.

Barrett, John Q. "No College, No Prior Clerkship: How Jim Marsh Became Justice Jackson's Law Clerk." In *Of Courtiers and Kings: More Stories of Supreme Court Law Clerks and the Justices,* edited by Todd C. Peppers and Clare Cushman. Charlottesville: University of Virginia Press, 2015.

Bass, Jack. *Unlikely Heroes.* New York: Simon & Schuster, 1981.

Bell, Derrick. "*Brown v. Board of Education* and the Interest-Convergence Dilemma." *Harvard Law Review* 93 (1980), 518.

————. *Silent Covenants:* Brown v. Board of Education *and the Unfulfilled Hopes for Racial Reform.* New York: Oxford University Press, 2004.

Bentley, Numan. *The Rise of Massive Resistance: Race and Politics in the South During the 1950s.* Baton Rouge: Louisiana State University Press, 1969.

Berger, Raoul. *Government by the Judiciary: The Transformation of the Fourteenth Amendment.* Cambridge, Mass.: Harvard University Press, 1977.

Berlin, Isaiah. *The Hedgehog and the Fox.* 2d ed. Princeton, N.J.: Princeton University Press, 2013.

Berry, Mary Frances. *Stability, Security, and Continuity: Mr. Justice Burton and Decision-Making in the Supreme Court, 1945–1958.* Westport, Conn.: Greenwood Press, 1978.

Bickel, Alexander. "The Court: An Indictment Analyzed." *New York Times Magazine* 16 (April 27, 1958).

———. "Frankfurter's Former Clerk Disputes Byrnes's Statement." *U.S. News & World Report* 132 (June 15, 1956).

———. *The Least Dangerous Branch: The Supreme Court at the Bar of Politics.* Indianapolis, Ind.: Bobbs-Merrill, 1962.

———. "The Original Understanding and the Segregation Decision." *Harvard Law Review* 69 (1955), 1.

———. *Politics and the Warren Court.* New York: Harper & Row, 1965.

———. "The Supreme Court, 1960 Term—Foreword: The Passive Virtues." *Harvard Law Review* 75 (1961), 40.

Black, Elizabeth. "Hugo Black: A Memorial Portrait." *Yearbook of the Supreme Court Historical Society* 1982 (1982), 72.

Black, Hugo. "Justice Black and the Bill of Rights." Interview by Eric Sevareid and Martin Agronsky, *CBS News* special, December 3, 1968. In *Southwestern University Law Review* 9 (1977), 937.

Black, Hugo L. *A Constitutional Faith.* New York: Knopf, 1968.

Black, Hugo, Jr. *My Father: A Remembrance.* New York: Random House, 1975.

Blandford, Linda A., and Patricia Russell Evans, eds. *Supreme Court of the United States, 1789–1980: An Index to Opinions Arranged by the Justice.* Volume 2, 1902–1980. New York: Kras International, 1983.

Bork, Robert H. *The Tempting of America: The Political Seduction of the Law.* New York: Free Press, 1990.

Boskey, Bennett. "Bob Jackson Remembered." *Albany Law Review* 68 (2004), 5.

Brandeis, Louis. *The Unpublished Opinions of Mr. Justice Brandeis.* Edited by Alexander M. Bickel. Cambridge, Mass.: Harvard University Press, 1957.

Brandwein, Pamela. *Reconstructing Reconstruction: The Supreme Court and the Production of Historical Truth.* Durham, N.C.: Duke University Press, 1999.

Breitel, Charles D. "Introduction" and "Mr. Justice Jackson and Individual Rights." In *Mr. Justice Jackson: Four Lectures in His Honor,* edited by Charles Desmond, Paul Freund, Potter Stewart, and Lord Shawcross. New York: Columbia University Press, 1965.

Brennan, William J., Jr. "The Constitution of the United States: Contemporary Ratification." In O'Brien, ed., *Judges on Judging.*

———. "A Remembrance of William O. Douglas." *Journal of Supreme Court History* 1991 (1991), 104.

Brenner, Saul. "The Memos of Supreme Court Law Clerk William Rehnquist: Conservative Tracts or Mirrors of His Justice's Mind?" *Judicature* 76 (1993), 77.

"The Bright Young Men Behind the Bench." *U.S. News & World Report* 45 (July 17, 1957).

"The Brooke Memorandum" (1971). In *The Record of Brown v. Board of Education,* edited by Mark Whitman. Princeton, N.J.: Markus Wiener, 1993.

Brownell, Herbert. "*Brown v. Board of Education* Revisited." *Journal of Supreme Court History* 1993 (1993), 21.

Bugliosi, Vincent. *The Betrayal of America: How the Supreme Court Undermined the Constitution and Chose Our President.* New York: Nation Books, 2009.

Byrnes, James F. *All in One Lifetime*. New York: Harper & Brothers, 1958.

————. "The Supreme Court Must Be Curbed." *U.S. News & World Report* 50 (May 18, 1956).

Cahn, Edmond. "Jurisprudence." *New York University Law Review* 30 (1957), 157.

Calabresi, Steven, ed. *Originalism: A Quarter-Century of Debate*. Washington, D.C.: Regnery, 2007.

Cardozo, Benjamin N. *The Nature of the Judicial Process*. New Haven, Conn.: Yale University Press, 1921.

Chen, Jim. "Poetic Justice." *Cardozo Law Review* 28 (2006), 581.

Chernack, Gregory. "The Clash of Two Worlds: Justice Robert H. Jackson, Institutional Pragmatism, and *Brown*." *Temple Law Review* 72 (1999), 51.

Choper, Jesse H. "Clerking for Chief Justice Earl Warren." In *In Chambers: Stories of Supreme Court Law Clerks and Their Justices,* edited by Todd Peppers and Artemus Ward. Charlottesville: University of Virginia Press, 2012.

Clark, Kenneth. "The Desegregation Cases: Criticism of the Social Scientist's Role." *Villanova Law Review* 5 (1969), 234.

Clark, Tom C., and Philip B. Perlman. *Prejudice and Prosperity: An Historic Brief Against Racial Covenants*. Washington, D.C.: Public Affairs Press, 1948.

Conference of Chief Justices. *Report of the Committee on Federal–State Relationships as Affected by Judicial Decisions*. Chicago: Conference of Chief Justices, 1958.

"Constitutionality of Anti-Miscegenation Statutes" [note], *Yale Law Journal* 58 (1949), 472.

Cooper, Phillip J. *Battles on the Bench: Conflict Inside the Supreme Court*. Lawrence: University Press of Kansas, 1995.

Corley, Pamela, Amy Steigerwalt, and Artemus Ward. "Revisiting the Roosevelt Court: The Critical Juncture from Consensus to Dissensus." *Journal of Supreme Court History* 38 (2013), 20.

Cortner, Richard C. *Civil Rights and Public Accommodations:* The Heart of Atlanta Motel *and* McClung *Cases*. Lawrence: University Press of Kansas, 2001.

Cottol, Robert, Raymond Diamond, and Leland Ware. Brown v. Board of Education: *Caste, Culture, and the Constitution*. Lawrence: University Press of Kansas, 2004.

Couch, Cullen. "Behind the Scenes of *Brown*, E. Barrett Prettyman, Jr., '53 Sensed History in the Making." *University of Virginia Lawyer* 1 (2004).

Cray, Ed. *Chief Justice: A Biography of Earl Warren*. New York: Simon & Schuster, 1997.

Crosskey, William W. "Charles Fairman, 'Legislative History,' and the Constitutional Limits on State Authority." *University of Chicago Law Review* 22 (1954), 1.

Danelski, David J. "The Influence of the Chief Justice in the Decisional Process of the Supreme Court." In *American Court Systems: Readings in Judicial Process and Behavior,* edited by Sheldon Goldman and Austin Sarat. 2d ed. White Plains, N.Y.: Longman, 1989.

Davidson, Gordon, Daniel Meador, Earl Pollock, and E. Barrett Prettyman Jr. "Supreme Court Law Clerks: Recollections of *Brown v. Board of Education II*." *St. John's Law Review* 79 (2005), 823.

Dean, John W. *The Rehnquist Choice: The Untold Story of the Nixon Appointment That Redefined the Supreme Court*. New York: Simon & Schuster, 2001.

Desmond, Charles, Paul Freund, Potter Stewart, and Lord Shawcross. *Mr. Justice Jackson: Four Lectures in His Honor.* New York: Columbia University Press, 1965.

Dickson, Del. "State Court Defiance and the Limits of Supreme Court Authority: *Williams v. Georgia* Revisited." *Yale Law Journal* 103 (1994), 1423.

———. *The Supreme Court in Conference (1940–1985).* New York: Oxford University Press, 2001.

Domnarski, William. *The Great Justices, 1941–1954: Black, Douglas, Frankfurter, and Jackson in Chambers.* Ann Arbor: University of Michigan Press, 2006.

Dorr, Gregory Michael. "Principled Expediency: *Naim v. Naim* and the Supreme Court." *Journal of Legal History* 42 (1988), 119.

———. *Segregation's Science: Eugenics and Society in Virginia.* Charlottesville: University of Virginia Press, 2008.

Douglas, William O. *Being an American.* New York: John Day, 1940.

———. *The Court Years, 1939–1975: The Autobiography of William O. Douglas.* New York: Random House, 1980.

———. *Points of Rebellion.* New York: Random House, 1969.

Dudziak, Mary. *Cold War Civil Rights: Race and the Image of American Democracy.* Princeton, N.J.: Princeton University Press, 2002.

Duke, Steven B. "Justice Douglas and Criminal Law." In *"He Shall Not Pass This Way Again": The Legacy of Justice William O. Douglas,* edited by Stephen L. Wasby. Pittsburgh, Pa.: University of Pittsburgh Press, 1990.

Dworkin, Ronald. *Justice for Hedgehogs.* Cambridge: Oxford University Press, 2011.

———. *Law's Empire.* Cambridge: Oxford University Press, 1986.

———. *A Matter of Principle.* Cambridge, Mass.: Harvard University Press, 1985

———. *Taking Rights Seriously.* Cambridge, Mass.: Harvard University Press, 1977.

Ellsberg, Daniel. *Secrets: A Memoir of Vietnam and the Pentagon Papers.* New York: Viking Press, 2003.

Elman, Philip, and Norman Silber. "The Solicitor General's Office, Justice Frankfurter, and Civil Rights Litigation, 1946–1960: An Oral History." *Harvard Law Review* 100 (1987), 817.

Epstein, Lee, Jeffrey Segal, Harold Spaeth, and Thomas Walker, eds. *The Supreme Court Compendium.* Washington, D.C.: CQ Press, 1994.

———. *The Supreme Court Compendium: Data, Decisions, and Developments.* 2d ed. Washington, D.C.: CQ Press, 2001.

Faigman, David. *Laboratory of Justice: The Supreme Court's 200-Year Struggle to Integrate Science and the Law.* New York: Times Books, 2004.

———. "Normative Constitutional Fact-Finding: Exploring the Empirical Component of Constitutional Interpretation." *University of Pennsylvania Law Review* 139 (1991), 541.

Fairman, Charles. "Does the Fourteenth Amendment Incorporate the Bill of Rights? The Original Understanding." *Stanford Law Review* 2 (1949), 5.

———. "Robert H. Jackson, 1892–1954: Associate Justice of the Supreme Court." *Columbia Law Review* 55 (1955), 445.

———. "The Supreme Court, 1955 Term—Foreword: The Attack on the Segregation Cases." *Harvard Law Review* 70 (1956), 83.

Fassett, John D. "Mr. Justice Reed and *Brown v. Board of Education.*" *Yearbook of the Supreme Court Historical Society* 1986 (1986), 48.

———. *New Deal Justice: The Life of Stanley Reed of Kentucky.* New York: Vantage Press, 1994.

Fassett, John, Earl Pollock, E. Barrett Prettyman Jr., and Frank Sander. "Supreme Court Law Clerks' Recollections of *Brown v. Board of Education.*" *St. John's Law Review* 78 (2004), 515.

Feldman, Noah. *Scorpions: The Battles and Triumphs of FDR's Great Supreme Court Justices.* New York: Twelve, 2010.

Fine, Sidney. *Frank Murphy: The Washington Years.* Ann Arbor: University of Michigan Press, 1984.

Finkelman, Paul. "Breaking the Back of Segregation: Why *Sweatt* Matters." *Thurgood Marshall Law Review* 36 (2010), 7.

Fisher, William W., III, Morton J. Horwitz, and Thomas A. Reed, eds. *American Legal Realism.* New York: Oxford University Press, 1993.

Frank, John P. *Clement Haynsworth, the Senate, and the Supreme Court.* Charlottesville: University of Virginia Press, 1991.

———. "Fred Vinson and the Chief Justiceship." *University of Chicago Law Review* 21 (1954), 212.

———. *The Marble Temple.* New York: Knopf, 1958.

Frank, John P., and Robert F. Munro. "The Original Understanding of 'Equal Protection of the Laws.'" *Washington University Law Quarterly* 1972 (1972), 421.

Frankfurter, Felix. "Chief Justices I Have Known." In *Felix Frankfurter on the Supreme Court,* edited by Philip Kurland. Chicago: University of Chicago Press, 1970.

———. "Foreword." *Columbia Law Review* 55 (1955), 435.

———. *From the Diaries of Felix Frankfurter.* Edited by Joseph P. Lash. New York: Norton, 1975.

———. *Law and Politics: Occasional Papers of Felix Frankfurter, 1913–1938.* Edited by E. F. Prichard Jr. and Archibald MacLeish. New York: Harcourt, Brace, 1939.

———. "Mr. Justice Jackson" (1955). In *Felix Frankfurter on the Supreme Court: Extrajudicial Essays on the Court and the Constitution,* edited by Philip Kurland. Cambridge, Mass.: Harvard University Press, 1970.

Franklin, John Hope. *From Slavery to Freedom: A History of African Americans.* 9th ed. New York: McGraw-Hill, 2010.

———. "Jim Crow Goes to School: The Genesis of Legal Segregation in Southern Schools." *South Atlantic Quarterly* 58 (1959), 225.

Freund, Paul. "Dedication—1964, Constitutional Dilemmas." *Boston University Law Review* 45 (1965), 13.

———. "Individual and Commonwealth in the Thought of Mr. Justice Jackson." In *On Law and Justice.* Cambridge: Belknap/Harvard University Press, 1968.

———. "Mr. Justice Black and the Judicial Function." *U.C.L.A. Law Review* 14 (1967), 467.

———. "Mr. Justice Jackson and Individual Rights." In *Mr. Justice Jackson: Four Lectures in His Honor,* edited by Charles S. Desmond, Paul A. Freund, Potter Stewart, and Lord Shawcross. New York: Columbia University Press, 1965.

———. *On Law and Justice.* Cambridge, Mass.: Harvard University Press, 1968.

————. *The Supreme Court of the United States: Its Business, Purposes, and Performance.* Cleveland, Ohio: World, 1961.

Friedman, Leon, ed. Brown v. Board: *The Landmark Oral Argument Before the Supreme Court.* New York: New Press, 2004.

Gardner, Warner W. "Robert Jackson: Government Attorney." *Columbia Law Review* 55 (1955), 438.

Gerhart, Eugene. *America's Advocate: Robert H. Jackson.* New York: Bobbs-Merrill, 1958.

————. *Lawyer's Judge.* Albany, N.Y.: Albany Q. Corporation, 1961.

————. "The Legacy of Robert H. Jackson." *Albany Law Review* 68 (2004), 19.

————. *Robert H. Jackson: Country Lawyer, Supreme Court Justice, and America's Advocate* [combining Gerhart's *America's Advocate* and *Lawyer's Judge*]. Foreword by Chief Justice William H. Rehnquist. Buffalo, N.Y.: William S. Hein, 2003.

Goluboff, Risa. *The Lost Promise of Civil Rights.* Cambridge, Mass.: Harvard University Press, 2007.

Gralia, Lino. *Disaster by Decree.* Ithaca, N.Y.: Cornell University Press, 1976.

Greenberg, Jack. Brown v. Board of Education: *Witness to a Landmark Decision.* New York: Twelve Tables, 2004.

————. *Race Relations and American Law.* New York: Columbia University Press, 1959.

Gronlund, Mimi Clark. *Supreme Court Justice Tom C. Clark: A Life of Service.* Austin: University of Texas Press, 2010.

Gugin, Linda, and James E. St. Clair. *Sherman Minton: New Deal Senator, Cold War Justice.* Bloomington: Indiana Historical Society, 1997.

Gunther, Gerald. *Learned Hand: The Man and the Judge.* New York: Knopf, 1994.

————. "The Subtle Vices of the 'Passive Virtues.'" *Columbia Law Review* 64 (1964), 1.

Hand, Learned. *The Bill of Rights.* Cambridge, Mass.: Harvard University Press, 1958.

————. "The Spirit of Liberty" (1944). In *The Spirit of Liberty: Papers and Addresses of Learned Hand,* collected and edited by Irving Dillard. New York: Knopf, 1952.

Harbaugh, William. *Lawyer's Lawyer: The Life of John W. Davis.* New York: Oxford University Press, 1973.

Harlan, John M. "A Glimpse of the Supreme Court at Work." *University of Chicago Law School Record* 11 (1963), 1.

Harris, Robert. *Decision: The Intense Minute by Minute Account of the Senate's Defeat of the Nomination of G. Harrold Carswell.* New York: Ballantine Books, 1972.

Haynie, Stacia L. "Leadership and Consensus on the U.S. Supreme Court." *Journal of Politics* 54 (1992), 1158.

Hockett, Jeffrey. "Justice Robert H. Jackson and Segregation: A Study of the Limitations and Proper Basis of Judicial Action." In *Black, White, and* Brown: *The Landmark School Desegregation Case in Retrospective,* edited by Clare Cushman and Melvin Urofsky. Washington, D.C.: CQ Press, 2004.

————. *New Deal Justice: The Constitutional Jurisprudence of Hugo L. Black, Felix Frankfurter, and Robert H. Jackson.* Lanham, Md.: Rowman & Littlefield, 1996.

————. *A Storm over This Court: Law, Politics, and Supreme Court Decision Making in* Brown v. Board of Education. Charlottesville: University of Virginia Press, 2013.

Holmes, Oliver Wendell. *The Occasional Speeches of Justice Oliver Wendell Holmes.* Edited by Mark De Wolfe Howe. Cambridge, Mass.: Harvard University Press, 1962.

————. "The Path of Law" (1897). *Harvard Law Review* 110 (1997), 991.

Holmes, Oliver Wendell, and Harold J. Laski. *Holmes–Laski Letters.* 2 vols. Edited by Mark De Wolfe Howe. Cambridge, Mass.: Harvard University Press, 1953.

Holmes, Oliver Wendell, and Frederick Pollock. *Holmes–Pollock Letters: The Correspondence of Mr. Justice Holmes and Sir Frederick Pollock, 1874–1932.* Edited by Mark DeWolfe Howe. Cambridge, Mass.: Harvard University Press, 1946.

Horowitz, Donald. *The Courts and Social Policy.* Washington, D.C.: Brookings Institution, 1977.

Horwitz, Morton. *The Warren Court and the Pursuit of Justice.* New York: Hill & Wang, 1998.

Howe, Mark De Wolfe. *Justice Oliver Wendell Holmes: The Proving Years, 1870–1882.* Cambridge, Mass.: Harvard University Press, 1963.

————. *Justice Oliver Wendell Holmes: The Shaping Years, 1841–1870.* Cambridge, Mass.: Harvard University Press, 1957.

Hughes, Charles Evans. *The Autobiographical Notes of Charles Evans Hughes.* Edited by David Danelski and Joseph Tulchin. Cambridge, Mass.: Harvard University Press, 1973.

Hutchinson, Dennis J. "'The Achilles Heel' of the Constitution: Justice Jackson and the Japanese Exclusion Cases." *Supreme Court Review* 2002 (2002), 455.

————. "The Black–Jackson Feud." *Supreme Court Review* 1988 (1988), 203.

————. "*Brown v. Board of Education.*" In *The Oxford Companion to the Supreme Court of the United States,* edited by Kermit Hall, 2d ed. New York: Oxford University Press, 2005.

————. "Mr. Justice Frankfurter and the Business of the Supreme Court, 1949–1961." *Supreme Court Review* 1980 (1980), 143.

————. "Unanimity and Desegregation: Decisionmaking in the Supreme Court, 1948–1958." *Georgetown Law Journal* 68 (1979), 1.

Jackson, Robert H. "Advocacy Before the United States Supreme Court." *A.B.A. Journal* 37 (1951), 801.

————. *The Case Against the Nazi War Criminals.* New York: Knopf, 1946.

————. "Decline of Stare Decisis Is Due to Volume of Opinions." *Journal of the American Judicature Society* 28 (1944), 6.

————. *Full Faith and Credit: The Lawyer's Clause of the Constitution.* New York: Columbia University Press, 1945.

————. *The Nürnberg Case.* New York: Knopf, 1947.

————. *The Struggle for Judicial Supremacy.* New York: Knopf, 1941.

————. *The Supreme Court in the American System of Government.* Cambridge, Mass.: Harvard University Press, 1955.

————. "The Task of Maintaining Our Liberties: The Role of the Judiciary." *A.B.A. Journal* 39 (1953), 961.

————. "Tribute to Country Lawyers: A Review." *A.B.A. Journal* 138 (March 1944).

————. "Wartime Security and Liberty Under Law." *Buffalo Law Review* 1 (1951), 103.

Jackson, Robert H., and John Q. Barrett. *That Man: An Insider's Portrait of Franklin D. Roosevelt.* New York: Oxford University Press, 2003.

Jaffe, Louis. "Mr. Justice Jackson." *Harvard Law Review* 68 (1955), 940.

Jenkins, John A. *The Partisan: The Life of William Rehnquist.* New York: Public Affairs, 2012.

————. "The Partisan: A Talk with Justice Rehnquist." *New York Times Magazine* 3 (March 3, 1985).

Kaufman, Andrew L. *Cardozo.* Cambridge, Mass.: Harvard University Press, 1998.

Kennedy, Randall. *Interracial Intimacies: Sex, Marriage, Identity, and Adoption.* New York: Pantheon Books, 2003.

Klarman, Michael J. "*Brown*, Originalism, and Constitutional Theory: A Response to Professor McConnell." *Virginia Law Review* 81 (1995), 1881.

————. *From Jim Crow to Civil Rights: The Supreme Court and the Struggle for Racial Equality.* New York: Oxford University Press, 2004.

Kluger, Richard. *Simple Justice: The History of* Brown v. Board of Education, *the Epochal Supreme Court Decision That Outlawed Segregation, and of Black America's Struggle for Equality.* New York: Knopf, 1975.

Knox, John. *The Forgotten Memoir of John Knox: A Year in the Life of a Supreme Court Clerk in FDR's Washington.* Edited by Dennis Hutchinson and David Garrow. Chicago: University of Chicago Press, 2002.

Kozinski, Alex. "Conduct Unbecoming." Review of Edward Lazarus, *Closed Chambers: The First Eyewitness Account of the Epic Struggles Inside the Supreme Court. Yale Law Journal* 108 (1999), 835.

Kozlowski, Mark. *The Myth of the Imperial Judiciary: Why the Right Is Wrong About the Courts.* New York: New York University Press, 2003.

Kurland, Philip B. "Earl Warren, the 'Warren Court,' and the Warren Myth." *Michigan Law Review* 67 (1968), 353.

————. "Justice Robert H. Jackson—Impact on Civil Rights and Civil Liberties." *Law Forum* 1977 (1977), 551.

————. *Mr. Justice Frankfurter and the Constitution.* Chicago: University of Chicago Press, 1971.

————. *Politics, the Constitution, and the Warren Court.* Chicago: University of Chicago Press, 1970.

————. "Robert H. Jackson." In *The Justices of the United States Supreme Court, 1789–1969*, edited by Leon Friedman and Fred Israel. New York: Chelsea House, 1969.

Kurland, Philip B., ed. *Felix Frankfurter on the Supreme Court: Extrajudicial Essays on the Court and the Constitution.* Cambridge, Mass.: Belknap/Harvard University Press, 1970.

Kurland, Philip, and Gerard Casper, eds. *Landmark Briefs and Arguments of the Supreme Court of the United States*, Vols. 49–49A. Arlington, Va.: University Publications of America, 1975.

Larson, Carlton. "What If Chief Justice Fred Vinson Had Not Died of a Heart Attack in 1953? Implications for *Brown* and Beyond." *Indiana Law Review* 45 (2011), 131.

Lavergne, Gary M. *Before* Brown: *Herman Marion Sweatt, Thurgood Marshall, and the Long Road to Justice.* Austin: University of Texas Press, 2010.

Lazarus, Edward. *Closed Chambers: The First Eyewitness Account of the Epic Struggles Inside the Supreme Court.* New York: Times Books, 1998.

Lerner, Max. *Nine Scorpions in a Bottle.* New York: Arcade, 1994.

Levy, Beryl Harold, ed. *Cardozo and the Frontiers of Legal Thinking.* New York: Oxford University Press, 1938.

Levy, Leonard. *Against the Law: The Nixon Court and Criminal Justice.* New York: Harper & Row, 1974.

————. *Original Intent and the Framers' Constitution.* New York: Macmillan, 1988.

Lofgren, Charles. *The* Plessy *Case: A Legal-Historical Interpretation.* New York: Oxford University Press, 1987.

Lukas, J. Anthony. "*Playboy* Interview: Bob Woodard." *Playboy* 36 (February 1989), 51.

Maillard, Kevin, and Rose Cuison Villazor, eds. Loving v. Virginia *in a Post-Racial World: Rethinking Race, Sex, and Marriage.* New York: Cambridge University Press, 2012.

Marietta, Morgan, and Tyler Farley. "The Prevalence and Justification of Social Facts in Landmark Decisions of the Supreme Court." *Journal of Law and Courts* 4 (Fall 2016), 243.

Marsh, James M. "Affirm, If Possible: How a United States Supreme Court Justice's Confidence in This Clerk Turned a Tentative 5–4 Vote into an 8–1 Decision." *Philadelphia Lawyer* 62 (1997).

————. "The Genial Justice: Robert H. Jackson." *Albany Law Review* 68 (2004), 41.

————. "Robert H. Jackson." In *The Supreme Court Justices: Illustrated Bibliography, 1789–1993,* edited by Clare Cushman. Washington, D.C.: CQ Press, 1993.

————. "Supreme Court Justices Without a College Degree." *Philadelphia Lawyer* 63 (1999).

Marshall, Thurgood. "The Constitution: A Living Document." In O'Brien, ed., *Judges on Judging.*

Mason, Alpheus T. *Harlan Fiske Stone: Pillar of the Law.* New York: Viking Press, 1956.

McAllister, Stephen R. "Justice Byron White and *The Brethren.*" *Green Bag* 15 (2012), 159.

McConnell, Michael. "Originalism and the Desegregation Decisions." *Virginia Law Review* 81 (1995), 947.

————. "The Originalist Case for *Brown v. Board of Education.*" *Harvard Journal of Law and Public Policy* 19 (1996), 457.

————. "The Originalist Justification for *Brown*; A Reply to Professor Klarman." *Virginia Law Review* 81 (1995), 1937.

McElwain, Edwin. "The Business of the Supreme Court as Conducted by Chief Justice Hughes." *Harvard Law Review* 63 (1949), 9.

Mendelson, Wallace. *Justices Black and Frankfurter: Conflict in the Court.* 2d ed. Chicago: University of Chicago Press, 1966.

————. "On the Meaning of the First Amendment: Absolutes in the Balance." *California Law Review* 50 (1962), 821.

Miller, Merle. *Plain Speaking—An Oral Biography of Harry S. Truman.* New York: Berkley, 1973.

Morrison, Stanley. "Does the Fourteenth Amendment Incorporate the Bill of Rights? The Judicial Interpretation." *Stanford Law Review* 2 (1949), 140.

Motley, Constance Baker. "The Historical Setting of *Brown* and Its Impact on the Supreme Court's Decision." *Fordham Law Review* 61 (1942), 9.

Murphy, Bruce Allen. *The Brandeis/Frankfurter Connection: The Secret Political Activities of Two Supreme Court Justices.* New York: Oxford University Press, 1982.

————. *Wild Bill: The Legend and Life of William O. Douglas.* New York: Random House, 2003.

Murphy, Walter. *Elements of Judicial Strategy.* Chicago: University of Chicago Press, 1964.

Muse, Benjamin. *Ten Years of Prelude: The Story of Integration Since the Supreme Court's 1954 Decision.* New York: Viking, 1964.

————. *Virginia's Massive Resistance.* Bloomington: Indiana University Press, 1961.

Myrdal, Gunnar. *An American Dilemma: The Negro Problem and Modern Democracy.* New York: Harper & Brothers, 1944.

Neal, Phil. "Justice Jackson: A Law Clerk's Recollections." *Albany Law Review* 68 (2005), 549.

Newbeck, Phyl. *Virginia Hasn't Always Been for Lovers: Interracial Marriage Bans and the Case of Richard and Mildred Loving.* Carbondale: Southern Illinois University Press, 2008.

Newby, I. A. *Challenge to the Court: Social Scientists and the Defense of Segregation, 1954–1966.* Baton Rouge: Louisiana State University Press, 1967.

Newman, Roger K. *Hugo Black: A Biography.* New York: Pantheon, 1994.

Newton, Jim. *Justice for All: Earl Warren and the Nation He Made.* New York: Riverhead Trade, 2007.

Obermayer, Herman J. *Rehnquist: A Personal Portrait of the Distinguished Chief Justice of the United States.* New York: Threshold Editions, 2009.

O'Brien, David M. *Constitutional Law and Politics.* Volume 1, *Struggles for Power and Governmental Accountability.* 10th ed. New York: Norton, 2017.

————. *Constitutional Law and Politics.* Volume 2, *Civil Rights and Civil Liberties.* 10th ed. New York: Norton, 2017.

————. "Institutional Norms and Supreme Court Opinions: On Reconsidering the Rise of Individual Opinions." In *Supreme Court Decision-Making: New Institutionalist Approaches,* edited by Cornell Clayton and Howard Gilman. Chicago: University of Chicago Press, 1999.

————. "Justice John Marshall Harlan's Unpublished Opinions: Reflections on a Supreme Court at Work." *Journal of Supreme Court History* 1991 (1991), 27.

————. "Of Myths, Motivations, and Justifications: A Postscript on Social Science and the Law." *Judicature* 64 (1981), 285.

————. "The Seduction of the Judiciary: Social Science and the Courts." *Judicature* 64 (1980), 8.

————. *Storm Center: The Supreme Court in American Politics.* 11th ed. New York: Norton, 2017.

O'Brien, David M., ed. *Judges on Judging: Views from the Bench.* Washington, D.C.: Sage/CQ Press, 2016.

Oppenheimer, J. Robert. "Atomic Weapons and American Policy." *Foreign Affairs* 31 (1953), 52.

Orfield, Gary, and Carole Ashkinaze. *The Closing Door: Conservative Policy and Black Opportunity.* Chicago: University of Chicago Press, 1991.

Orfield, Gary, and Susan Eaton. *Dismantling Desegregation: The Quiet Reversal of Brown v. Board of Education.* New York: New Press, 1996.

Parrish, Michael. "Felix Frankfurter, the Progressive Tradition, and the Warren Court." In *The Warren Court in Historical and Political Perspective,* edited by Mark Tushnet. Charlottesville: University of Virginia Press, 1996.

Pascoe, Peggy. *What Comes Naturally: Miscegenation Law and the Making of Race in America.* New York: Oxford University Press, 2009.

Patterson, James T. *Brown v. Board of Education: A Civil Rights Milestone and Its Troubled Legacy.* New York: Oxford University Press, 2001.

Pearson, Drew, and Robert S. Allen. *The Nine Old Men.* Garden City, N.Y.: Doubleday, Doran, 1936.

Peltason, J. W. *Fifty-Eight Lonely Men: Southern Federal Judges and School Desegregation.* New York: Harcourt, Brace, & World, 1961.

Peppers, Todd C. *Courtiers of the Marble Palace: The Rise and Influence of the Supreme Court Law Clerk.* Stanford, Calif.: Stanford University Press, 2006.

Peppers, Todd C., and Artemus Ward, eds. *In Chambers: Stories of Supreme Court Law Clerks and Their Justices.* Charlottesville: University of Virginia Press, 2012.

Peppers, Todd C., and Christopher Zorn. "Law Clerk Influence on Supreme Court Decision Making: An Empirical Assessment." *De Paul Law Review* 58 (2008), 5.

Pittman, R. Carter. "The Fourteenth Amendment: Its Intended Effect on Anti-Miscegenation Laws." *North Carolina Law Review* 43 (1964), 92.

Posner, Richard A. "What Am I, a Potted Plant? The Case Against Strict Constructionism." *New Republic* 197 (1987), 23.

Pound, Roscoe. *An Introduction to the Philosophy of Law.* New Haven, Conn.: Yale University Press, 1922.

Powell, Lewis. "What the Justices Are Saying . . ." *A.B.A. Journal* 1454 (1976).

President's Committee on Civil Rights. *To Secure These Rights: The Report of the President's Committee on Civil Rights.* New York: Simon & Schuster, 1947.

Prettyman, E. Barrett, Jr. *Death and the Supreme Court.* New York: Harcourt, Brace & World, 1961.

————. "Robert Jackson: 'Solicitor General for Life.'" *Journal of Supreme Court History* 1992 (1992), 75.

Pritchett, C. Herman. *The Roosevelt Court: A Study in Judicial Politics and Values.* New York: Macmillan, 1948.

Pusey, Merlo J. "Justice Roberts' 1937 Turnaround." *Yearbook of the Supreme Court Historical Society* 1983 (1983), 102.

Radcliff, William F. *Sherman Minton: Indiana's Supreme Court Justice.* Bloomington: Guild Press of Indiana, 1996.

Rakove, Jack. *Original Meanings: Politics and Ideas in the Making of the Constitution.* New York: Knopf, 1997.

Ray, Laura K. "A Law Clerk and His Justice: What William Rehnquist Did Not Learn from Robert H. Jackson." *Indiana Law Review* 29 (1996), 535.

Rehnquist, William H. "Another View: Clerks Might 'Influence' Some Actions." *U.S. News & World Report* 116 (February 21, 1958).

———. "Letter to the Editor: A Reply to Two Editorials on the Carswell Nomination." *Washington Post* (February 14, 1971), A14.

———. "The Making of a Supreme Court Justice." *Harvard Law Record* 7 (October 8, 1959), 10.

———. "The Notion of a Living Constitution." *Texas Law Review* 54 (1976), 693.

———. "Robert H. Jackson: A Perspective Twenty-Five Years Later." *Albany Law Review* 44 (1980), 533.

———. *The Supreme Court: How It Was, How It Is.* New York: Morrow, 1987.

———. "Who Writes Decisions of the Supreme Court?." *U.S. News & World Report* 74 (December 13, 1957).

Rehnquist, William H., with William Wayne Justice. "A Relativistic Constitution." *University of Colorado Law Review* 52 (1980), 19.

Rogers, William D. "Clerks' Work Is 'Not Decisive of Ultimate Result,'" *U.S. News & World Report* 114 (February 21, 1958).

Rosen, Paul. *The Supreme Court and Social Science.* Champaign: University of Illinois Press, 1972.

Rosenberg, Gerald. *The Hollow Hope: Can Courts Bring About Social Change?* 2d ed. Chicago: University of Chicago Press, 2009.

Rudenstine, David. *The Day the Presses Stopped: A History of the Pentagon Papers.* Berkeley: University of California Press, 1996.

Rumble, Wilfred. *American Legal Realism: Skepticism, Reform, and the Judicial Process.* Ithaca, N.Y.: Cornell University Press, 1968.

Sarat, Austin, ed. *Race, Law, and Culture: Reflections on* Brown v. Board of Education. New York: Oxford University Press, 1997.

Scalia, Antonin. "The Dissenting Opinion." *Journal of Supreme Court History* 1994 (1994), 33.

Schubert, Glendon, ed. *Dispassionate Justice: A Synthesis of the Judicial Opinions of Robert H. Jackson.* New York: Bobbs-Merrill, 1969.

Schwartz, Bernard. "Chief Justice Earl Warren: Super Chief in Action." *Journal of Supreme Court History* 1 (1998), 112.

———. "Chief Justice Rehnquist, Justice Jackson, and the *Brown* Case." *Supreme Court Review* 1988 (1988), 245.

———. "Felix Frankfurter and Earl Warren: A Study in Deteriorating Relationship." *Supreme Court Review* 1980 (1980), 115.

———. *Main Currents in American Legal Thought.* Durham, N.C.: Carolina Academic Press, 1993.

———. *Super Chief: Earl Warren and His Supreme Court—A Judicial Biography.* New York: New York University Press, 1983.

———. *The Unpublished Opinions of the Warren Court.* New York: Oxford University Press, 1985.

Schwartz, Bernard, ed. *The Warren Court: A Retrospective*. New York: Oxford University Press, 1996.

Senate Committee on the Judiciary. U.S. Congress, 92th Cong., 1st Sess. *Hearings on the Nominations of William H. Rehnquist of Arizona and Lewis F. Powell, Jr., of Virginia to Be Associate Justices of the Supreme Court of the United States, November 3, 4, 8, 9, and 10, 1971*. Washington, D.C.: Government Printing Office, 1971.

————. U.S. Congress, 99th Cong., 2d Sess. *Hearings before the Committee on the Judiciary on the Nomination of Justice William Hubbs Rehnquist to the Chief Justiceship of the United States, July, 29, 30, 31, and August 1, 1986*. Washington, D.C.: Government Printing Office, 1987.

Senate Judiciary Committee. *Nomination of William H. Rehnquist, S. Exec. Doc. No. 16*. In *The Supreme Court of the United States: Hearings and Reports on Successful and Unsuccessful Nominations of Supreme Court Justices by the Senate Judiciary Committee, 1916–1975*, volume 8, edited by Roy M. Mersky and J. Myron Jacobstein. Buffalo, N.Y.: Hein, 1975.

Silber, Norman I. *With All Deliberate Speed: The Life of Philip Elman——An Oral History Memoir*. Ann Arbor: University of Michigan Press, 2004.

Simon, James F. *Antagonists: Hugo Black, Felix Frankfurter, and Civil Liberties in Modern America*. New York: Simon & Schuster, 1990.

————. *FDR and Chief Justice Hughes: The President, the Supreme Court, and the Epic Battle over the New Deal*. New York: Simon & Schuster, 2012.

————. *Independent Journey: The Life of William O. Douglas*. New York: Harper & Row, 1980.

————. *In His Own Image: The Supreme Court in Nixon's America*. Philadelphia: McKay, 1974.

Small, Marshall L. "William O. Douglas Remembered: A Collective Memory by WOD Law Clerks." *Journal of Supreme Court History* 32 (2007), 297.

Snyder, Brad. "How the Conservatives Canonized *Brown v. Board of Education*." *Rutgers Law Review* 52 (2000), 383.

————. "The Judicial Genealogy (and Mythology) of John Roberts: Clerkships from Gray to Brandeis to Friendly to Roberts." *Ohio State Law Journal* 17 (2010), 1149.

————. "What Would Justice Holmes Do? Rehnquist's *Plessy* Memo, Majoritarianism, and *Parents Involved*." *Ohio State Law Journal* 69 (2008), 873.

Snyder, Brad, and John Q. Barrett. "Rehnquist's Missing Letter: A Former Law Clerk's 1955 Thoughts on Justice Jackson and *Brown*." *Boston College Law Review* 53 (2012), 631.

Sollars, Werner. *Interracialism: Black–White Intermarriage in American History, Literature, and Law*. New York: Oxford University Press, 2000.

St. Clair, James E., and Linda Gugin. *Chief Justice Fred M. Vinson of Kentucky: A Political Biography*. Lexington: University Press of Kentucky, 2002.

Stennis, John C. May 6, 1958, Senate speech, reprinted as "Investigate Supreme Court 'Law Clerk' System?" *U.S. News & World Report* 117 (May 16, 1958).

Strauss, David A. *The Living Constitution*. New York: Oxford University Press, 2010.

Thelin, John R. *A History of American Higher Education*. Baltimore, Md.: Johns Hopkins University Press, 2004.

Truman, Harry S. *Off the Record: The Private Papers of Harry S. Truman.* Edited by R. Ferrell. New York: Harper & Row, 1980.

Tushnet, Mark. *A Court Divided: The Rehnquist Court and the Future of Constitutional Law.* New York: Norton, 2005.

———. *Making Civil Rights Law: Thurgood Marshall and the Supreme Court, 1936–1961.* New York: Oxford University Press, 1994.

———. *The NAACP's Legal Strategy Against Segregated Education, 1925–1950.* Chapel Hill: University of North Carolina Press, 1988.

Tushnet, Mark, ed. *I Dissent: Great Opposing Opinions in Landmark Supreme Court Cases.* Boston: Beacon Press, 2008.

Tushnet, Mark, with Katya Lezin. "What Really Happened in *Brown v. Board of Education?*" *Columbia Law Review* 91 (1991).

Ulmer, S. Sidney. "Bricolage and Assorted Thoughts on Working in the Papers of Supreme Court Justices." *Journal of Politics* 35 (1973), 286.

———. "Earl Warren and the *Brown* Decision." *Journal of Politics* 33 (1971), 689.

———. "Further Reflections on Working in the Papers of Supreme Court Justices." *Judicature* 73 (1990), 193, 1867.

Urofsky, Melvin I. *Division and Discord: The Supreme Court Under Stone and Vinson, 1941–1953.* Columbia: University of South Carolina Press, 1997.

———. *Louis D. Brandeis: A Life.* New York: Pantheon, 2009.

———. "William O. Douglas and His Law Clerks." *Western Legal History* 3 (1990), 1.

Van den Haag, Ernst. "Social Science Testimony in the Desegregation Cases—A Reply to Professor Kenneth Clark." *Villanova Law Review* 6 (1960), 69.

Waddington, Walter. "The *Loving* Case: Virginia's Anti-Miscegenation Statute in Historical Perspective." *Virginia Law Review* 52 (1966), 1189.

Walker, Thomas, Lee Epstein, and William Dixon. "On the Mysterious Demise of Consensual Norms in the United States Supreme Court." *Journal of Politics* 50 (1988), 362.

Wallenstein, Peter. "Race, Marriage, and the Law of Freedom: Alabama and Virginia, 1860s–1960s." *Chicago-Kent Law Review* 70 (1994), 371.

———. "Race, Marriage, and the Supreme Court from *Pace v. Alabama* (1883) to *Loving v. Virginia* (1967)." *Journal of Supreme Court History* 1998 (1998), 65.

———. *Race, Sex, and the Freedom to Marry: Loving v. Virginia.* Lawrence: University Press of Kansas, 2014.

———. *Tell the Court I Love My Wife: Marriage and Law—An American History.* New York: Palgrave Macmillian, 2002.

Ward, Artemus, and David Weiden. *Sorcerers' Apprentices: 100 Years of Law Clerks at the United States Supreme Court.* New York: New York University Press, 2006.

Warren, Earl. *The Memoirs of Chief Justice Earl Warren.* New York: Doubleday, 1977.

Wasby, Stephen, Anthony D'Amato, and Rosemary Metrailer. *Desegregation from Brown to Alexander: An Exploration of Supreme Court Strategies.* Carbondale: Southern Illinois University Press, 1977.

Wechsler, Herbert. *Principles, Politics, and Fundamental Law: Selected Essays.* Cambridge, Mass.: Harvard University Press, 1961.

———. "Toward Neutral Principles of Constitutional Law." *Harvard Law Review* 73 (1959), 1.

White, Edward Douglas. "The Supreme Court of the United States." *A.B.A. Journal* 7 (1921), 341.

White, G. Edward. *Earl Warren: A Public Life*. New York: Oxford University Press, 1982.

Whitman, Mark, ed. *Removing the Badge of Slavery: The Record of* Brown v. Board of Education. Princeton, N.J.: Markus Wiener, 1993.

Wilkinson, J. Harvey, III. *From* Brown *to* Bakke: *The Supreme Court and School Integration, 1954–1978*. New York: Oxford University Press, 1979.

Wilson, Paul. "The Genesis of *Brown v. Board of Education*." *Kansas Journal of Law and Public Policy* 6 (1996), 7.

————. "A Time to Lose." *Journal of Supreme Court History* 24 (1999), 170.

————. *A Time to Lose: Representing Kansas*. Lawrence: University Press of Kansas, 1995.

Wohl, Alexander. *Father, Son, and Constitution: How Justice Tom Clark and Attorney General Ramsey Clark Shaped American Democracy*. Lawrence: University Press of Kansas, 2013.

Yarbrough, Tinsley E. *Mr. Justice Black and His Critics*. Durham, N.C.: Duke University Press, 1988.

Zelden, Charles L. Smith v. Allwright *and the Defeat of the Texas All-White Primary*. Lawrence: University Press of Kansas, 2005.

Zook, George Frederick. The President's Commission on Higher Education. *Higher Education for American Democracy: Report of the President's Commission on Higher Education*, Vol. II. Washington, D.C.: Government Printing Office, 1947.

Index of Cases

Index of Names and Subjects

and relationships with fellow justices, 33–34, 44, 47, 85
in Roosevelt administration, 7, 12, 13, 143
as Roosevelt Supreme Court appointee, 7–8, 15 (photo), 21–22, 26, 45–46, 81, 97 (photo)
segregation issue and, 2, 8, 62, 76, 77, 78–80, 81–85, 95–96, 109, 111–112, 115–118
in *Struggle for Judicial Supremacy*, 16, 17, 20, 24–25, 26, 85, 107, 119
in *Terry v. Adams*, 74
at Vinson's funeral, 49 (photo)
See also Jackson's unpublished *Brown* opinion
Jackson, William E., 56
Jackson's unpublished *Brown* opinion
and constitutional interpretation, 3, 71, 82–83, 84–86, 93, 119
criticisms and misunderstandings of, 115–118, 185n17
and decision to withhold publication, 78–80
Fourteenth Amendment in, 3–4, 18–19, 77, 78–80, 84–91, 105–106, 125–127
and judicial responsibility to address segregation issue, 3, 84, 115, 184nn1–2
Prettyman memo on, 79–80, 148
and racial classification, 105, 115, 116–118, 131–132
"separate but equal" in, 79, 98–99, 104–105, 118, 127–128, 132
significance of, 55
text of, 123–132
Jamestown, New York, 8, 9, 10, 11 (photo), 12, 13, 142–143, 154n3
Javits, Jacob, 68
Jefferson, Thomas, 30
Jenkins, John, 73–74
Jim Crow laws, 112, 142
Johnson, Lyndon B., 49
Jones, Walter, 154n18

Kennedy, Anthony, 106, 107
Kennedy, Edward, 68, 75
Kennedy, John F., 33
Kleindienst, Richard, 65, 67
Kluger, Richard, 2, 71–73, 74, 76, 80, 93, 177n29
Krock, Arthur, 33–34
Kurland, Philip, 15, 58, 59, 64, 67, 76, 170n34

legislative versus judicial powers, 14, 19, 84, 89, 90, 93–94, 95–96, 102, 128, 141
Lerner, Max, 158n13
Lewis, Anthony, 69, 71–72, 73

Marsh, James M., 56, 58–59
Marshall, John, 27
Marshall, Thurgood, 40, 51, 70, 76–77, 90, 113
McReynolds, James, 32, 33, 37, 40, 45–46, 143
Metzenbaum, Howard M., 75
Mickum, George, 40
Milton, John, 24
Minow, Newton, 48
Minton, Sherman, 31, 33, 37, 45, 48, 49, 50–51
Mitchell, John, 65, 67, 69
Mott, Frank, 7, 10
Murphy, Frank, 22, 30, 35, 41, 44, 45, 48, 54, 56
Myrdal, Gunnar, 72, 76–77, 91, 92, 93, 94, 106, 110–111, 115

NAACP, 51, 70, 90–92, 113, 144, 145
Neal, Phil C., 56, 58
New Deal. *See* Roosevelt, Franklin D.
Newsweek, 67, 69
New York Times, 63, 64, 69, 71–72, 73, 91
"nine scorpions in a bottle," Supreme Court as, 27, 158n13
Nixon, Richard M., 64, 65, 67, 69, 88
Nuremberg trials, Jackson as chief prosecutor at, 12, 47, 56, 58, 111, 143

O'Connor, Sandra Day, 106

Pearson, Drew, 61–62
Plessy, Homer, 108
Pollock, Earl E., 92
Pound, Roscoe, 90
Powell, Lewis F., Jr., 65, 67, 91
Prettyman, E. Barrett, Jr., 56, 60–61,
  78–80, 115, 116–117, 148,
  169n19
Pritchett, C. Herman, 27–28

racial classification, 50–51, 81, 105, 108,
  115–118, 131–132
Reagan, Ronald, 67, 73
Reed, Stanley
  in *Adamson v. California*, 35
  and *Brown*, 31, 32, 36, 39–40, 43–44,
    45, 83, 109, 111–112
  as cultural conservative, 38
  in *District of Columbia v. John R.
    Thompson*, 38–39
  Frankfurter's relationship with, 41
  as judicial restraint advocate, 30
  in *McLaurin v. Oklahoma State Regents*,
    38
  in *Missouri ex rel. Gaines v. Canada*, 38
  in *Morgan v. Virginia*, 46
  in *Ray v. Blair*, 94–95
  and role of law clerks, 54, 63–64
  as Roosevelt Supreme Court
    appointee, 10, 29–30, 37–38
  segregation issue and, 38–40, 43–44,
    45, 46, 82, 83, 103, 109, 111–112
  in *Smith v. Allwright*, 38, 143, 146
  in *Sweatt v. Painter*, 38
  in *Terry v. Adams*, 146
Rehnquist, William H.
  and *Brown* 1952 memo, 62, 64–65, 66
    (figure), 67–77
  and chief justice nomination and
    confirmation, 2, 55, 67–68, 69,
    71, 73, 74–76
  conservatism of, 67, 74
  and Fourteenth Amendment, 64, 72,
    76–77

on Jackson in letter to Frankfurter,
  59–61
as Jackson law clerk, 54, 55, 57–58,
  59–60, 60 (photo), 67, 145, 147,
  170n32
and law clerks in opinion-writing
  process, 54, 55, 63–64
as "the Lone Ranger" in solo dissents,
  73
in Nixon administration, 64, 65
as Nixon Supreme Court nominee,
  65, 67
in *Planned Parenthood v. Casey*, 107
segregation issue and, 67–68, 76
in *Terry v. Adams*, 74, 76
in *The Supreme Court: How It Was, How It
  Is*, 59–60
on Warren's chief justice
  appointment, 59
Rehnquist Choice, The (Dean), 69
Reston, James, 91
restrictive housing covenants, 48, 111,
  143, 144
Roberts, John G., Jr., 14, 55
Roberts, Owen, 26, 32, 33, 46, 56
Rogers, William D., 47, 63–64
Roosevelt, Franklin D.
  Court-packing plan of, 16, 26, 32–
    33, 49–50
  death of, 46
  and divided Supreme Court, 35, 47
  Fair Employment Practice
    Commission created by, 81
  Jackson in administration of, 7, 13,
    16, 45, 143
  Murphy as attorney general to, 44,
    45
  New Deal and, 2, 7–8, 12, 13, 17,
    26, 32–33, 37–38, 40–41, 54, 62,
    85
  Supreme Court appointments by,
    7–8, 10–11, 21–22, 26, 29–30,
    32–33, 37–38, 40–41, 44, 45–46,
    62, 81, 143
Rutledge, Wiley, 21–22, 30, 35, 41, 46,
  48, 143, 144